AP U.S. H
REVIEW

PRACTICE QUESTIONS AND ANSWER EXPLANATIONS

Dennis Urban, Ph.D.

Island Prep Publishing

Designed for the new AP U.S. History Exam

All Inquiries should be addressed to:
Island Prep Publishing, Inc.
P.O. Box 1021
Bellmore, NY 11710
info@longislandregentsprep.com

ISBN: 978-1537371498

CONTENTS

ABOUT THE AUTHOR

Dennis Urban teaches social studies at John F. Kennedy High School in Bellmore, New York. Since 2003, he has taught many courses, including AP U.S. History, Participation in Government, Historical Research, Sociology, Economics, and Writing Applications. He has also taught social studies methods classes at Teachers College, Columbia University, and graduate courses in elementary education, social studies, and philosophy at Touro College, where he is currently an Adjunct Professor. Dr. Urban received his undergraduate degree in history from Salisbury University in Maryland, and his M.A., M.Phil., and Ph.D. in social studies education from Columbia University. Dr. Urban is also co-founder and co-owner of Long Island Regents Prep, which offers NY State Regents, AP, and SAT review classes in Farmingdale, New York.

INTRODUCTION

Advanced Placement United States History

Over the past decade, the number of students participating in the AP U.S. History program has doubled, with nearly half a million students across the United States taking the exam in 2014. This trend is not unique to U.S. History. In recent years, student participation in the Advanced Placement program has increased in every subject across every demographic. Simply put, students are taking more AP exams in an effort to prepare for and gain admission to selective colleges. This book is designed to help relieve some of the pressure associated these high-stakes courses, and to provide students with the essential strategies, skills, and content to excel on the AP U.S. History exam.

The AP U.S. History curriculum, which underwent a complete redesign for the 2014-15 academic year, emphasizes content in United States history, overarching thematic strands, and historical thinking skills. The content covers the years 1491–Present, and is divided into nine time periods that we have used to organize this book. In addition, there are seven themes that are woven throughout the course and this review book. They include Work, Exchange, and Technology; Identity; Ideas, Beliefs, and Culture; America in the World; Environment and Geography; Politics and Power; and Peopling. Finally, the course requires students to recognize and employ four broad historical thinking skills. In this way, the AP U.S. history course is about more than learning facts about the past. Rather, it requires familiarity with the skills that professional historians use to present complex, contested portraits of the past. These skills include chronological reasoning, comparison and contextualization, crafting historical arguments from historical evidence, and historical interpretation and synthesis. In the answer section of this book, we have identified the specific historical thinking skills associated with each document-based multiple-choice question.

The newly redesigned AP U.S. History exam includes 55 multiple-choice questions, 4 short-answer questions, 1 document-based essay question, and 1 long essay question. This book, which includes over 445 practice questions with detailed explanations, will help students review the essential content, themes, and skills to master the AP U.S. History exam.

QUESTIONS

Period 1491-1607

PART A

DIFFICULTY LEVEL 1

1. How did the Great Ice Age account for the origins of human history in North America?

    (A) It allowed for the linking of Africa and South America.

    (B) It exposed a land bridge connecting Eurasia with North America.

    (C) It permitted early settlers to sail across the Atlantic Ocean.

    (D) It prevented dangerous animals from migrating to North America.

2. Before the Europeans arrived in the Americas, Indians in the Great Basin and Western Plains regions

    (A) traded with migrants from Africa and Asia.

    (B) created complex permanent civilizations.

    (C) developed nomadic lifestyles in response to the lack of steady resources.

    (D) cultivated potatoes and maize for sustenance.

DIFFICULTY LEVEL 2

3. Prior to 1492, the peoples of South and Central America relied on

    (A) the cultivation of crops such as corn and potatoes.

    (B) predetermined reservations to sustain their lifestyles.

    (C) the importation of slaves from Africa.

    (D) the domestication of pigs and horses.

Questions 4-6 refer to the image below.

The Kincaid Site in southern Illinois as it may have looked at its peak.

4. The artist's rendering of the city of Kincaid best reflects which of the following developments in Native American societies prior to European arrival?

   (A) Broad-reaching and complex political economies.

   (B) Mandated sanctification of nature.

   (C) Egalitarianism in pre-Columbian societies.

   (D) The adoption of the three-sister farming by native peoples.

5. Which Native cultural group is the most similar to the one found in the above artistic rendition?

   (A) Hopewell.

   (B) Mississippian.

   (C) Adena.

   (D) Hohokam.

6. Which of the following caused the social complexities displayed in the artistic depiction of Kinkaid?

    (A) Agriculture, especially corn growing, by native peoples.

    (B) The extinction of megafauna by Paleo-Indians in North America.

    (C) Migration over the Bering land bridge during the last Ice Age.

    (D) The development of matrilineal lines of kinship by native societies.

Questions 7-8 refer to the map below.

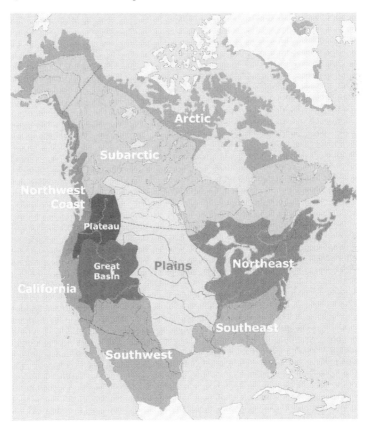

Cultural areas of North American Indigenous peoples at the time of European contact, 1492

7. Which of the following was a significant cause of the trend shown in the map?

(A) The retreat of glaciers after the end of the Ice Age.

(B) The ability of Native Americans to adapt to different geographical conditions.

(C) The development of sophisticated trading networks.

(D) The development of complex cities.

8. Prior to 1492, Native American tribes

(A) forged alliances to prevent Europeans from taking their lands.

(B) shared a written language.

(C) established trade and communication networks over large areas.

(D) embarked on transatlantic travel.

PART B

DIFFICULTY LEVEL 1

1. As a result of European contact with Native Americans,

    (A) millions of Native Americans died because of European diseases.
    (B) Europe introduced potatoes, tomatoes, and beans into the New World.
    (C) the Native American population grew at a steady rate.
    (D) Native Americans began cultivating and using tobacco.

2. Which of the following best characterizes the impact of European exploration on the Native American populations?

    (A) Europeans did not interact with the Native Americans.
    (B) Spain had a positive relationship with the Native Americans, but the French did not.
    (C) Native Americans were killed or subjugated by the European settlers.
    (D) Portugal created a lasting alliance with the Native Americans.

DIFFICULTY LEVEL 2

Questions 3-5 refer to the excerpt below.

"They afterwards came to the ship's boats where we were, swimming and bringing us parrots, cotton threads in skeins, darts, and many other things; and we exchanged them for other things that we gave them, such as glass beads and small bells. In fine, they took all, and gave what they had with good will.... They neither carry nor know anything of arms, for I showed them swords and they took them by the blade and cut themselves through ignorance. They have no iron... They should be good servants and intelligent, for I observe that they quickly took in what was said to them, and I believe that they would easily become Christians, as it appeared to me that they had no religion."

— Christopher Columbus, *Journal of His First Voyage*, 1492

3. In his journal, why did Columbus mention the Native Americans' interest in weapons, glass beads, and iron?

   (A) It demonstrated the different worldviews of Europeans and Native Americans.
   (B) It served to prove the existence of early forms of capitalism in the Americas prior to European contact.
   (C) It provided an example of Native Americans' nomadic lifestyles.
   (D) It demonstrated the economic superiority of the Native Americans.

4. After Columbus' arrival in the West Indies, the Spanish used conversion to Christianity to justify

   (A) the redistribution of land.
   (B) enslaving the Native Americans.
   (C) destroying the native environment.
   (D) oppressing the Native Americans.

5. Based on the document above, the beliefs of Columbus best support which Spanish goal?

   (A) Defeating England in the quest for global dominance.
   (B) Changing the Native Americans' religious beliefs.
   (C) Embracing a mercantilist economic system.
   (D) Working in harmony with the Native Americans.

PART C

DIFFICULTY LEVEL 1

1. What was the *encomienda* system?

    (A) A system of labor that relied on African slaves.

    (B) A system of indentured servitude for European immigrants.

    (C) A matriarchal labor system.

    (D) A system that required conquered Indians to serve as laborers.

DIFFICULTY LEVEL 2

2. Spain's most enduring legacy from the conquest and exploration of the Americas has been

    (A) its dominance as a global superpower.

    (B) its maintenance of a large empire.

    (C) its missionary success in promoting Christianity.

    (D) its status among the world's wealthiest nations.

Questions 3-4 refer to the map below.

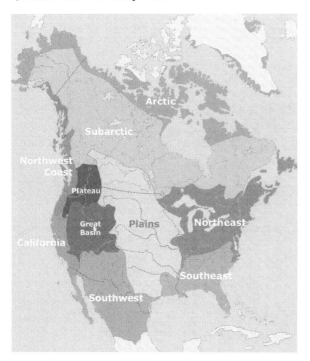

Cultural areas of North American Indigenous peoples at the time of European contact, 1492 (*http://en.wikipedia.org/wiki/Aboriginal_peoples_in_Canada#mediaviewer/File:Nordamerikanische_Kulturareale_en.png*)

3. How did most Native Americans' views of land ownership differ from those of the Europeans?

(A) They believed they could use the land without actually owning it.

(B) They believed individuals should be permitted to own land.

(C) They believed in tribal ownership of land.

(D) They believed all people could settle wherever they wanted, even when land was occupied.

4. Before contact with Europeans, Native American cultures

    (A) developed ploughs pulled by livestock.

    (B) experienced frequent devastating disease epidemics.

    (C) had frequent contact with African societies.

    (D) engaged in conflicts with other Native American tribes.

Questions 5-6 refer to the map below.

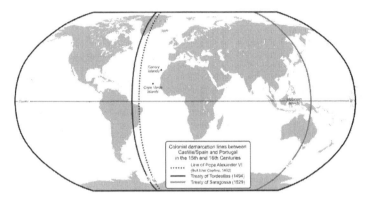

Colonial demarcation lines between Castille/Spain and Portugal in the 15th and 16th Centuries
(*http://en.wikipedia.org/wiki/Treaty_of_Tordesillas#mediaviewer/File:Spain_and_Portugal. png*)

5. According to the Treaty of Tordesillas,

    (A) Spain and Portugal shared the territory west of the line of demarcation.

    (B) The Pope declared the New World for the Holy Roman Empire.

    (C) England was permitted to colonize North America.

    (D) Lands east of the demarcation line would belong to Portugal and the lands west of the line would belong to Spain.

6. Who would most likely oppose the Treaty of Tordesillas in the 16ᵗʰ Century?

   (A) Ferdinand and Isabella of Spain.
   (B) Charles VIII of France.
   (C) Pope Alexander VI.
   (D) Elizabeth I of England.

DIFFICULTY LEVEL 3

7. England began settling the New World in the sixteenth century after

   (A) a peaceful treaty with the King of Spain.
   (B) the success the Roanoke Island colony.
   (C) the defeat of the Spanish Armada in 1588.
   (D) the French Revolution.

Period 1491-1607

Period 1607-1754

PART A

DIFFICULTY LEVEL 1

1. How did the English secure the financial means for establishing their first permanent colonies in North America?

    (A) joint-stock companies.
    (B) royal charters.
    (C) land grants from Queen Elizabeth II.
    (D) the headright system.

2. The Mayflower Compact (1620) was an early example of

    (A) a dictate from the King of England.
    (B) a document promoting gender equality.
    (C) a Bill of Rights.
    (D) a step toward self-government.

3. New England's poor soil resulted in all of the following *EXCEPT*

    (A) an emphasis on a "Puritan Work Ethic."
    (B) an economically diverse society.
    (C) reliance on cash crops for economic success.
    (D) early forms of manufacturing and trade.

4. Although slavery began in America for economic reasons,

    (A) it was not a profitable institution.
    (B) racism did not play a role.
    (C) it was perpetuated by race and heredity.
    (D) Native Americans provided the main source of labor.

DIFFICULTY LEVEL 2

5. Why did the Dutch settle New Netherland in the 17th century?

    (A) to establish a society based on principles of religious freedom.
    (B) to develop trade relationships with the Native Americans.
    (C) to expand their economy through commerce and mercantilism.
    (D) to secure a strategic naval base.

6. The Middle Colonies, such as New York and Pennsylvania, were similar in that they

    (A) had ethnically diverse populations.
    (B) lacked economic diversity.
    (C) had large Catholic populations.
    (D) had poor soil.

7. As a result of his defense of the principle of Liberty of Conscience, Roger Williams

    (A) became governor of Massachusetts Bay colony.
    (B) won support from the Native American tribes.
    (C) was banished from Massachusetts Bay colony.
    (D) solidified his role as a prominent Puritan minister.

8. By the early 1700s, slavery was legal in

    (A) the Southern colonies only.

(B) colonies in the Chesapeake region.

(C) the Middle and Southern colonies.

(D) All of the colonies.

Questions 9-12 refer to the excerpt below.

For we must consider that we shall be as a City upon a Hill. The eyes of all people are upon us. So that if we deal falsely with our God in this work we have undertaken, and so cause him to withdraw his present help from us, we shall be made a story and a by-word throughout the world. We shall open the mouths of enemies to speak evil of the ways of God, and all professors for God's sake. We shall shame the faces of many of God's worthy servants, and cause their prayers to be turned into curses upon us till we be consumed out of the good land whither we are a-going."

— John Winthrop, A Modell for Christian Charity, 1630.

9. The Plymouth and Massachusetts Bay Colonies were founded primarily by

   (A) English conquerors looking to exploit native populations.

   (B) Puritans seeking to establish communities where they would be free to practice their religion.

   (C) Dutch settlers who were culturally tolerant.

   (D) English planters looking cultivate cash crops.

10. Which of the following was an important effect of viewpoint described in the passage above?

   (A) Massachusetts Bay executed nonbelievers.

   (B) John Winthrop was excommunicated from the church.

   (C) Native Americans were accepted into the Massachusetts Bay colony.

   (D) Individuals with divergent views such as Roger Williams and Anne Hutchinson were banished from the colony.

11. The passage above best serves as evidence of which of the following?

   (A) Demographic diversity.

(B) A shortage of indentured servitude.

(C) Adherence to a strict Protestant orthodoxy.

(D) Acceptance of Native American groups.

12. The ideas expressed by Winthrop demonstrate which of the following continuities in American history?

(A) Westward expansion.

(B) Roman Catholic influence.

(C) American exceptionalism.

(D) The pursuit of social reform.

Questions 13-15 refer to the excerpt below.

It seems, in the first rise of the War, this Gentleman [Bacon] had made some overtures unto the Governor for a Commission, to go and put a stop to the Indian proceedings. But the Governor, at present, either not willing to commence the quarrel till' more suitable reasons presented, for to urge his more severe prosecution of the same, against the heathen: or that he doubted Bacon's temper; being generally discontented, for want of timely provisions against the Indians, or for Annual impositions [taxes] laid upon them, too great for them to bear, and against which they had some considerable time complained, without the least redress. For these, or some other reason, the Governor refused to comply with Bacon s proposals.

— Anonymous, The History of Bacon's and Ingram's Rebellion, 1676

13. Which of the following was a major cause of Bacon's Rebellion?

(A) Slaves were discontent with their status in society.

(B) Young men on the Virginia frontier were frustrated by frequent Indian attacks.

(C) Governor Berkeley resigned from office.

(D) The King of England established the Dominion of New England.

14. As a result of Bacon's Rebellion,

(A) African slavery was reduced.

15

(B) Chesapeake planters begin to purchase more African slaves.

(C) Governor Berkeley resigned from office.

(D) Native Americans were increasingly used as slaves.

15. Which of the following resembles the circumstances of Bacon's Rebellion?

(A) Paxton Boys' Rebellion.

(B) Leisler's Rebellion.

(C) Regulator Movement.

(D) All of the Above.

PART B

DIFFICULTY LEVEL 1

1. Early European settlers believed that Native Americans were

   (A) inferiors who could be exploited for economic gain.
   (B) equals with whom that could peacefully coexist.
   (C) savages who intended to murder them.
   (D) Africans whom they could enslave.

2. French immigrants to the New World tended to inhabit

   (A) Canada.
   (B) Florida.
   (C) territory east of the Appalachian Mountains.
   (D) Southern colonies.

3. Following their initial failures in the early 1600s, Jamestown settlers eventually prospered as a result of

   (A) the establishment of the House of Burgesses.
   (B) the election of Governor John Winthrop.
   (C) the cultivation of tobacco.
   (D) the elimination of malaria.

DIFFICULTY LEVEL 2

4. The English colony of Jamestown nearly failed for all of the following reasons EXCEPT

   (A) Indian wars led to a decrease in English population.
   (B) an outbreak of malaria within the colony.
   (C) the inhabitants focused on finding gold instead of food.
   (D) English settlers were ill-equipped to adapt to the environment.

5. Georgia was considered a "Buffer Colony" because

   (A) it had frequent conflict with Native Americans.

   (B) it supported the British economy.

   (C) it had a strong militia.

   (D) it protected the Carolinas from Spanish invasion.

Questions 6-7 are based on the following song.

"In excelsis gloria.
Within a lodge of broken bark
The tender babe was found
A ragged robe of rabbit skin
En-wrapped His beauty round
But as the hunter braves drew nigh
The angel song rang loud and high

Jesus your King is born
Jesus is born
The earliest moon of wintertime
Is not so round and fair
As was the ring of glory
On the helpless Infant there
The chiefs from far before Him knelt
With gifts of fox and beaver pelt"

Huron Carol or *"Twas in the moon of wintertime,"* composed by Jean de Brébeuf in the Native American language of the Huron people in 1643, translated by Jesse Edgar Middleton

6. Historians would most likely use this song to research

   (A) the relationship between French missionaries and Native Americans.

   (B) the origins of the Huron Indians.

   (C) the impact of Spanish colonialism on Mesoamerica.

   (D) the political hierarchy of Huron civilization.

7. This song best reflects which of the following historical trends in Colonial America?

   (A) The need to create a "City upon a Hill" in New England.

(B) A desire for new sources of wealth, increased power and status, and converts to Christianity.

(C) The death of Native Americans as a result of diseases and violence.

(D) The implementation of the *encomienda* system in Central America.

Questions 8-9 are based on the following image.

Taos Pueblo, located about 1 mile north of the modern city of Taos, New Mexico, served as a base for Popé during the Pueblo Revolt of 1680.
(*http://en.wikipedia.org/wiki/Pueblo_Revolt#mediaviewer/File:USA_09669_Taos_Pueblo_L uca_Galuzzi_2007.jpg*)

8. The image above is *least* consistent with which of the following?

    (A) The environment in New Mexico made crop irrigation challenging.

    (B) The Pueblo resided in stone or mud brick dwellings.

    (C) The Pueblo were unable to unite against the Spanish.

    (D) The Pueblo dealt with extreme drought and other hostile natives.

9. The Pueblo Revolt of 1680 represents a *change* in relations between the Spanish and Native Americans in that

    (A) The Spanish easily defeated the Pueblo.

(B) The Pueblo united under Popé to drive the Spanish from New Mexico.

(C) The Spanish were able to reconquer New Mexico.

(D) The Spanish aggressively forced the Pueblos to convert to Christianity.

DIFFICULTY LEVEL 3

10. The most important result of King Philip's War was that

(A) The British lost territory in the Ohio Valley.

(B) New England settlers faced fewer serious threats from local Native Americans.

(C) Native Americans gained land in French Canada.

(D) Chesapeake settlers defeated Spanish incursions.

PART C

DIFFICULTY LEVEL 1

1. Why was the "Act Concerning Religion," or the Maryland Toleration Act, instituted in 1649?

   (A) To protect Lord Baltimore.
   (B) To protect Jews and atheists.
   (C) To protect all Christians, including Catholics.
   (D) To protect Native Americans in their traditional beliefs.

2. One of reasons Quakers left England to settle in North America was

   (A) their search for a more tolerant environment.
   (B) their tolerance of aboriginal peoples.
   (C) their denial of God's existence.
   (D) their refusal to run for public office.

DIFFICULTY LEVEL 2

3. Why were Harvard and Yale colleges established during the Colonial Era?

   (A) to train doctors.
   (B) to advance scientific discovery.
   (C) to educate students to become ministers.
   (D) to preserve Greco-Roman traditions.

4. Why did Southern colonies usually allow married women to retain property rights?

   (A) Women in the South were seen as men's political equals.
   (B) English tradition demanded it.
   (C) The mortality rate of Southern men was high.
   (D) Women outnumbered men in the South.

5. What was the Dominion of New England?

   (A) A union of English colonies in the New England region of North America.
   (B) An attempt by the English government to streamline the administration of its colonies.
   (C) A union that eventually included the Middle Colonies of New York and New Jersey.
   (D) All of the above.

6. The Great Awakening led to which of the following?

   (A) The persecution of witches in Salem.
   (B) The spread of Enlightenment ideas throughout the colonies.
   (C) An emphasis on emotional, evangelical sermons.
   (D) The successful conversion of Native Americans to Christianity.

Questions 7-9 refer to the following excerpt.

"…if God should let you go, you would immediately sink and swiftly descend plunge into the bottomless gulf, and your healthy constitution, and your own care and prudence, and best contrivance, and all your righteousness, would have no more influence to uphold you and keep you out of Hell, than a spider's web would have stop a fallen rock."

— Jonathan Edwards, excerpt from his sermon "Sinners in the Hands of an Angry God"

7. The sermon above represents which of the following 18th century movements?

   (A) The American Revolution.
   (B) The First Great Awakening.
   (C) The Regulator Movement.
   (D) The Second Great Awakening.

8. Which of the following was a major cause of the movement described above?

   (A) The American Revolution.
   (B) The Enlightenment.
   (C) The Glorious Revolution in England.

(D) The lack of religious freedom in the colonies.

9. A major result of the movement represented by the document above was the

(A) failure of many in colonial society to achieve salvation in any substantial way.

(B) end of religious toleration.

(C) division of Congregationalists into New Lights and Old Lights.

(D) excommunication of Roger Williams and Anne Hutchinson.

Questions 10-11 refer to the following excerpt.

"The Question before the Court…is not the Cause of the poor Printer, nor of New-York alone…No! It may in its Consequence, affect every Freeman that lives under a British Government on the Main of America…. It is the Cause of Liberty….Every Man who prefers Freedom to a Life of Slavery will bless and honour You, as Men who have…given us a Right…both of exposing and opposing arbitrary Power (in these Parts of the World, at least) by speaking and writing Truth."

— Andrew Hamilton, attorney defending John Peter Zenger, accused of libel by royal governor of New York, William Cosby, 1735

10. The idea expressed by Andrew Hamilton best illustrates which development in 18th century colonial America?

(A) Colonial concern for the lack of justice in British colonial courts.

(B) Concern over British control of trade and taxation.

(C) Disagreement between the colonies and the British regarding slavery.

(D) The colonial view of the British exercising arbitrary power.

11. The ideas about justice expressed in the excerpt are most consistent with those of which of the following documents?

(A) Anne Hutchinson's trial transcripts from the Massachusetts Bay Colony.

(B) Jonathan Edwards' "Sinners in the Hands of an Angry God" sermon.

(C) William Lloyd Garrison's *Liberator* newspaper.

(D) George Washington's Farewell Address.

Questions 12-13 refer to the following excerpt.

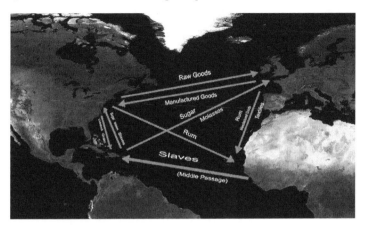

Detailed model of the Triangular Trade.
(http://commons.wikimedia.org/wiki/File:Detailed_Triangle_Trade.jpg)

12. Which of the following was the most important factor in the development of the exchange of raw materials shown in the map?

(A) Slavery.

(B) Mercantilism.

(C) Self-government.

(D) Native American resistance.

13. The map above is best understood in the context of what 17th-century British action?

(A) The Stamp Act.

(B) The Navigation Acts.

(C) The Toleration Act.

(D) The Dominion of New England.

14. According to Thomas Jefferson, "the best school of political liberty the world ever saw" was

    (A) Harvard College.
    (B) the House of Burgesses.
    (C) the New England town meeting.
    (D) England's Parliament.

15. In Colonial New England, what was the Half-Way Covenant?

    (A) It provided a partial church membership for the children of church members.
    (B) It banned Quakers from church membership.
    (C) It opened church membership to nonbelievers.
    (D) It led to a decrease in ministers.

16. In 1692, most of those accused as witches during the Salem Witch Trials were

    (A) proven to be in communion with Satan.
    (B) from Salem's poor, backcountry population.
    (C) Native Americans.
    (D) people who participated in Salem's growing eastern market economy.

Period 1754-1800

PART A

DIFFICULTY LEVEL 1

1. Why did the Colonists in British North America object to the Stamp Act of 1765?

    (A) It was passed by Parliament without consent of the colonists.
    (B) It was prohibitively expensive.
    (C) The colonists opposed all taxes.
    (D) The colonists believed they were independent from Britain.

2. During the 17th and 18th centuries, Enlightenment philosophers believed that

    (A) God is the primary authority for government.
    (B) people should convert to Christianity.
    (C) sovereignty resides with absolute rulers.
    (D) a fundamental purpose of government is to protect people's rights.

3. President George Washington issued his Proclamation of Neutrality in 1793 in response to

    (A) England's encroachment on American shorelines.
    (B) France's efforts to gain American support for its war against Britain.
    (C) Spain's attempts to cede Louisiana.
    (D) The Netherlands' overtures to forge a transatlantic alliance.

4. What was the main purpose of the Albany Congress of 1754?

   (A) Arrive at peace agreement with France.
   (B) Declare independence from Great Britain.
   (C) Propose a common defense against the French and certain Native American tribes.
   (D) Overturn the Navigation Acts.

5. Which of the following was a result of the French and Indian War?

   (A) The British gained control of Louisiana.
   (B) Great Britain became the dominant power in North America.
   (C) France annexed the island of Cuba.
   (D) The Dutch gained exclusive control of the slave trade.

6. The main purpose of the Proclamation of 1763 was to

   (A) prevent conflicts with Native Americans.
   (B) levy new taxes on the colonists.
   (C) prevent the French from gaining control of North America.
   (D) provide a safe haven for Puritans.

7. Which of the following colonial actions helped unite the colonists against Great Britain during the 1760s?

   (A) The Albany Plan of Union.
   (B) The Proclamation of 1763.
   (C) Committees of correspondence.
   (D) Declaration of Independence.

Period 1754-1800

Questions 8-10 refer to the map below.

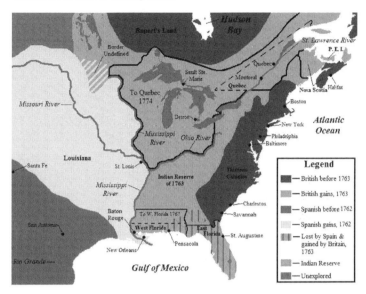

Map showing territorial gains of Britain and Spain following the French and Indian War.

8. According to the map, which of the following was a result of the French and Indian War?

    (A) The British Empire dramatically increased in size.

    (B) New France claimed new land north of the Great Lakes.

    (C) Spain lost Louisiana.

    (D) New England dominated colonial America.

9. The map above best reflects which of the following historical trends in 18th century North America?

(A) Native American tribes commanded large portions of the continent.

(B) North America east of the Mississippi River was largely claimed by either Great Britain or France.

(C) Great Britain shifted its settlements to the southwest.

(D) The Dutch remained a major force in North American through the 1700s.

10. The American Revolution was a long-term effect of the French and Indian War because of

(A) Colonial dissatisfaction with lack of American Indian assimilation.

(B) England's infringement on colonists' rights to migrate west.

(C) King George III's dissolution of the Navigation Acts.

(D) Britain's occupation of Canada.

Questions 11-12 refer to the document below.

"This Town has received the Copy of an Act of the British Parliament, wherein it appears that we have been tried and condemned, and are to be punished, by the shutting up of the harbor and other marks of revenge, until we shall disgrace ourselves by servilely yielding up, in effect, the just and righteous claims of America....The people receive this cruel edict with abhorrence and indignation. They consider themselves as suffering the stroke ministerial...I hope they will sustain the blow with a becoming fortitude, and that the cursed design of intimidating and subduing the spirits of all America, will, by the joint efforts of all, be frustrated."

— Samuel Adams, letter to James Warren (May 14, 1774)

11. The excerpt above is best understood in the context of which of the following historical events?

(A) The Stamp Act.

(B) The Boston Massacre.

(C) The Boston Tea Party.

(D) The Sugar Act.

12. Based on this excerpt, Samuel Adams would most likely have supported which of the following actions?

(A) The Molasses Act.

(B) The Proclamation of 1763.

(C) The Olive Branch Petition.

(D) The publication of Thomas Paine's *Common Sense.*

Questions 13-14 refer to the document below.

"Why, by interweaving our destiny with that of any part of Europe, entangle our peace and prosperity in the toils of European ambition, rivalship, interest, humor or caprice? It is our true policy to steer clear of permanent alliances with any portion of the foreign world; so far, I mean, as we are now at liberty to do it; for let me not be understood as capable of patronizing infidelity to existing engagements. I hold the maxim no less applicable to public than to private affairs, that honesty is always the best policy. I repeat it, therefore, let those engagements be observed in their genuine sense. But, in my opinion, it is unnecessary and would be unwise to extend them."

— George Washington's Farewell Address, 1796

13. The advice described in the excerpt above most likely resulted from the fact that

(A) Spain was attempting to reclaim its colonies in Latin America.

(B) Haiti attempted an unsuccessful revolution against France.

(C) France wanted to sell the Louisiana Territory to the United States.

(D) Britain and France were at war.

14. Which of the following continuities in United States history is best reflected in the document above?

(A) Debates over the proper role of the United States in world affairs.

(B) Debates over the relationship between federal and state governments.

(C) Debates over the proper interpretation of the United States Constitution.

(D) Debates over power of the presidency.

DIFFICULTY LEVEL 3

15. The 18ᵗʰ century war between Britain and France for control of North America resulted from a dispute over which territory?

(A) Florida.

(B) The Great Lakes.

(C) The Mississippi River.

(D) The Ohio River Valley.

16. Which of the following would provide historians with insight into the causes of the American Revolution?

(A) John Dickinson's Letter from a Farmer.

(B) Benjamin Franklin's Poor Rickard's Almanack.

(C) Jonathan Edwards's "Sinners in the Hands of an Angry God".

(D) The Albany Plan of Union.

PART B

DIFFICULTY LEVEL 1

1. What was the purpose of the Olive Branch Petition?

    (A) To attempt reconciliation with King George III.

    (B) To declare America's independence.

    (C) To make peace with the Native Americans.

    (D) To accept Parliament's policies of taxation.

2. The Declaration of Independence

    (A) Established a written Constitution for the United States.

    (B) Elected George Washington as the first President of the United States.

    (C) Listed the colonists' grievances against King George III.

    (D) Repealed the Stamp Act.

3. Which individual urged John Adams to "remember the ladies" during the Continental Congress?

    (A) Betsy Ross.

    (B) Thomas Jefferson.

    (C) Benjamin Franklin.

    (D) Abigail Adams.

4. The United States Constitution that was adopted at the Constitutional Convention in 1787

    (A) Included a Bill of Rights.

    (B) Required a voting age of 21 years.

    (C) Was built on a series of compromises.

    (D) Established guidelines for the formation of political parties.

5. What was the motivation for adding the Bill of Rights to the United States Constitution?

    (A) To strengthen the power of the state governments.

    (B) To reinforce the Constitution's delegated powers.

    (C) To protect freedoms not specified in the Constitution.

    (D) To establish a federal judiciary.

6. What was the main purpose of the Alien and Sedition Acts?

    (A) To punish the Federalist Party.

    (B) To capture French and British spies.

    (C) To silence and punish critics of the Adams Administration.

    (D) To secure Americans' civil liberties.

DIFFICULTY LEVEL 2

7. During the 17th and 18th centuries, the North American colonies took advantage of Great Britain's policy of salutary neglect to

    (A) Introduce slavery to the Caribbean.

    (B) Form republican systems of local government.

    (C) Form a Continental Army.

    (D) Make territorial agreements with France.

8. The Articles of Confederation

    (A) Established a strong central government.

    (B) Established a bicameral legislature.

    (C) Denied the national government the ability to levy taxes.

    (D) Formed a powerful judiciary.

9. One of the few lasting achievements of the government under the Articles of Confederation was

   (A) A system for federal taxation.
   (B) The abolition of slavery throughout the United States.
   (C) Post-Revolutionary War economic prosperity.
   (D) The organization of the Northwest Territory.

10. During the debate over ratifying the Constitution, the authors of *The Federalist* argued it was

    (A) Impossible to protect the rights of all citizens in a large republic.
    (B) Possible to establish a large, commercial republic.
    (C) Probable that slavery would be abolished within twenty years.
    (D) Necessary to maintain the Articles of Confederation.

11. What were the historical circumstances leading to the Whiskey Rebellion of the 1790s?

    (A) Congress levied an excise tax on whiskey.
    (B) Congress tried to prohibit the sale of whiskey.
    (C) Congress allowed the import of foreign whiskey.
    (D) Congress prohibited the manufacturing of whiskey.

12. In response to the Alien and Sedition Acts, the Kentucky and Virginia Resolutions argued that

    (A) State governments could nullify federal laws and decide whether or not an act of Congress was unconstitutional.
    (B) Only the Supreme Court could determine the constitutionality of a law.
    (C) The Democratic-Republican Party was overstepping its constitutional authority.
    (D) Foreign policy issues should be left up to the states to decide.

Questions 13-15 refer to the excerpt below.

We hold these truths to be self-evident, that all men are created equal, that they are endowed by their Creator with certain unalienable Rights, that among these are Life, Liberty and the pursuit of Happiness.--That to secure these rights, Governments are instituted among Men, deriving their just powers from the consent of the governed, --That whenever any Form of Government becomes destructive of these ends, it is the Right of the People to alter or to abolish it, and to institute new Government, laying its foundation on such principles and organizing its powers in such form, as to them shall seem most likely to effect their Safety and Happiness. Prudence, indeed, will dictate that Governments long established should not be changed for light and transient causes; and accordingly all experience hath shewn, that mankind are more disposed to suffer, while evils are sufferable, than to right themselves by abolishing the forms to which they are accustomed. But when a long train of abuses and usurpations, pursuing invariably the same Object evinces a design to reduce them under absolute Despotism, it is their right, it is their duty, to throw off such Government, and to provide new Guards for their future security.

— Declaration of Independence, 1776

Period 1754-1800

13. The document above is evidence that the basic ideas in the Declaration of Independence were influenced by

   (A) The divine right of monarchs of Europe.
   (B) The laws of Spanish colonial governments in North America.
   (C) Laws used by the Holy Roman Empire.
   (D) The philosophies of John Locke.

14. Which of the following most directly led to the drafting of the Declaration of Independence?

   (A) Failed attempts to reconcile differences with King George III.
   (B) The Battles of Lexington and Concord.
   (C) The Boston Massacre.
   (D) The French and Indian War.

15. Which of the following represents a continuation of the ideas described in the excerpt above?

    (A) The Seneca Falls Convention's "Declaration of Sentiments".
    (B) Martin Luther King Jr.'s "I Have a Dream Speech".
    (C) France's "Declaration of the Rights of Man and Citizen".
    (D) All of the above.

Questions 16-17 refer to the following excerpts.

"It would reduce the whole instrument to a single phrase, that of instituting a Congress with power to do whatever would be for the good of the United States; and as they would be the sole judges of the good or evil, it would be also a power to do whatever evil they please. Certainly no such universal power was meant to be given them. It [the Constitution] was intended to lace them up straightly within the enumerated powers and those without which, as means, these powers could not be carried into effect."

— Thomas Jefferson, Opinion on a National Bank, February 15, 1791

"It is not denied that there are implied well as express powers, and that the former are as effectually delegated as the latter."

— Alexander Hamilton, Opinion on the National Bank, 1791

16. The excerpts above are best understood in the context of the debate over

    (A) Whether to levy taxes.
    (B) How to safeguard the rights of the people.
    (C) The necessity of the Bill of Rights.
    (D) How to interpret the United States Constitution.

17. As a result of the disagreement between Hamilton and Jefferson regarding the National Bank,

    (A) Jefferson won the election of 1800.
    (B) The nation's capital was moved from New York to Washington, D.C.
    (C) The first political parties were formed in the United States.
    (D) The National Bank was destroyed.

Question 18 refers to the political cartoon below.

Federalist poster, 1800. Washington (in heaven) tells partisans to keep the pillars of
Federalism, Republicanism, and Democracy.
http://upload.wikimedia.org/wikipedia/commons/f/f1/~party3.JPG

18. The political poster above is best understood in the context of

   (A) debates about infrastructure development in the early republic.

   (B) George Washington's warnings against the formation of political parties.

   (C) the Louisiana Purchase.

   (D) debates over American support for the French Revolution.

DIFFICULTY LEVEL 3

19. Between 1787 and 1789, which of the following groups was most likely to oppose the
ratification of the Constitution?

   (A) Backcountry farmers.

   (B) Northern merchants.

   (C) Southern planters.

   (D) Ministers.

20. Which of the following groups benefitted most from Alexander Hamilton's financial program?

(A) Western farmers.

(B) War veterans.

(C) Southern planters.

(D) Northeastern merchants.

PART C

DIFFICULTY LEVEL 1

1. In his inaugural address of 1801, when Thomas Jefferson said, "We are all republicans—we are all federalists," he meant that

   (A) Americans would never ally themselves with monarchical governments.

   (B) Federalists would be appointed to his cabinet.

   (C) The two parties' platforms were identical.

   (D) The principles of American government were above party politics.

DIFFICULTY LEVEL 2

2. What was a major issue of dispute leading up to Shays' Rebellion?

   (A) The jailing of individuals or seizure of property for failure to pay taxes.

   (B) Involvement in the American Revolution.

   (C) The failure of Massachusetts authorities to protect its residents from Indian raids.

   (D) The publication of *Common Sense.*

3. Alexander Hamilton and his Federalist Party approved of Jay's Treaty because it

   (A) adhered to Washington's Proclamation of Neutrality.

   (B) Also reflected the ideas of the Democratic-Republican party.

   (C) united public opinion in support of the treaty.

   (D) provided a framework for peaceful United States relations with Great Britain.

4. Why was Pinckney's Treaty with Spain considered a diplomatic highlight of Washington's administration?

(A) The United States gained control of Florida.

(B) It allowed the United States to use the port of New Orleans and to navigate the Mississippi River.

(C) The United States gained territory in the American Southwest.

(D) Spain withdrew its military forces from the Caribbean.

Questions 5-7 refer to the document below.

"In the years of the early republic there developed the consensus that a mother could not be a citizen but that she might serve a political purpose. Those who said that women ought to play no political role at all had to meet the proposal that women might play a deferential political role through the raising of a patriotic child. The concept of Republican Motherhood began to fill the gap left by the political theorist of the Enlightenment…. It provided a context in which skeptics could easily maintain that women should be content to perform this limited political role permanently and ought not to wish fuller participation."

— Linda K. Kerber, "The Republican Mother: Women and the Enlightenment—An American Perspective," *American Quarterly*, 1976.

5. Which of the following best supports the argument expressed in the excerpt above?

(A) Throughout United States history, women have been considered men's equals.

(B) Women received national voting rights shortly after the Constitution was ratified.

(C) Women would be permitted to receive greater access to education than had been previously allowed.

(D) Women were granted full citizenship when the Constitution was ratified.

6. In contrast to women's roles during the Colonial Era, the document above demonstrates that women were now seen as

   (A) responsible for maintaining the domestic sphere.
   (B) morally superior to their husbands.
   (C) deserving of the same legal rights as men.
   (D) politically active citizens.

7. Which of the following was a direct effect of ideas expressed in this excerpt?

   (A) Women refused to educate their children about the rights and responsibilities of citizenship.
   (B) Women began fighting for suffrage, or the right to vote.
   (C) Women began demanding property rights.
   (D) Women were expected to focus on the domestic sphere, a trend that continued under the Victorian-era "Cult of Domesticity."

Questions 8-9 refer to the following quotation.

"The national dignity and justice require that the arms of the Union should be called forth in order to chastise the Creek nation of Indians, for refusing to treat with the United States on reasonable terms, and for their hostile invasion of the State of Georgia.… But, in future, the obligations of policy, humanity, and justice, together with that respect which every nation sacredly owes to its own reputation, unite in requiring a noble, liberal, and disinterested administration of Indian affairs.…In the administration of the Indians, every proper expedient that can be devised to gain their affections, and attach them to the interest of the Union, should be adopted.…Missionaries…should be appointed to reside in their nation… [and] be their friends and fathers."

Secretary of War Henry Knox to George Washington, July 7, 1789.

8. The excerpt above was most likely a reaction to the fact that

(A) Native America tribes repeatedly changed alliances with Europeans and other tribes.

(B) the United States Constitution failed to define the relationship between Native American tribes and the federal government.

(C) Native American tribes had vastly different views on gender roles than did the Europeans.

(D) competition for land in the Northeast was becoming violent.

9. During the late 1700s, the most difficult challenge facing Native American tribes was

(A) gaining navigation rights on the Mississippi river.

(B) negotiating conflicts between England, Spain, and the United States.

(C) solving treaty disputes and the preventing the seizure of Indian lands.

(D) the United States government's attempts to assimilate Native Americans into American society.

DIFFICULTY LEVEL 3

10. Episodes such as Bacon's Rebellion, the Boston Tea Party, and Shays' Rebellion demonstrate that

(A) most violence occurred in urban areas.

(B) violent conflict subsided after the American Revolution.

(C) rebellions were often directed at representatives of distant authority.

(D) foreign intervention was necessary to quell rebellions.

11. How did the Haitian Revolution of the 1790s affect the United States?

(A) The revolution had little impact on the United States.

(B) It strained the Unites States' relationship with France.

(C) The United States began trading with Haiti.

(D) Slave owners worried that similar uprisings could take place in the American South.

12. Which of the following statements is true about the relations between Native Americans and white Americans during the 1790s?

(A) Federal and state governments generally respected Native American land claims.

(B) Native Americans tribes in the Old Northwest Territory ceded much of their land to the United States.

(C) Many Native American leaders supported the assimilation of Native Americans into white civilization.

(D) Native Americans enjoyed the advantage of superior numbers because white westward settlement was gradual.

Period 1754-1800

Period 1800-1848

PART A

DIFFICULTY LEVEL 1

1. The 1803 Supreme Court decision of *Marbury v. Madison* established the principle of

    (A) Judicial review.
    (B) Separation of powers.
    (C) Federalism.
    (D) States' rights.

2. Andrew Jackson's signature policy towards the Native Americans involved

    (A) Forcibly moving them west of the Mississippi River.
    (B) Giving them citizenship.
    (C) Setting aside native land in Georgia and Florida.
    (D) Placing them on reservations in Upstate New York.

3. The 1848 women's rights convention in Seneca Falls, New York, proposed

    (A) Equal access to educational facilities for women.
    (B) Full voting rights for women.
    (C) The right of women to own and keep property.
    (D) All of the above.

4. Why did the Whig Party form in the 1830s?

    (A) To repeal the Bank of the United States.
    (B) To oppose the policies of Andrew Jackson.
    (C) To dismantle public education.
    (D) To promote agrarian reform.

5. Under Chief Justice John Marshall, the decisions of the Supreme Court tended to

    (A) Allow the Executive Branch to exercise greater authority over states' issues.
    (B) Expand the power of the federal government at the expense of states' rights.
    (C) Espouse a strict construction of the U.S. Constitution.
    (D) Disregard the sanctity of contract.

6. During his presidency, Thomas Jefferson advocated which of the following changes as a way to restore republican ideals?

    (A) Repealing the Bank of the United States.
    (B) Reducing the size and scope of the federal government.
    (C) Reenacting the Alien and Sedition Acts.
    (D) Increasing funding for United States military.

7. Which of the following factored into the United States decision to declare war against Great Britain in 1812?

    (A) France's alliance with Great Britain.
    (B) British attacks on the capitol building.
    (C) The impressment of American seamen.
    (D) The desire for American independence.

8. Which of the following statements is true about Henry Clay's proposed "American System"?

    (A) It was strongly promoted by Andrew Jackson.
    (B) It was established by the Treaty of Ghent at the end of the War of 1812.
    (C) It restricted seditious speech about the United States government.
    (D) It was designed to promote economic progress and self-sufficiency.

Period 1800-1848

9. How did South Carolina respond to the Tariff of 1828?

   (A) It endorsed the tariff.
   (B) It proposed the tariff.
   (C) It attempted to nullify the tariff.
   (D) It seceded from the United States.

10. What was the "cult of domesticity"?

   (A) An aspect of the Salem witchcraft trials, in which middle-aged matrons were accused of practicing evil magic.
   (B) The idealization of women in their roles as wives and mothers during the nineteenth century.
   (C) The defense given by antebellum apologists for slavery, who argued that bondage was a "positive good."
   (D) The continued influence of the Puritans' insistence on the importance of family as the cornerstone of social their order.

11. What were the central tenets of American Transcendentalism?

   (A) Belief in the value of individualism, self-reliance, and nature.
   (B) Belief in the concept of sin and the necessity for forgiveness from God and from fellow worshippers.
   (C) The expectation that Christ would descend to earth during the nineteenth century.
   (D) Rejection of reason and Cartesian dualism.

12. What was a typical theme of the Second Great Awakening?

   (A) The Calvinist doctrine of predestination.
   (B) Deistic rationalism.
   (C) Perfectionism.
   (D) Transubstantiation.

Questions 13-15 refer to the graph below.

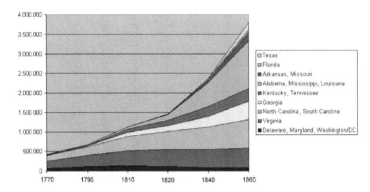

Slave Population in the Southern United States of the U. S., 1770-1860
(http://commons.wikimedia.org/wiki/File:US_Slavery_Statistics_1770_thru_1860_South.jpg)

13. Which of the following most directly contributed to the information shown in the graph?

(A) The abolition of slavery.

(B) Eli Whitney's invention of the cotton gin.

(C) Nat Turner's rebellion.

(D) The end of slave importation in 1808.

14. The graph presented above best illustrates the fact that

(A) antebellum social reform effectively addressed the issue of slavery in America.

(B) despite the emergence of the Abolition Movement, slavery continued to flourish and grow.

(C) expanding democracy included new and greater economic opportunities for African-Americans.

(D) The economic benefits of slavery diminished over time.

15. The information shown in the graph best reflects which of the following continuities in United States History?

(A) Debates about federalism.

(B) Debates about access to voting rights.

(C) Debates about the meaning of freedom and equality.

(D) Debates about the proper role of political parties.

Questions 16-18 refer to the excerpt below.

Amongst the novel objects that attracted my attention during my stay in the United States, nothing struck me more forcibly than the general equality of conditions. I readily discovered the prodigious influence which this primary fact exercises on the whole course of society, by giving a certain direction to public opinion, and a certain tenor to the laws; by imparting new maxims to the governing powers, and peculiar habits to the governed. I speedily perceived that the influence of this fact extends far beyond the political character and the laws of the country, and that it has no less empire over civil society than over the Government; it creates opinions, engenders sentiments, suggests the ordinary practices of life, and modifies whatever it does not produce.

— *Democracy in America* - Alexis de Tocqueville, 1831

16. This excerpt most directly reflects which of the following characteristics of American society in the early 1800's?

(A) Rugged individualism.

(B) Expansion of democracy.

(C) Puritan work ethic.

(D) Manifest Destiny.

17. The except above is best understood in the context of

(A) Antebellum reform movements.

(B) Native American removal.

(C) The abolition of slavery.

(D) Women suffrage.

18. Which of the following examples from antebellum America would best *refute* Tocqueville's sentiments?

(A) slavery.

(B) Indian removal.

(C) nativism.

(D) All of the above.

Questions 19-20 refer to the following excerpt.

"Compare his condition with the tenants of the poor houses in the more civilized portions of Europe—look at the sick, and the old and infirm slave, on one hand, in the midst of his family and friends, under the kind superintending care of his master and mistress, and compare it with the forlorn and wretched condition of the pauper in the poorhouse. But I will not dwell on this aspect of the question; I turn to the political; and here I fearlessly assert that the existing relation between the two races in the South, against which these blind fanatics are waging war, forms the most solid and durable foundation on which to rear free and stable political institutions. It is useless to disguise the fact. There is and always has been in an advanced stage of wealth and civilization, a conflict between labor and capital. The condition of society in the South exempts us from the disorders and dangers resulting from this conflict; and which explains why it is that the political condition of the slaveholding States has been so much more stable and quiet than that of the North. . . ."

— John C. Calhoun, Speech before the United States Senate, 1837

19. Calhoun's sentiments in the excerpt above can best be understood as

(A) supportive of the continuation of the international slave trade.

(B) opposition to the continued restrictions against citizenship for slaves.

(C) an expression of Southern pride in the institution of slavery.

(D) an argument for the gradual emancipation of slaves.

20. Calhoun's speech was most likely a response to which of the following?

    (A) The formation of a temporary national truce over the issue of slavery.

    (B) The abolitionist criticism of the treatment of slaves in the South.

    (C) The creation of free African American communities.

    (D) The outlawing of the international slave trade.

Questions 21-22 refer to the following excerpt.

"There were no beds given the slaves, unless one coarse blanket be considered such, and none but the men and women had these. This, however, is not considered a very great privation. They find less difficulty from the want of beds, than from the want of time to sleep; for when their day's work in the field is done, the most of them having their washing, mending, and cooking to do, and having few or none of the ordinary facilities for doing either of these, very many of their sleeping hours are consumed in preparing for the field the coming day; and when this is done, old and young, male and female, married and single, drop down side by side, on one common bed,—the cold, damp floor,—each covering himself or herself with their miserable blankets; and here they sleep till they are summoned to the field by the driver's horn. At the sound of this, all must rise, and be off to the field. There must be no halting; every one must be at his or her post; and woe betides them who hear not this morning summons to the field; for if they are not awakened by the sense of hearing, they are by the sense of feeling: no age nor sex finds any favor. Mr. Severe, the overseer, used to stand by the door of the quarter, armed with a large hickory stick and heavy cowskin, ready to whip any one who was so unfortunate as not to hear, or, from any other cause, was prevented from being ready to start for the field at the sound of the horn."

— Frederick Douglass, Narrative of the Life of Frederick Douglass, 1945

21. Douglass's excerpt is best understood in the context of

    (A) African-American involvement in the abolitionist movement.

    (B) sectional tensions over the institution of slavery.

    (C) continued restrictions on African American citizenship in Northern states.

    (D) the growth of the internal slave trade in the United States.

22. Before the Civil War, which of the following groups shared the most similar experience to that described in the excerpt above?

    (A) Native Americans.

(B) White women.

(C) German immigrants.

(D) Abolitionists.

Questions 23-24 refer to the image below

A political cartoon about the Embargo Act of 1807
(*http://en.wikipedia.org/wiki/Embargo_Act_of_1807#mediaviewer/File:Ograbme.jpg*)

23. Which of the following was the most direct cause of the situation depicted in the image?

(A) The Louisiana Purchase.

(B) Violations of American neutrality.

(C) The Barbary Wars.

(D) The XYZ Affair.

24. As a result of the Embargo Act,

(A) the American economy prospered.

(B) the United States went to war with France.

(C) the American economy suffered.

(D) Thomas Jefferson was impeached.

DIFFICULTY LEVEL 3

25. What was the Hartford Convention of 1814?

(A) A manifestation of New England Federalist opposition to the War of 1812.

(B) A meeting of War Hawks to discuss expanding the War of 1812.

(C) A military strategy for invading Canada.

(D) A congress of Western farmers to address British-backed American Indian attacks.

PART B

DIFFICULTY LEVEL 1

1. During his presidency, Andrew Jackson supported

   (A) the right of nullification.
   (B) rechartering the Bank of the United States.
   (C) Annexing the state of Texas.
   (D) Indian removal.

2. In addition to the cotton gin, what was Eli Whitney's major contribution to American technology?

   (A) The stead engine.
   (B) The factory system.
   (C) The mechanical reaper.
   (D) Interchangeable parts.

DIFFICULTY LEVEL 2

3. During the antebellum era, New England farm girls who worked in textile mills were eventually replaced by

   (A) German Immigrants.
   (B) Freed African Americans from the South.
   (C) Irish immigrants.
   (D) Chinese immigrants.

4. What was the significance of the 1825 opening of the Erie Canal?

   (A) It led to the passage of the Homestead Act.

   (B) It made the steamboat obsolete.

   (C) It eliminated the incentives to build canals elsewhere in the country.

   (D) It stimulated trade between the industrializing Northeast and the agricultural Midwest.

Questions 5-8 refer to the following map.

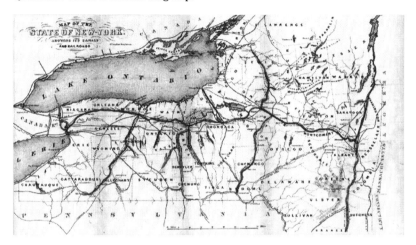

Map of Erie Canal and other New York canals, 1853.
(*http://en.wikipedia.org/wiki/Erie_Canal#mediaviewer/File:Erie_Canal_Map_1853.jpg*)

5. The expansion of canals detailed in the map above best exemplify

   (A) The growth of a national market economy in the 1840s.

   (B) The development of political parties during the 1830s.

   (C) The proliferation of American Antebellum reform movements.

   (D) The growth of urban cities in the American south.

6. The expansion of the U.S. transportation network by 1853, as shown in the map above, benefitted MOST from which of the following technological advances?

   (A) Interchangeable parts.
   (B) The cotton gin.
   (C) The steam engine.
   (D) The telegraph.

7. The lack of developed infrastructure in the South is best understood in the context of

   (A) The failure of many cotton crops in the 1840s.
   (B) The impact of geographically dispersed plantations and dearth of urban centers.
   (C) The violence associated with slavery.
   (D) The strength of the Democratic Party's influence on federal politics.

8. The opening of canals and new roads in the United States, as depicted in the map above, had an impact on all of the following EXCEPT

   (A) European immigration to the United States.
   (B) Westward migration of American citizens.
   (C) The market revolution.
   (D) Regional economic specialization.

Questions 9-10 refer to the following excerpt.

"The Northern or New England States are endowed by nature with a mountainous and sterile soil, which poorly rewards the labor of the [farmer]. However, its wooded slopes, and tumbling streams...showed the first settlers the direction in which their industry was to be employed.... The mountain torrents of New England have become motors, by which annually improving machinery has been driven. These machines require only the attendance of females, but a few years since a non-producing class, to turn out immense quantities of textile fabrics...[With] every extension of national territory, the New England States gained a larger market for their wares, while the foreign competing supply has been restricted by high duties on imports."

— Thomas Kettell, Southern Wealth and Northern Profits, 1860

9. According to the author, the New England states were environmentally suited for manufacturing due to their

(A) Abundant coal supplies.

(B) Mountainous and barren soil.

(C) Ability to harness moving water as an energy source.

(D) Natural tendency towards cotton production.

10. Southern discontent with federal support for "high duties on imports" is evidence of which of the following continuities in American history?

(A) Debates over interpretations of the Constitution.

(B) Debates over federalism and states' rights.

(C) Debates over presidential authority.

(D) Debates over civil liberties found in the Bill of Rights.

Question 11 refers to the following image.

Samuel F. B. Morse plaque on First Telegraph Office, Washington D.C.
(*http://en.wikipedia.org/wiki/Samuel_Morse#mediaviewer/File:Samuel_Morse_plaque.jpg*)

11. As a result of the invention described in the image above,

    (A) transcontinental transportation was possible.
    (B) regional tensions diminished.
    (C) communication lines linked major metropolitan centers across the country.
    (D) slavery became less profitable.

DIFFICULTY LEVEL 3

12. Between 1790 and 1830, which of the following transportation developments opened the West to settlement and trade between 1790 and 1830?

    (A) Roads and canals.
    (B) Steamships and railroads.
    (C) Railroads and canals.
    (D) Automobiles and railroads.

13. Why did Andrew Jackson veto the Maysville Road bill of 1830?

    (A) He opposed transportation developments.
    (B) He supported state and local funding for internal improvements.
    (C) He wanted the federal government to focus on providing land grants for railroad companies.
    (D) He held stock in the leading canal contracting corporation.

14. During the 1830s, Cherokee efforts to retain their tribal lands in Georgia received support from

    (A) Residents of Georgia.
    (B) The United States Supreme Court.
    (C) President Andrew Jackson.
    (D) The United States Congress.

PART C

DIFFICULTY LEVEL 1

1. Why did President Thomas Jefferson purchase the Louisiana Territory from France?

    (A) It opened the Mississippi river permanently to western farmers.

    (B) It ended the threat of American Indian raids on western settlements.

    (C) It forced British troops out of the frontier.

    (D) It renewed the Alliance Treaty of 1778.

2. The main purpose of the Monroe Doctrine of 1823 was to

    (A) encourage Latin American revolutions.

    (B) rule out United States involvement in South America.

    (C) provide a warning to European nations against further colonial ventures in the Western Hemisphere.

    (D) encourage Spain to retake its former colonies.

3. In the 1840s, the view that the United States had the God-given right to expand across North America was called

    (A) Divine Right.

    (B) isolationism.

    (C) Manifest Destiny.

    (D) imperialism.

4. Why did Spain sell Florida to the United States in 1819?

   (A) Spain wanted to help America rival Britain in North America.

   (B) Spain could not defend the area and would have lost it.

   (C) Spain received America's promise to give up claims to Oregon.

   (D) The United States had recently defeated Mexico in a war.

5. Which of the following is true about the Monroe Doctrine?

   (A) It reaffirmed George Washington's goal of United States neutrality.

   (B) It secured the presidency for Secretary of State John Quincy Adams in 1824.

   (C) It established the United States colonies in South America.

   (D) It provided the basis for resolving Anglo-American border disputes in North America.

6. How did the United States take possession of the Oregon Territory?

   (A) The United States was granted the territory in a post-war treaty with Britain.

   (B) The United States bought it from the Native Americans.

   (C) The United States bought it from France.

   (D) Great Britain ceded it to the United States as part of a negotiated treaty.

Questions 7-9 refer to the map below.

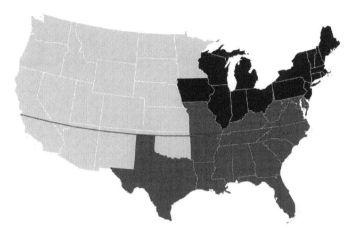

Congress discussed extension of the Missouri Compromise Line westward during the Texas Annexation in 1845, during the Compromise of 1850, and as part of the proposed Crittenden Compromise in 1860, but the line never reached the Pacific. States in RED allowed slavery as of 1850 and states in BLUE prohibited slavery.
(*http://en.wikipedia.org/wiki/Missouri_Compromise#mediaviewer/File:Missouri_Compromise_Line.svg*)

7. Based on the map above, historians might conclude that by the mid-nineteenth century,

    (A) the United States had abolished slavery.
    (B) members of Congress generally agreed about the status of slavery in the United States.
    (C) the United States was becoming increasingly divided over the issue of slavery.
    (D) the North was actively promoting the expansion of slavery.

8. Which of the following resulted in the 36°-30' line of demarcation shown in the map?

    (A) Texas's annexation into the United States.
    (B) The Webster-Ashburton Treaty.

(C) The Missouri Compromise.

(D) The Louisiana Purchase.

9. In 1819, why was the South was becoming increasingly concerned about the fate of slavery in the nation?

(A) The Senate was under Northern control.

(B) Abolitionists had won seats in the House of Representatives.

(C) European nations had been forbidden to engage in the slave trade.

(D) Relative to the North, the South was falling behind in population and wealth.

Questions 10-13 refer to the following quotation.

"This momentous question like a fire-bell in the night, awakened and filled me with terror. I considered it at once as the knell of the Union. It is hushed, indeed, for the moment. But this is a reprieve only, not a final sentence. A geographical line, coinciding with a marked principle, moral and political, once conceived and held up to the angry passions of men, will never be obliterated; and every new irritation will mark it deeper and deeper.... But as it is, we have the wolf by the ears, and we can neither hold him, nor safely let him go. Justice is in one scale, and self-preservation in the other."

— Thomas Jefferson, Letter to John Holmes, 1820

10. Jefferson's letter above was written in response to

(A) the Emancipation Proclamation.

(B) passage of the Missouri Compromise.

(C) the War of 1812.

(D) the Indian Removal Act.

11. Jefferson's letter can best be understood in the context of

(A) state efforts to remove Native American populations.

(B) Manifest Destiny.

(C) debates over the expansion of slavery.

(D) concerns about federal funding for the American System.

Question 12 refers to the excerpt below.

"Our ... destiny [is] to overspread the continent allotted by Providence for the free development of our yearly multiply millions ... The Anglo-Saxon foot is already on [California's] borders. Already the advance guard of the irresistible army of Anglo-Saxon emigration has begun to pour down upon it, armed with the [plow] and the rifle, and marking its trail with schools and colleges, courts and representative halls, mills, and meeting houses. A population will soon be in actual occupation of California ... Their right to independence will be the natural right of self-government belonging to any community strong enough to maintain it."

— John L. O'Sullivan, 1845

12. The ideas expressed in the passage above most clearly show the influence of which of the following?

   (A) Models of limited government inherent in the *Articles of Confederation.*
   (B) Beliefs in separation of powers articulated in the *United States Constitution.*
   (C) Concerns about foreign alliances expressed in Washington's *Farewell Address.*
   (D) Concepts of republican self-rule found in the *Declaration of Independence.*

Question 13 refers to the map below.

States and Territories of the United States of America
November 10 1842 to March 3 1845

13. The map above is best understood in the context of which of the following developments in the United States in the mid-1840s.

    (A) Several boundary disputes between the United States and other nations.
    (B) The expansion of slavery to Northern states.
    (C) The successful annexation of Alaska.
    (D) Debates over slavery in the Mexican Cession.

DIFFICULTY LEVEL 3

14. Jefferson's purchase of the Louisiana faced domestic opposition because it

    (A) removed the French from forts along the Mississippi Valley.
    (B) was designed to expand slavery.
    (C) violated strict constructions of the United States Constitution.
    (D) demonstrated friendship with Britain in the Napoleonic Wars.

15. Opposition to the idea of Manifest Destiny would most likely have come from

    (A) Supporters of James K. Polk in the 1844 presidential election.
    (B) Supporters of the Treaty of Guadalupe-Hidalgo of 1848.
    (C) Supporters of the abolitionist movement.
    (D) Supporters of the Ostend Manifesto calling for annexation of Cuba.

Period 1800-1848

Period 1844-1877

PART A

DIFFICULTY LEVEL 1

1. The Homestead Act was designed to

   (A) raise government revenue.

   (B) conserve natural resources.

   (C) guarantee shipments for the railroads.

   (D) promote frontier settlement.

2. The Gold Rush of the 1840s and 1850s, along with the development of the mining frontier, resulted in

   (A) bringing law and order to the West.

   (B) attracting population to the West.

   (C) influencing the government to continue the gold standard.

   (D) bringing prosperity to the Native American populations.

DIFFICULTY LEVEL 2

3. Which transcendentalist defended his refusal to pay taxes to support the Mexican War in his "Essay on Civil Disobedience"?

   (A) Herman Melville.

   (B) Henry David Thoreau.

   (C) Ralph Waldo Emerson.

   (D) Nathaniel Hawthorne.

4. What were the terms of the Treaty of Guadalupe-Hidalgo, which ended the Mexican-American War?

   (A) The United States promised to respect Mexican sovereignty.
   (B) The United States ceded Texas and Oklahoma.
   (C) The United States agreed to prohibit slavery in the southwest.
   (D) The United States gained the territories of New Mexico and Upper California.

5. The platform of the American Party, or Know-Nothing party, in the 1850s was

   (A) nativism.
   (B) popular sovereignty.
   (C) abolitionism.
   (D) Manifest Destiny.

6. The targets of the Know-Nothing party in the 1850s were primarily

   (A) Freemasons.
   (B) Irish and German immigrants.
   (C) Republicans.
   (D) Slaveholders.

7. During the nineteenth century, all of the following were true of railroad expansion EXCEPT

   (A) It opened new territories to westward settlement.
   (B) It led to the rise of new cities in the Midwest and West.
   (C) Government played little or no role in the process.
   (D) It led to the near extinction of the American bison.

8. All of the following encouraged Westward settlement during the mid-1800s EXCEPT the

   (A) Homestead Act.
   (B) Dawes Act.
   (C) Transcontinental Railroad.
   (D) Morrill Land Grant Act.

Questions 9-10 refer to the excerpt below.

I propose in this letter to present such considerations as seem to me pertinent and feasible, in favor of the speedy construction of a railroad, connecting at some point our eastern network of railways with the waters of the Pacific ocean. . . . The social, moral, and intellectual blessings of a Pacific railroad can hardly be glanced at within the limits of an article. Suffice it for the present that I merely suggest them.... Our mails are now carried to and from California by steamships, via Panama, in twenty to thirty days, starting once a fortnight. The average time of transit from writers throughout the Atlantic states to their correspondents on the Pacific exceeds thirty days. With a Pacific railroad, this would be reduced to ten; for the letters written in Illinois or Michigan would reach their destinations in the mining counties of California quicker than letters sent from New York or Philadelphia would reach San Francisco. With a daily mail by railroad from each of our Atlantic cities to and from California, it is hardly possible that the amount of both letters and printed matter transmitted, and consequently of postage, should not be speedily quadrupled. . . .

— Horace Greeley, An Overland Journey from New York to San Francisco, in The Summer of 1859, C. M. Saxton, Barker & Co., 1860.

9. This article can be best understood in the context of Abraham Lincoln's passage of

   (A) The Morrill Land Grant Act.
   (B) The Chinese Exclusion Act.
   (C) The Pacific Railroad Acts.
   (D) The Emancipation Proclamation.

10. Which of the following was a long-term consequence of the action Horace Greely is describing in the passage above?

   (A) The Chinese Exclusion Act.
   (B) The forcible takeover of Native American lands.
   (C) The Homestead Act.
   (D) The Spanish-American War.

Questions 11-12 refer to the song below.

> The Mexicans are on our soil,
> In war they wish us to embroil ;
> They've tried their best and worst to vex us
> By murdering our brave men in Texas.
> Chorus — We're on our way to Rio Grande,
> On our way to Rio Grande,
> On our way to Rio Grande,
> And with arms they'll find us handy.

— "On our Way to Rio Grande," George Washington Dixon, 1846.

11. The song above can be understood in the context of

(A) Manifest Destiny.

(B) Texas independence.

(C) The Mexican War.

(D) All of the above.

12. One political consequence of the Mexican War (1846-48) discussed in the song above was

(A) territorial acquisitions in the Pacific Northwest.

(B) growing restriction on immigration.

(C) a nation women's suffrage amendment.

(D) a debate over the necessity of the war.

Questions 13-14 refer to the following excerpt.

Arrived at Bannack, and now my friends, I suppose you want to hear what I've to say about this place. Well, I would now stop, if it was not for your gratification for that alone, [1] will I continue my narrative, which is already too long. My greatest difficulty has been to condense and shorten my journal. The half is not told, only the particular event of each day. We are thankful to our Heavenly Father that he has brought us safe to our journey's end. Many were attacked by Indians just before and after us. From the time we left Ft Larimie till we reached Black Foot we never even saw one. A few persons were killed, and other wounded and much stock run off – - But enough of this -. We are now camped on " Yankee Flats ", the part of Bannack lying on the South and west bank of Grass Hopper ;- on the other side is Bannack proper, where the stores, hotels and shops are kept. One half mile down in the canon is another village, called Marysville , but also belonging to Bannack. At this latter place are the quartz mills, and on the mountains are the leads of gold.

— The Diary of Kate Dunlap, 1864-65.

13. The ideas expressed in the excerpt above reflect which of the following continuities in United States history?

    (A) Individuals challenging authority figures in government.
    (B) The role of Christianity in the lives of Americans.
    (C) Battles between business interests and conservationists over unspoiled wilderness.
    (D) The conflict between Native Americans and white settlers in the West.

14. The excerpt above best serves as evidence of which of the following?

    (A) Mining towns developed out West as a result of the discovery of precious metals and minerals.
    (B) African Americans increasingly found more economic opportunities in the United States.
    (C) Conflict between Native Americans and white settlers resulted in a halt to westward settlement.
    (D) The Civil War disrupted westward expansion.

Questions 15-16 refer to the following excerpt.

The issue of yesterday's News, containing the following dispatch, created considerable of a sensation in this city, particularly among the Thirdsters and others who participated in the recent campaign and the battle on Sand creek:

Washington, December 20, 1864

"The affair at Fort Lyon, Colorado, in which Colonel Chivington destroyed a large Indian village, and all its inhabitants, is to be made the subject of congressional investigation. Letters received from high officials in Colorado say that the Indians were killed after surrendering, and that a large proportion of them were women and children."

Indignation was loudly and unequivocally expressed, and some less considerate of the boys were very persistent in their inquiries as to who those "high officials" were, with a mild intimation that they had half a mind to "go for them." This talk about "friendly Indians" and a "surrendered" village will do to "tell to marines," but to us out here it is all bosh.

— "The Fort Lyon Affair," editorial from *Rocky Mountain News*, 1864

15. The newspaper editorial above is best understood in the context of

    (A) debates over federal supremacy and states' rights.

    (B) debates about whether to expand to new territories.

    (C) the desirability of going to war with Mexico.

    (D) a sense of American cultural and racial superiority over Native Americans.

16. The excerpt quoted above would be most helpful to historians analyzing the

    (A) public response to the Sand Creek Massacre.

    (B) U.S. government interaction and conflict with American Indians.

    (C) attempts to assimilate Native Americans.

    (D) western fronts in the Civil War.

DIFFICULTY LEVEL 3

17. Which of the following is true about the Mexican government's policies toward the United States in the 19th century?

    (A) It favored annexation of Texas by the United States.

    (B) It tried to sell Texas to the United States after the Louisiana Purchase.

    (C) It encouraged American settlement in Texas in the 1820s and early 1830s.

    (D) It encouraged Texas independence in the mid-1830s.

PART B

DIFFICULTY LEVEL 1

1. John Brown's intended goal in raiding Harpers Ferry was to

    (A) retaliate against the South for the *Dred Scott* decision.

    (B) provoke a slave rebellion.

    (C) force the North and South to compromise on the slavery issue.

    (D) overthrow the federal government.

DIFFICULTY LEVEL 2

2. As a result of the Compromise of 1850, the questions of slavery in the territories of New Mexico and Utah would be determined by

    (A) Popular sovereignty.

    (B) A national election.

    (C) Congressional legislation.

    (D) A Supreme Court decision.

3. Most Northerners disliked which of the following provisions of the Compromise of 1850?

    (A) Slavery in the District of Columbia.

    (B) The new Fugitive Slave Law.

    (C) Settlement of the Texas-New Mexico boundary dispute.

    (D) California's admission as a free state.

4. What impact did Harriet Beecher Stowe's book *Uncle Tom's Cabin* have on Northern readers?

    (A) They opposed its exaggerated portrayal of slavery's horrors.
    (B) They threatened to secede from the union.
    (C) They opposed enforcement of the new Fugitive Slave Law.
    (D) They joined the Republican Party.

5. During the 1850s, the main plank of the Republican Party platform involved

    (A) Limiting immigration.
    (B) Halting the spread of slavery.
    (C) Abolishing slavery.
    (D) Promoting secession.

6. Which of the following groups supported the Supreme Court's decision in *Dred Scott v. Sandford*?

    (A) abolitionists.
    (B) Republicans.
    (C) popular-sovereignty proponents.
    (D) proslavery southerners.

7. Which of the following was a major issue of Lincoln-Douglas debates for Illinois' Senate seat?

    (A) Southern secession.
    (B) Expansion of slavery.
    (C) *Uncle Tom's Cabin.*
    (D) Senator Crittendon's Compromise.

8. As a result of Stephen A. Douglas's "Freeport Doctrine," concerning the legislative action banning slavery in the territories,

   (A) he won support from abolitionists.

   (B) he angered proslavery southerners.

   (C) Lincoln dropped out of the Senate race.

   (D) Congress reopened the Atlantic slave trade.

Questions 9-10 refer to the following excerpt.

"If we could first know where we are and whither we are tending, we could better judge what to do and how to do it. We are now far into the fifth year since a policy was initiated with the avowed object and confident promise of putting an end to slavery agitation. Under the operation of that policy, that agitation has not only not ceased but has constantly augmented. In my opinion, it will not cease until a crisis shall have been reached and passed. "A house divided against itself cannot stand." I believe this government cannot endure, permanently, half slave and half free. I do not expect the Union to be dissolved; I do not expect the house to fall; but I do expect it will cease to be divided. It will become all one thing, or all the other. Either the opponents of slavery will arrest the further spread of it and place it where the public mind shall rest in the belief that it is in the course of ultimate extinction, or its advocates will push it forward till it shall become alike lawful in all the states, old as well as new, North as well as South."

— Abraham Lincoln, "A House Divided" speech, 1858

9. The excerpt above was most likely written in response to

   (A) the *Dred Scott* decision.

   (B) the Compromise of 1850.

   (C) the Missouri Compromise.

   (D) John Brown's raid on Harpers Ferry.

10. Which of the following events during the 1860s would compare most closely to the ideas expressed in the excerpt?

(A) The secession of Southern states.

(B) The Election of 1860.

(C) The Emancipation Proclamation.

(D) The Thirteenth Amendment to the Constitution.

Questions 11-13 refer to the following map.

Presidential electoral votes by state,1860.

11. The election results depicted in the map most likely resulted from

(A) Northern dissatisfaction with the Democratic President James Buchanan.

(B) Southern fears that Republican candidate Abraham Lincoln would abolish slavery.

(C) Southern beliefs that Stephen Douglas best represented their interests.

(D) Widespread dissatisfaction with Republicans in the West.

12. As a result of Abraham Lincoln's victory in the presidential election of 1860,

(A) Democrat Andrew Johnson became Vice President.

(B) South Carolina seceded from the United States.

(C) John Brown was executed for treason.

(D) Abraham Lincoln was assassinated.

13. Following the presidential election of 1860, what was Abraham Lincoln's principal goal for his presidency?

(A) To go to war with the Confederacy.

(B) To free the slaves.

(C) To preserve the Union.

(D) To resign from the presidency after two years.

Questions 14-16 refer to the following excerpt.

Published under such auspices, the [Hinton Helper's] 'Impending Crisis' became at once an authoritative exposition of the principles of the Republican party. The original, as well as a compendium, were circulated by hundreds of thousands, North, South, East, and West. No book could be better calculated for the purpose of intensifying the mutual hatred between the North and the South. This book, in the first place, proposes to abolish slavery in the slaveholding States by exciting a revolution among those called 'the poor whites,' against their rich slaveholding neighbors. To accomplish this purpose, every appeal which perverse ingenuity and passionate malignity could suggest, was employed to excite jealousy and hatred between these two classes. The cry of the poor against the rich, the resort of demagogues in all ages, was echoed and reechoed.... Mr. Helper proceeds to still greater extremities, and exclaims: 'But, sirs, slaveholders, chevaliers, and lords of the lash, we are unwilling to allow you to cheat the negroes out of all the rights and claims to which, as human beings, they are most sacredly entitled. Not alone for ourself as an individual, but for others also, particularly for five or six millions of southern non-slaveholding whites, whom your iniquitous Statism has debarred from almost all the mental and material comforts of life, do we speak, when we say, you must sooner or later emancipate your slaves, and pay each and every one of them at least sixty dollars cash in hand.'

James Buchanan, Mr. Buchanan's Administration on the Eve of Rebellion, 1866.

14. Which of the following most directly supports the assertion expressed in the excerpt above?

(A) Attempts by Abraham Lincoln to abolish slavery.

(B) The defense of slavery by Southerners as a positive good.

(C) The intensified sectionalism of the 1850s.

(D) The increase in slave rebellions in the 1850s.

15. The excerpt above was most likely a response to which of the following historical trends?

(A) The rise of minstrel shows in the South.

(B) Regional economic and demographic changes between the North and South.

(C) The emergence of the Republican Party.

(D) The growing importance of the abolitionist movement.

16. What was Buchanan's most likely purpose for writing the excerpt above?

    (A) To acknowledge culpability in failing to prevent the outbreak of war.

    (B) To deflect criticism against his administration.

    (C) To credit Hinton Helper for the abolition of slavery.

    (D) To discredit Abraham Lincoln's preservation of the Union.

DIFFICULTY LEVEL 3

17. Stephen A. Douglas's Kansas-Nebraska Act required repeal of the

    (A) Gag Rule.

    (B) Fugitive Slave Act.

    (C) Northwest Ordinance.

    (D) Missouri Compromise.

18. With the publication of *The Liberator*, William Lloyd Garrison and his fellow abolitionists advocated

    (A) radicalism.

    (B) moral suasion.

    (C) violent resistance.

    (D) colonization.

19. During the Panic of 1857, the South

    (A) suffered very little.

    (B) saw the weakness of its economic system.

    (C) supported government gifts of homesteads.

    (D) moved toward manufacturing.

PART C

DIFFICULTY LEVEL 1

1. As a result of sharecropping, the crop lien system, and tenant farming in the South after the Civil War,

    (A) land ownership was equal among whites and blacks.

    (B) cotton became less significant in the South.

    (C) freedmen were stuck in cycles of debt.

    (D) northern bankers increased loans to the South.

DIFFICULTY LEVEL 2

2. In 1861, why did Abraham Lincoln take the North to war against the Confederacy?

    (A) To end slavery.

    (B) To preserve the union.

    (C) To exact vengeance on the South.

    (D) To prevent a Southern invasion of the North.

3. At the outbreak of the Civil War, the North's advantages over the South included all of the following EXCEPT

    (A) more experienced generals.

    (B) more substantial industrial resources.

    (C) dominance in foreign trade.

    (D) naval supremacy.

4. How did President Lincoln control public opinion during the Civil War?

   (A) He disbanded Congress.
   (B) He suspended the writ of habeas corpus and applied martial law in critical areas.
   (C) He prohibited all free elections during the war.
   (D) He sent all dissenters to the South.

5. What effect did the Emancipation Proclamation have on the Civil War?

   (A) It abolished slavery.
   (B) It ended the Civil War.
   (C) It freed slaves held in the Border States.
   (D) It strengthened the moral cause and military strength of the Union.

6. After the Civil War, both President Lincoln's and President Johnson's plans for Reconstruction aimed to

   (A) punish the South for causing the Civil War.
   (B) grant equal voting rights for both white and black males in the South.
   (C) provide economic aid to rebuild the South.
   (D) encourage swift readmission of ex-Confederate states into the Union.

7. During Reconstruction, Radical Republicans in Congress implemented all of the following programs EXCEPT

   (A) providing 40 acres to each freedman.
   (B) enacting the 14th amendment.
   (C) military occupation of the South.
   (D) punishment of the Confederate leaders.

8. During Reconstruction, what was a carpetbagger?

   (A) A white Southern Republicans.
   (B) Southern white Democrats who moved North.
   (C) African Americans who took advantage of the Homestead Act.
   (D) Northerners who came to the South to benefit economically.

9. Why did Congressional Reconstruction end in 1877?

(A) African Americans no long needed federal protection of civil rights.

(B) It was part of a compromise to resolve the disputed election of 1876.

(C) The Supreme Court struck down Congressional acts.

(D) The Union army had succeeded in dismantling the Ku Klux Klan.

Questions 10-11 refer to the excerpt below.

"With malice toward none, with charity for all, with firmness in the right as God gives us to see the right, let us strive on to finish the work we are in, to bind up the nation's wounds, to care for him who shall have borne this battle for his widow and orphans, to do all which may achieve and cherish a just and lasting peace among ourselves and all nations."

— Abraham Lincoln, Second Inaugural Address, 1865

10. Which of the following provides evidence for the sentiment expressed in the above excerpt?

    (A) Emancipation Proclamation.

    (B) Ten Percent Plan.

    (C) Freedman's Bureau.

    (D) Reconstruction Act of 1867.

11. Which of the following Reconstruction proposals most closely resembles the Lincoln's approach expressed in the excerpt?

    (A) Military Reconstruction Act of 1877.

    (B) Civil Rights Act of 1866.

    (C) Johnson's Amnesty Plan.

    (D) Fifteenth Amendment.

Questions 12-15 refer to the following Reconstruction-Era Amendments.

Amendment 13

Section 1.
Neither slavery nor involuntary servitude, except as a punishment for crime whereof the party shall have been duly convicted, shall exist within the United States, or any place subject to their jurisdiction.

Amendment 14

Section 1.
All persons born or naturalized in the United States, and subject to the jurisdiction thereof, are citizens of the United States and of the state wherein they reside. No state shall make or enforce any law which shall abridge the privileges or immunities of citizens of the United States; nor shall any state deprive any person of life, liberty, or property, without due process of law; nor deny to any person within its jurisdiction the equal protection of the laws.

Amendment 15

Section 1.
The right of citizens of the United States to vote shall not be denied or abridged by the United States or by any state on account of race, color, or previous condition of servitude.

Section 2.
The Congress shall have power to enforce this article by appropriate legislation.

12. What was the immediate result of these amendments to the Unites States Constitution?

    (A) African Americans remained slaves.

    (B) African Americans had new opportunities to serve in public office.

    (C) African Americans left the South in large numbers.

    (D) African Americans purchased land from their former owners.

13. Which of the following groups was most disappointed by the passage of the Fifteenth Amendment?

   (A) Freed slaves.
   (B) Northern whites.
   (C) Abolitionists.
   (D) Advocates of women's rights.

14. Why did Republican members of Congress require Southern states to ratify the Fourteenth Amendment before gaining readmission to the Union?

   (A) To protect the Black Codes passed by Southern states.
   (B) To prevent the South from practicing racial discrimination.
   (C) To ensure that Southern states would agree to enter the Union.
   (D) To gain Southern support for the Republican Party.

15. Which of the following was the main cause behind the creation of the Ku Klux Klan in 1865?

   (A) The admittance of Southern states back into the Union.
   (B) The fact that the South had lost the Civil War.
   (C) The election of Ulysses Grant.
   (D) The increased government support of African American civil rights.

Questions 16-17 refer to the following excerpts.

"The late war between two acknowledged belligerents...broke all the ties that bound them together. The future condition of the conquered power depends on the will of the conqueror. They must come in as new states or remain as conquered provinces. Congress . . . is the only power that can act in the matter. Congress alone can do it. . . . Congress must create States and declare when they are entitled to be represented. Then each House must judge whether the members presenting themselves from a recognized State possess the requisite qualifications of age, residence, and citizenship; and whether the election and returns are according to law."

— Thaddeus Stevens, speech in the House of Representatives, 1865

"As eleven States are not at this time represented in either branch of Congress, it would seem to be [the President's] duty on all proper occasions to present their just claims to

Congress…[I]f they are all excluded from Congress, if in a permanent statute they are declared not to be in full constitutional relations to the country, they may think they have cause to become a unit in feeling and sentiment against the Government."

— President Andrew Johnson, 1866

16. The statements of both Stevens and Johnson share the same goal of

(A) Reinstating southern representatives to their seats in Congress.

(B) Reuniting the nation following the Civil War.

(C) Creating a new Constitution to replace the existing one.

(D) Allowing the States to determine their own course of action.

17. The ideas about government expressed by Stevens and Johnson are most consistent with those of which of the following individuals?

(A) Rousseau's ideas about the social contract.

(B) John Locke' belief in natural rights.

(C) Baron de Montesquieu's writings on separation of powers.

(D) Adam Smith's *laissez-faire* approach to government interference in the economy.

Questions 18-21 refer to the following cartoon.

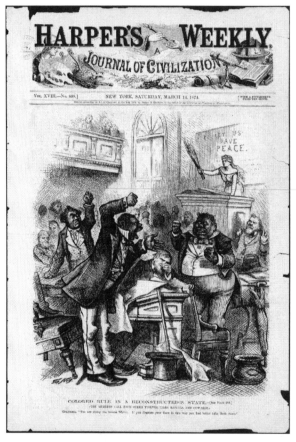

"Colored rule in a reconstructed state," caption for a cartoon showing members of the South Carolina Legislature in argument in the House, with Columbia rebuking them. Woodcut illustration in *Harper's Weekly*, 1874 March 14, page 229. (*http://upload.wikimedia.org/wikipedia/commons/2/29/Colored_rule_in_a_reconstructed_state.jpg*)

18. The image above is best understood in the context of

(A) passage of the Fifteenth Amendment.

(B) the crop lien system.

(C) the Emancipation Proclamation.

(D) the Reconstruction Acts of 1867.

19. The cartoon above provides evidence that white Southerners

(A) favored a stronger national government.

(B) opposed the Jim Crow legal system.

(C) disliked the Reconstruction programs of the Republicans.

(D) led efforts to advance civil rights.

20. Which of the following best supports the argument, "Although important strides were made, Reconstruction failed to provide lasting guarantees of the civil rights of the freedmen"?

(A) passage of Jim Crow laws in the latter part of the 19th century.

(B) refusal of Southern States to allow sharecropping.

(C) ratification of the 13th, 14th, and 15th amendments.

(D) passage of the Civil Rights Acts of 1866.

21. As a result of the Southern ideas reflected in the above image, Southern states passed poll taxes and literacy tests to

(A) extend suffrage to women and 18-year-old citizens.

(B) raise money for political campaigns.

(C) deny African Americans the right to vote.

(D) prevent immigrants from becoming citizens.

Questions 22-23 refer to the following excerpt.

CHAPTER LIX. An Act to amend an Act entitled an Act to establish a Code of Criminal Procedure for the State of Texas, approved August 26th, 1866, and to repeal certain portions thereof.

SECTION Be it enacted by the Legislature of the State of Texas, That Article 143 of the above named Code, be so amended as to hereafter read as follows : . . .

3rd. Persons of color shall not testify, except where the prosecution is against a person who is a person of color ; or where the offence is charged to have been committed against the person or property of a person of color. . . .

CHAPTER LXXX. An Act regulating Contracts for Labor.

SECTION Be it enacted by the Legislature of the State of Texas, That all persons desirous of engaging as laborers for a period of one year or less, may do so under the following regulations : All contracts for labor for a longer period than one month shall be made in writing, and in the presence of a Justice of the peace, County Judge, County Clerk, Notary Public, or two disinterested witnesses, in whose presence the contract shall be read to the laborers, and, when assented to, shall be signed in triplicate b both parties, and shall then be considered binding, for the time therein prescribed.

Texas Black Codes, 1866 (*The American Black Codes, 1865-1866,*
http://home.gwu.edu/~jjhawkin/BlackCodes/BlackCodes.htm)

22. Which of the following groups would most likely oppose the legislation above?

   (A) Members of the Republican Party.
   (B) The Supreme Court justices.
   (C) New international migrants.
   (D) Supporters of slavery.

23. The legislation above is best understood in the context of

   (A) American exceptionalism.
   (B) changing relationships between the states and the federal government.
   (C) Southern secession.
   (D) Southern resistance to the abolition of slavery.

DIFFICULTY LEVEL 3

24. During the Civil War, what was meant by King Cotton diplomacy?

   (A) Attempts to annex land south of the Rio Grande.

(B) Southern efforts to win British support for the Confederacy.

(C) Ongoing trade between the Confederacy and Northern "Copperheads."

(D) The compromise that led to the admission of Missouri to the Union as a slave state.

25. After a series of early Union defeats, Lincoln feared that

(A) The Union might run out of money.

(B) European nations might recognize Southern independence.

(C) California would secede.

(D) Military recruitment would become more difficult.

26. Why was President Andrew Johnson impeached?

(A) He vetoed the Civil Rights Act of 1866.

(B) He refused to support the Thirteenth Amendment.

(C) He removed a Radical Republican from his cabinet.

(D) He attempted to break up the Republican Party.

Period 1865-1898

PART A

DIFFICULTY LEVEL 1

1. Under the leadership of Samuel Gompers, the American Federation of Labor organized

   (A) skilled workers to achieve "pure and simple" gains.
   (B) skilled and unskilled workers to fight for social justice.
   (C) unskilled workers along industrial lines.
   (D) workers into a new Populist Party.

2. Which of the following individuals was the most influential American investment banker in the late nineteenth and early twentieth centuries?

   (A) Jay Gould.
   (B) J. P. Morgan.
   (C) Cornelius Vanderbilt.
   (D) James Hill.

3. What was the main cause of urbanization in the nineteenth century?

   (A) completion of the Transcontinental Railroad.
   (B) internal migration from rural areas.
   (C) natural reproduction among urban families.
   (D) industrial expansion.

4. Social Darwinists advocated which of the following?

   (A) federal enforcement of business regulations.

   (B) relief for the unemployed.

   (C) a minimum wage.

   (D) a laissez-faire approach to business regulation.

DIFFICULTY LEVEL 2

5. During the late nineteenth century, the American labor movement was

   (A) allied with the Republican party.

   (B) confined to factory workers.

   (C) protected by federal laws.

   (D) involved in a number of violent strikes.

6. The formation of trusts, pools, and holding companies in American industry that occurred at the end of the nineteenth century was primarily a response to

   (A) economic competition.

   (B) high tariffs.

   (C) powerful labor unions.

   (D) federal monetary policy.

7. Which of the following was the first major union to welcome African Americans, women, and immigrants into its ranks?

   (A) American Federation of Labor.

   (B) Industrial Workers of the World.

   (C) International Ladies Garment Workers Union.

   (D) Knights of Labor.

8. During the late nineteenth century, a period in the United States known as the Gilded Age, the American economy was characterized by all of the following EXCEPT

(A) acceptance of labor unions.

(B) advances in technology.

(C) a growing gap between rich and poor.

(D) business combinations such as trusts and holding companies.

Questions 9-10 refer to the image below.

1869 poster advertising Transcontinental Railroad.
(*http://commons.wikimedia.org/wiki/File:TranscontinentalPoster.jpg*)

9. The purpose of the poster above was to

(A) Persuade people to travel West via rail line.

(B) Promote Manifest Destiny.

(C) To promote international migration.

(D) Attract workers for the Transcontinental Railroad.

10. The event depicted in the poster above resulted in

(A) genocide against of Native Americans.

(B) The expansion of American industry.

(C) The industrialization of the South.

(D) A decrease in urbanization.

Questions 11-13 refer to the image below.

Political cartoon by Grant Hamilton, 1896, satirizing William Jennings Bryan's 'Cross of Gold' speech at the Democratic National Convention in Chicago, which won Bryan the presidential nomination.

11. The cartoon above is best understood in the context of which of the following trends?

    (A) Increased demand for farm products in Europe.

    (B) The ability of perishable farm products to be shipped east in refrigerated railroad cars.

    (C) The appropriation of Indian land by white settlers.

    (D) The decline in farm prices due to the mechanization of agriculture.

12. Which of the following was a major contrast between supporters of Populist Party and the intended audience of the cartoon above?

    (A) Populists believed that labor unions should be illegal.

    (B) Populists believed that the government should take a strong role in regulating the American economy.

    (C) Populists believed that land grants to railroad companies were a good idea.

    (D) Populists generally supported child labor.

13. The rise and fall of the Populist Party in American politics demonstrates which of the following continuities in United States history?

    (A) The tension between federal supremacy and states' rights.

    (B) The growing power of the presidency during the twentieth century.

    (C) The failure of third parties, or minor political parties, to win national elections.

    (D) The success of labor movements in the late nineteenth century.

Questions 14-15 are based on the excerpt below.

The problem of our age is the proper administration of wealth, so that the ties of brotherhood may still bind together the rich and poor in harmonious relationship. The conditions of human life have not only been changed, but revolutionized, within the past few hundred years. In former days there was little difference between the dwelling, dress, food, and environment of the chief and those of his retainers.... The contrast between the palace of the millionaire and the cottage of the laborer with us today measures the change which has come with civilization.

This change, however, is not to be deplored, but welcomed as highly beneficial. It is well, nay, essential for the progress of the race, that the houses of some should be homes for all that is highest and best in literature and the arts, and for all the refinements of civilization, rather than that none should be so. Much better this great irregularity than universal squalor.

— Andrew Carnegie, "The Gospel of Wealth," 1889

14. The excerpt above is best understood in the context of

(A) The migration of many Americans to cities.

(B) The growing wealth gap in the United States.

(C) Changes in federal legislation that aided economic growth.

(D) The influx of new international migrants.

15. As a result of the ideas expressed in this excerpt,

(A) Carnegie endowed many public libraries.

(B) the federal government abandoned laissez-faire policies.

(C) socialism became a viable alternative to capitalism.

(D) Carnegie closed his steel mills.

Question 16 is based on the image below.

Rockefeller as an industrial emperor, 1901 cartoon from *Puck* magazine.
(*http://en.wikipedia.org/wiki/John_D._Rockefeller#mediaviewer/File:Jdr-king.JPG*)

16. The cartoon above depicts ideas most consistent with

    (A) Laissez-faire capitalism.
    (B) Social Darwinism.
    (C) Vertical integration.
    (D) All of the above.

DIFFICULTY LEVEL 3

17. Shortly after the Sherman Antitrust was passed in 1890, it was primarily used to

    (A) regulate the railroad industry.
    (B) break up business monopolies.
    (C) protect American industry from foreign competition.
    (D) weaken labor unions.

18. Horatio Alger's novels and short stories of the Gilded Age typically emphasized

    (A) urban pollution.
    (B) "rags to riches" success.
    (C) "pure and simple' unionism.
    (D) conspicuous consumption.

PART B

DIFFICULTY LEVEL 1

1. Which if the following individuals was a prominent leader in the settlement house movement?

   (A) Carry Nation.
   (B) Jane Addams.
   (C) Alice Paul.
   (D) Margaret Sanger.

DIFFICULTY LEVEL 2

2. During the latter half of the nineteenth century, Native Americans and white settlers

   (A) began an extended period of rapprochement.
   (B) renewed their struggle for territory in the Great Plains.
   (C) respected each others' autonomy.
   (D) agreed to set aside territory in Arizona and New Mexico for Native American settlement.

3. What was the intent of the Dawes Severalty Act of 1887?

   (A) To assimilate Native Americans into the mainstream American culture.
   (B) To recognize the tribal cultures of Native Americans.
   (C) To place Native Americans on reservations.
   (D) To restore to Native Americans land seized unjustly.

4. Helen Hunt Jackson's *A Century of Dishonor*, published in 1881, had a significant impact on American history because it exposed

(A) the injustices of the Mexican War.

(B) the plight of sharecroppers.

(C) the federal government's oppressive policies against American Indians.

(D) the hardships endured by Chinese laborers whiled building the Transcontinental Railroad.

5. The federal government's first restrictive immigration policy targeted which of the following groups of international migrants?

(A) Mexicans.

(B) Italians.

(C) Japanese.

(D) Chinese.

6. During the Gilded Age, most international migrants arriving in the United States arrived from

(A) Northern Africa.

(B) Northern and Western Europe.

(C) Southern and Eastern Europe.

(D) Southeast Asia.

7. In the late nineteenth century, urban political machines and city bosses did which of the following?

(A) They became actively involved in the settlement house movement.

(B) They provided some welfare for poor immigrants in exchange for political support.

(C) They encouraged racial integration of residential neighborhoods.

(D) They discouraged railroad and highway construction to prevent people from moving out of urban areas.

Questions 8-9 refer to the song below.

No matter how poor I may be,
No drunkard's home e'er can be mine,
Cold water the one draught for me
I never will drink of the wine;
And maidens, be cautious and wise,
No matter what Miss Grundy thinks,
Old topers and tipplers despise,
And marry no man if he drinks.

— E.A. Parkhurst, "I'll Marry No Man If He Drinks," 1866

8. The sentiment expressed in the song above contributed to

   (A) passage of the Eighteenth Amendment, banning alcohol nationwide.

   (B) formation of the Women's Christian Temperance Union.

   (C) a ban on alcohol consumption in Washington, DC.

   (D) a backlash against premarital sexual intercourse.

9. Which of the following trends resulted in the ideas expressed in the song above?

   (A) sectional conflict.

   (B) a growing middle class.

   (C) an influx of new immigrants.

   (D) the rise of sharecropping and tenant farming.

Questions 10-11 refer to the excerpt below.

Into this favored section of the earth's surface have been introduced ever increasing numbers of the lower classes of foreign nations. What has been their effect upon the prevailing standard of living? As a major premise, it will be granted that the standard of living of the working classes of the United States has been and still is superior to that of the nations which have furnished the bulk of the immigrants.... As regards the new immigrants – those who have come during the last thirty years – the one great reason for their coming is that they believe...they can establish a higher standard than the one to which they have been accustomed. And this wage for which they are willing to sell their labor is in general appreciable below that which the native American workman requires to support his standard.... It means...that the American workman is continually underbid in the labor market by vast numbers of alien laborers....

— Henry P. Fairchild, *Immigration*, 1913

10. The passage above represents which of the following continuities in American history?

    (A) Discrimination against African Americans.
    (B) Hostility toward international migrants to America.
    (C) The gradual expansion of democracy in the United States.
    (D) The violation of treaties with Native Americans.

11. The arguments made in the passage above are most similar to those made by

    (A) Federalists in the 1790s.
    (B) supporters of Manifest Destiny in the 1840s.
    (C) labor unions in the 1890s.
    (D) advocates for equal pay for women in the 1970s.

Question 12 refers to the cartoon below.

— A cartoon in *Puck* magazine from 1888 attacked businessmen for welcoming large numbers of low paid immigrants, leaving the American men unemployed. (*http://upload.wikimedia.org/wikipedia/en/3/3a/Immigrants1888.jpg*)

12. The cartoon above best reflects which of the following trends from the late nineteenth century?

   (A) The United States passed restrictive quotas on migrants coming into the country.

   (B) The United States experienced the greatest influx of immigrants in its history.

   (C) The United States banned immigrants from Eastern European countries.

   (D) Anti-Semitism and anti-Catholicism were widespread in the United States.

Questions 13-14 refer to the excerpts below.

Eyewitness Accounts from Wounded Knee Massacre, 1890:

"I did not know then how much was ended. When I look back now from this high hill of my old age, I can still see the butchered women and children lying heaped and scattered all along the crooked gulch as plain as when I saw them with eyes young. And I can see that something else died there in the bloody mud, and was buried in the blizzard. A people's dream died there. It was a beautiful dream ... the nation's hope is broken and scattered. There is no center any longer, and the sacred tree is dead."

— Black Elk, medicine man, Oglala Lakota, 1891.

"General Nelson A. Miles who visited the scene of carnage, following a three day blizzard, estimated that around 300 snow shrouded forms were strewn over the countryside. He also discovered to his horror that helpless children and women with babies in their arms had been chased as far as two miles from the original scene of encounter and cut down without mercy by the troopers. ... Judging by the slaughter on the battlefield it was suggested that the soldiers simply went berserk. For who could explain such a merciless disregard for life? ... As I see it the battle was more or less a matter of spontaneous combustion, sparked by mutual distrust"

— Hugh McGinnis, First Battalion, Co. K, Seventh Cavalry, 1891

13. The actions described in the passages above are best understood in the context of

(A) efforts by the Lakota to escape to Canada.

(B) an armed attack by the Lakota against the United States military.

(C) the Lakota revival of the Ghost Dance.

(D) General Custer's defeat at Little Big Horn.

14. The passages above best serve as evidence of which of the following?

(A) The number of Lakota deaths has been widely exaggerated.

(B) The Lakota were their denied cultural and territorial autonomy.

(C) The American troops were provoked by the Lakota.

(D) The Lakota were a well-armed military force.

DIFFICULTY LEVEL 3

15. In his Frontier Thesis, Frederick Jackson Turner argued that the American frontier had a significant impact on all of the following EXCEPT

(A) new opportunities for Native Americans.

(B) the growth of nationalism.

(C) formation of the American character.

(D) the expansion of American democracy.

PART C

DIFFICULTY LEVEL 2

1. At the turn of the twentieth century, what was the major goal of the Social Gospel movement?

   (A) To gain support for Social Darwinism.
   (B) To draw the attention of Christian churches to the plight of the urban poor.
   (C) To send missionaries overseas to convert people, especially those in East Asia.
   (D) To promote Anglo-Saxon values along the frontier.

2. Public intellectuals such as Walt Whitman and Henry Adams responded to the new industrial civilization by

   (A) Moving to Europe.
   (B) Viewing it as evidence of the continuing progress of the human race.
   (C) Denouncing it as leading to inequality and materialism.
   (D) Admiring it uncritically and optimistically.

3. In the Supreme Court decision *Wabash v. Illinois* (1886), the court ruled that

   (A) only the federal government could regulate interstate commerce.
   (B) "Granger Laws" controlling grain elevators were unconstitutional.
   (C) railroads must submit to public regulation.
   (D) railroad practices like pooling and rebates were constitutional.

Questions 4-6 refer to the excerpt below.

We consider the underlying fallacy of the plaintiff's argument to consist in the assumption that the enforced separation of the two races stamps the colored race with a badge of inferiority. If this be so, it is not by reason of anything found in the act, but solely because the colored race chooses to put that construction upon it....

When the government, therefore, has secured to each of its citizens equal rights before the law, and equal opportunities for improvement and progress, it has accomplished the end for which it was organized, and performed all of the functions respecting social advantages with which it is endowed.' Legislation is powerless to eradicate racial instincts, or to abolish distinctions based upon physical differences, and the attempt to do so can only result in accentuating the difficulties of the present situation. If the civil and political rights of both races be equal, one cannot be inferior to the other civilly or politically. If one race be inferior to the other socially, the constitution of the United States cannot put them upon the same plane....

— *Plessy v. Ferguson* Supreme Court decision, 1896

4. The excerpt above is best understood in the context of

   (A) attempts by Southern states to obstruct the Fifteenth Amendment with poll taxes and literacy tests.

   (B) the establishment of segregationist Jim Crow laws in Southern States.

   (C) the expansion of railroads and other common carriers during the late nineteenth century.

   (D) the denial of full citizenship to African Americans in the *Dred Scott* decision.

5. The excerpt above seems to contradict which of the following amendments to the Constitution?

   (A) Thirteenth Amendment.

   (B) Fourteenth Amendment.

   (C) Fifteenth Amendment.

   (D) First Amendment.

6. Which of the following Supreme Court cases overturned the *Plessy* decision above?

   (A) *Lochner v. New York.*

   (B) *Gideon v. Wainwright.*

   (C) *Brown v. Board of Education.*

   (D) *Miranda v. Arizona.*

"No American travels abroad without blushing for shame for his country on this subject. And whatever the excuse that passes current in the United States, it avails nothing abroad. With all the powers of government in control; with all laws made by white men, administered by white judges, jurors, prosecuting attorneys, and sheriffs; with every office of the executive department filled by white men--no excuse can be offered for exchanging the orderly administration of justice for barbarous lynchings and "unwritten laws." Our country should be placed speedily above the plane of confessing herself a failure at self-government. This cannot be until Americans of every section, of broadest patriotism and best and wisest citizenship, not only see the defect in our country's armor but take the necessary steps to remedy it. Although lynchings have steadily increased in number and barbarity during the last twenty years, there has been no single effort put forth by the many moral and philanthropic forces of the country to put a stop to this wholesale slaughter. Indeed, the silence and seeming condonation grow more marked as the years go by."

— Ida B. Wells-Barnett, "Lynch Law in America," 1900.

Period 1865-1898

7. The excerpt above is best understood in the context of

   (A) African Americans' actively protesting against lynching in the United States.

   (B) high incidences of lynching with little action on behalf of government.

   (C) white lawmakers actively passing anti-lynching laws.

   (D) a decline in lynchings in the United States.

8. Which of the following evidence would best support Wells-Barnett's argument in the excerpt above?

   (A) First-hand accounts of witnesses to lynching.

   (B) A newspaper article reporting on a lynching in a local town.

   (C) Letters written by lawmakers debating the importance of a federal anti-lynching law.

   (D) A graph showing the number of lynchings in the US over a period of time.

Questions 9-10 refer to the following quotation.

"New York is, I firmly believe, the most charitable city in the world. Nowhere is there so eager a readiness to help. When it is known that the help is worthily wanted; nowhere are such armies of devoted workers, nowhere such abundance of means ready to the hand of those who know the need and how rightly to supply it. Its poverty, its slums, and its suffering are the result of unprecedented growth with the consequent disorder and crowding, and the common penalty of metropolitan greatness....The Day Nurseries, the numberless Kindergartens and charitable schools in the poor quarters, the Fresh Air Funds, the thousands and one charities that in one way or another reach the homes and the lives of the poor with sweetening touch..."

— Jacob Riis, How the Other Half Lives, 1890

9. Who carried out many of the reforms described in the passage?

    (A) working-class men.

    (B) labor unions.

    (C) wealthy industrialists.

    (D) middle-class women.

10. The activities described above were most closely associated with which of the following reform movements?

    (A) Social Darwinism.

    (B) The Social Gospel.

    (C) The Gospel of Wealth.

    (D) Populism.

11. Prominent African-American leaders W.E.B. DuBois and Booker T. Washington disagreed over

    (A) which social injustices the federal government should address.
    (B) whether African Americans should emigrate to Africa.
    (C) what role African-American churches should play in the struggle for civil rights.
    (D) whether African-Americans should first seek social or economic equality.

12. During Ulysses S. Grant's Administration, the Whiskey Ring

    (A) Was a network of large whiskey distillers and U.S. Treasury agent who defrauded the government of millions of dollars of excise taxes on liquor.
    (B) Discredited the president but did not result in any convictions.
    (C) Revealed the president's own alcoholism.
    (D) Involved a network of Department of the Interior officials who cheated Native Americans out of their lands and money.

13. The Crédit Mobilier scandal involved

    (A) A dummy corporation that helped to defraud the U.S. Treasury Department of millions of dollars of excise taxes on tobacco.
    (B) A dummy corporation that shielded illegal or fraudulent purchases and investments by stockholders of the Union Pacific Railroad.
    (C) A bona fide though corrupt French corporation that purchased bankrupt American railroads.
    (D) A bona fide though corrupt French corporation that helped railroad companies scam Native Americans out of their land.

14. After the assassination of James Garfield, civil service reform was enacted with the

    (A) Interstate Commerce Act.
    (B) Dawes Act.

(C) Pendleton Act.

(D) Sherman Antitrust Act.

15. In his book *Progress and Poverty*, social critic Henry George advocated

(A) the "single-tax".

(B) laissez-faire economics.

(C) social Darwinism.

(D) the Social Gospel.

Period 1890-1945

PART A

DIFFICULTY LEVEL 1

1. In 1913, the passage of the Federal Reserve Act

   (A) Provided insurance for bank deposits.

   (B) Regulated the stock market and financial securities.

   (C) Allowed for elasticity in currency circulation and credit rates.

   (D) Controlled exchange rates for the dollar.

2. Jacob Riis's *How the Other Half Lives* exposed problems associated with

   (A) The impact of segregation on African Americans.

   (B) Immigrant urban poverty in the 1890s.

   (C) The plight of farmers of the Great Plains in the 1890s.

   (D) The corruption in city political machines in the 1890s.

3. As a result of the publication of Upton Sinclair's novel *The Jungle*, Congress passed

   (A) the Pure Food and Drug Act.

   (B) the Mann Act.

   (C) the Elkins Act.

   (D) the Keating-Owen Child Labor Act.

4. The muckrakers of the late nineteenth and early twentieth centuries

   (A) Highlighted the horrors of the Jim Crow laws.

   (B) Were recent immigrants to America.

   (C) Were the leading critics of business and political corruption.

   (D) Wrote the earliest textbooks in America.

5. Which of the following amendments to the U.S. Constitution was NOT passed during the Progressive Era, 1890-1920?

   (A) Establishment of an income tax.

   (B) Banning of poll taxes.

   (C) Extension of suffrage to women.

   (D) Prohibition of the sale of alcoholic beverages.

6. Which of the following progressive reforms allowed voters, rather than party leaders, to select candidates to run for office?

   (A) Referendum.

   (B) Secret ballot.

   (C) Direct primary.

   (D) Initiative.

7. Progressive reformers at the turn of the twentieth century wanted all of the following EXCEPT

   (A) greater democracy in the American politics.

   (B) implementation of child labor laws.

   (C) expansion of women's rights.

   (D) creation of a socialist commonwealth.

8. Which of the following did NOT lead to start of the Great Depression in 1929?

   (A) A lack of business regulation.

   (B) Overproduction in the agricultural sector of the economy.

   (C) The abandonment of the gold standard.

   (D) Excessive speculation on the stock market.

9. President Herbert Hoover responded to the Great Depression by

(A) Enacting dozens of public works programs.

(B) Emphasizing the importance of private charities.

(C) Establishing a social safety net for Americans.

(D) Modernizing the American welfare system.

10. During is first "Hundred Days" in office, President Roosevelt addressed all of the following EXCEPT

(A) Agricultural relief.

(B) Unemployment relief.

(C) Social Security legislation.

(D) Banking regulation.

11. The goal of President Franklin D. Roosevelt's National Industrial Recovery Act of 1933 was to

(A) Regulate the stock market.

(B) Discourage the unionization of workers.

(C) Authorize cooperation between business and government.

(D) Establish a public works program.

12. Which of the following is true about the Agricultural Adjustment Act of 1933?

(A) It authorized the federal government to confiscate land from farmers.

(B) It paid farmers to cut production and destroy crops.

(C) It instituted a retirement program for farmers over the age of 50.

(D) It subsidized the cultivation of grain crops, such as wheat and corn.

13. How did Franklin D. Roosevelt respond to a series of unfavorable Supreme Court rulings concerning New Deal programs?

(A) He encouraged the public to protest the Supreme Court.

(B) He proposed new amendments to the Constitution.

(C) He began a espousing a laissez-fair approach to solving the problems of the Great Depression.

(D) He proposed legislation that would increase the number of justices in the Supreme Court.

Questions 14-16 refer to the photograph below.

Ford assembly line, Highland Park, Michigan, 1913.
(*http://en.wikipedia.org/wiki/Assembly_line#mediaviewer/File:Ford_assembly_line_-_1913.jpg*)

14. The photograph above is best understood in the context of

    (A) an early twentieth-century decline in manufacturing.
    (B) new economic opportunities for African Americans.
    (C) the development of new manufacturing technologies and techniques.
    (D) the aftermath of two devastating world wars.

15. Industries such as the one in the photograph above contributed to

    (A) a backlash against international migrants.
    (B) improved race relations in the North.
    (C) an overall rise in standard of living.
    (D) the onset of the Great Depression.

16. Progressive reformers attempted to improve the lives of industrial workers by

    (A) pushing for a return to rural ideals.
    (B) calling for less government intervention in the economy.
    (C) focusing their reform efforts exclusively at the state and local levels.
    (D) urging the government to address social problems associated with an industrial society.

Questions 17-18 refer to the following excerpt.

"The supreme duty of the Nation is the conservation of human resources through an enlightened measure of social and industrial justice. We pledge ourselves to work unceasingly in State and Nation for:

Effective legislation looking to the prevention of industrial accidents, occupational diseases, overwork, involuntary unemployment, and other injurous effects incident to modern industry;

The fixing of minimum safety and health standards for the various occupations, and the exercise of the public authority of State and Nation, including the Federal Control over interstate commerce, and the taxing power, to maintain such standards;

The prohibition of child labor; Minimum wage standards for working women, to provide a "living wage" in all industrial occupations...."

— Progressive Party Platform, 1912

17. The excerpt above was most likely a response to which of the following historical trends?

    (A) discrimination against African Americans.

    (B) lack of government regulation of business and industry.

    (C) unionization of workers during the Gilded Age.

    (D) denying the franchise to women.

18. Which of the following policies represents the continuation of the ideas presented in this excerpt?

    (A) Woodrow Wilson's New Freedom.

    (B) Herbert Hoover's rugged individualism.

    (C) Franklin Roosevelt's New Deal.

    (D) Ronald Reagan's trickle-down economics.

Questions 19-21 refer to the quotation below.

"So, also, security was attained in the earlier days through the interdependence of members of families upon each other and of the families within a small community upon each other. The complexities of great communities and of organized industry make less real these simple means of security. Therefore, we are compelled to employ the active interest of the Nation as a whole through government in order to encourage a greater security for each individual who composes it."

— Franklin D. Roosevelt, Message to Congress, June 8, 1934

19. Franklin Roosevelt's approach to dealing with the problems of the Great Depression is most consistent with the previous efforts of

    (A) union organizers of the late nineteenth century.

    (B) Radical Republicans during Reconstruction.

    (C) Progressive reformers of the early twentieth century.

    (D) abolitionists of the mid-nineteenth century.

20. The principles advocated in the speech above most directly challenged

    (A) American exceptionalism.

    (B) Laissez-faire economic policies of the Roaring Twenties.

    (C) Progressivism.

(D) Cooperation between business and government.

21. Which of the following groups benefitted greatly from the principles expressed in Roosevelt's speech?

    (A) women.
    (B) Native Americans.
    (C) African Americans.
    (D) labor unions.

Questions 22-23 refer to the excerpt below.

"I contend, my friends, that we have no difficult problem to solve in America, and that is the view of nearly everyone with whom I have discussed the matter here in Washington and elsewhere throughout the United States – that we have no very difficult problem to solve.

It is not the difficulty of the problem which we have; it is the fact that the rich people of this country – and by rich people I mean the super-rich – will not allow us to solve the problems, or rather the one little problem that is afflicting this country, because in order to cure all of our woes it is necessary to scale down the big fortunes, that we may scatter the wealth to be shared by all of the people...."

— Huey P. Long, "Every Man a King" speech, 1934

22. The speech above is most consistent with which of the following economic philosophies?

    (A) laissez-faire capitalism.
    (B) socialism.
    (C) Keynesianism.
    (D) corporatism.

23. Long's speech is best understood in the context of

    (A) the lead up to the Second World War.
    (B) growing opposition to Franklin Roosevelt's New Deal.
    (C) the failure of Herbert Hoover's solutions to the Great Depression.

(D) a resurgent conservative movement in the United States.

DIFFICULTY LEVEL 3

24. In what way was the Underwood Tariff of 1913 a significant change in trade policy?

(A) It was the first significant tariff reduction in half a century.

(B) It raised the tariff by 50%.

(C) It ran contrary to President Woodrow Wilson's New Freedom philosophy.

(D) It was opposed by Progressives in Congress.

25. Keynesian economic theories influenced Franklin D. Roosevelt's New Deal programs by promoting

(A) abandonment of the gold standard.

(B) a balanced federal budget.

(C) deficit spending in times of depression.

(D) abolition of the Federal Reserve.

PART B

DIFFICULTY LEVEL 1

1. What was a major problem facing American farmers in the 1920s?

    (A) Outdated farm equipment.

    (B) Overproduction of crops.

    (C) Passage of the McNary-Haugen bill.

    (D) Deregulation of railroads.

2. Prohibition failed in the United States because

    (A) it resulted in an increase in immigration.

    (B) it was unenforceable.

    (C) it resulted in widespread drinking among minors.

    (D) it led to threats of violence against women's groups.

3. The Harlem Renaissance can best be described as

    (A) a Back-to-Africa movement of the 1920s.

    (B) an attempt to build economic stability in urban centers.

    (C) an outpouring of African American artistic and literary creativity.

    (D) a reaction to the racial violence that erupted after World War I.

4. In what way did the "flappers" of the 1920s challenge traditional American attitudes about women?

    (A) They flaunted the use of birth control.

    (B) They fought for an Equal Rights Amendment.

    (C) They took greater liberty with fashion and behavior.

    (D) They took jobs as stockbrokers.

5. Which of the following did NOT contribute to the economic prosperity of the 1920s?

    (A) The use of assembly-line production.

    (B) The availability of consumer credit.

    (C) Government stimulation of the economy.

    (D) The growth of the advertising industry.

6. What was the Teapot Dome Scandal?

    (A) A bribery incident that involved the leasing of naval oil reserves.

    (B) President Harding's sale of presidential pardons.

    (C) A mishandling of the Bureau of Indian Affairs.

    (D) The theft of European war-debt payments.

7. Which of the following was a cause of the Palmer Raids in 1919?

    (A) Increased immigration from Mexico in the aftermath of World War I.

    (B) The Bolshevik Revolution in Russia and the fear that communism could spread to the United States.

    (C) The outbreak of racial riots in the North after World War I.

    (D) The murder trial of Sacco and Vanzetti, which stirred anti-immigrant feelings.

8. Marcus Garvey was responsible for founding which of the following organizations?

    (A) National Association for the Advancement of Colored People.

    (B) Universal Negro Improvement Association.

    (C) Congress of Racial Equality.

    (D) Southern Christian Leadership Conference.

9. The assembly-line production of Henry Ford's Model T automobile resulted in

    (A) A decline in automobile purchases.

    (B) The majority of Americans moving to the suburbs.

    (C) The overproduction and under-consumption of automobiles.

(D) An increase in purchases of automobiles by ordinary Americans.

10. The Great Migration of African Americans from the South to Northern cities occurred during which of the following periods?

(A) Reconstruction.

(B) The First World War and 1920s.

(C) The Great Depression and World War II.

(D) The 1960s.

11. The Great Depression of the 1930s led to

(A) A higher birth rate.

(B) A mass internal migration of Americans looking for work.

(C) A decrease in labor union membership.

(D) An increase in international migration.

Questions 12-15 refer to the following cartoon.

"COME UNTO ME, YE OPPREST!"

"An anarchist attempts to destroy the Statue of Liberty," *Memphis Commercial Appeal*, 1919.

12. In the political cartoon above, the cartoonist is most likely depicting which of the following groups?

    (A) Labor Unions.

    (B) Chinese Immigrants.

    (C) Irish Immigrants.

    (D) Russian Immigrants.

13. Which of the following actions most directly resulted from the situation depicted in the cartoon above?

    (A) American entry into World War I.

    (B) Emergency Quota Act.

    (C) Harlem Renaissance.

    (D) Wagner Act.

14. The sentiment reflected in the political cartoon above most closely relates to which of the following Supreme Court decisions?

    (A) *Schenck v. United States.*

    (B) *McCulloch v. Maryland.*

    (C) *Dred Scott v. Sanford.*

    (D) *Gibbons v. Ogden.*

15. Which of the following groups would likely support the assertions expressed in the cartoon above?

    (A) Labor unions.

    (B) Immigrants.

    (C) The Ku Klux Klan.

    (D) Supporters of Sacco and Vanzetti.

Questions 16-17 refer to the following image.

Photo of an American family in the 1920s listening to a crystal radio. From a 1922 advertisement for Freed-Eisemann radios in *Radio World* magazine.

16. The advertisement depicted above reflects which of the following continuities in United States history?

    (A) The intransigence of family values.

    (B) The significance of mass culture.

    (C) The influence of advertising.

    (D) The subjugation of women.

17. Which of the following events became a national media sensation as a result of the technological development depicted in the advertisement above?

    (A) The Red Scare.

    (B) The Sacco and Vanzetti Trial.

    (C) The Scopes "Monkey" Trial.

    (D) Passage of the Nineteenth Amendment.

Questions 18-19 refer to the following poem.

The night is beautiful,
So the faces of my people.
The stars are beautiful,
So the eyes of my people
Beautiful, also, is the sun.
Beautiful, also, are the souls of my people.

— "My People," Langston Hughes, published in *The Crisis*, 1923

18. The sentiments expressed in the poem above are best understood in the context of

(A) the Jim Crow laws.

(B) World War I.

(C) the Harlem Renaissance.

(D) the debut of the film *Birth of a Nation*.

19. The sentiments express in the poem above contributed to which of the following?

(A) Rising liberalism during the Great Depression.

(B) The decline of the Ku Klux Klan after World War I.

(C) The Civil Rights Movement of the 1950s and 1960s.

(D) The Great Migration of African Americans during the 1930s.

DIFFICULTY LEVEL 3

20. Prominent writers of the 1920s, such as F. Scott Fitzgerald and Sinclair Lewis, were best known for their

(A) Support of Protestant fundamentalism.

(B) Sympathy for the plight of farmers.

(C) Collaboration with writers and artists of the Harlem Renaissance.

(D) Criticism of middle-class values and materialism.

PART C

DIFFICULTY LEVEL 1

1. As a result of Theodore Roosevelt's Corollary to the Monroe Doctrine, the United States expanded its role in

   (A) Western Europe.
   (B) East Asia.
   (C) North Africa.
   (D) Central America.

2. Although President Woodrow Wilson declared United States neutrality at the start of the First World War,

   (A) The United States openly attacked German submarines.
   (B) The president privately sided with Germany.
   (C) The United States increased trade with Britain and France.
   (D) President Wilson engaged in secret diplomacy with Mexico.

3. Why did the United States Senate refuse to ratify the Treaty of Versailles?

   (A) Senators disagreed with the reparations Germany was required to pay.
   (B) Senators feared further involvement in foreign wars.
   (C) President Wilson's own Democratic Party rebelled against him.
   (D) President Wilson was unable to argue effectively because of his recent stroke.

4. Why were Japanese-Americans placed in concentration camps during World War II?

   (A) They committed numerous acts of sabotage.
   (B) As retaliation for the placement of Americans in concentration camps by the Japanese.
   (C) As a result of anti-Japanese prejudice and fear.
   (D) Many remained loyal to Japan.

5. In the late nineteenth century, all of the following encouraged American imperialism EXCEPT

(A) The "closing" of the American frontier.

(B) Alfred T. Mayhan's new naval policy.

(C) Social Darwinism.

(D) The need for African slaves.

6. Which of the following was NOT a cause of the Spanish-American War?

(A) Cuban nationalism.

(B) Philippine independence.

(C) yellow journalism.

(D) the sinking of the *Maine*.

7. As a result of the Spanish-American War, the United States gained control of which of the following territories?

(A) Alaska.

(B) Hawaii.

(C) The Panama Canal Zone.

(D) The Philippines.

8. Why did the United States remove Hawaii's Queen Lili'uokalani from power?

(A) She was a corrupt ruler.

(B) She refused to convert to Christianity.

(C) She insisted that native Hawaiians should retain control of Hawaii.

(D) She declared war against the United States.

9. Which of the following was a major reason for the construction of the Panama Canal?

    (A) A desire to improve American trade and military defense.
    (B) The Panamanian Revolution.
    (C) Britain's rejection of the Hay-Pauncefote Treaty.
    (D) American economic interests in Western Europe.

10. President Taft's foreign policy of Dollar Diplomacy

    (A) required deficit spending by the United States government.
    (B) overturned the existing Open Door Policy with China.
    (C) promoted American commercial interests in Latin America.
    (D) repealed Theodore Roosevelt's Corollary to the Monroe Doctrine.

11. Which of the following best describes the United States Open Door policy in China?

    (A) It challenged Japan's territorial interests in China.
    (B) It divided China into spheres of influence.
    (C) It resulted in a protracted war between the United States and China.
    (D) It bolstered American commercial interests in China.

12. What was the main function of American war boards during the First World War?

    (A) To manufacture supplies for the Allies.
    (B) To raise taxes on the wealthy.
    (C) To increase cooperation among business, labor and government.
    (D) To nationalize major industries.

13. Which of the following was NOT included in Woodrow Wilson's Fourteen Points?

    (A) national self-determination.
    (B) freedom of the seas.
    (C) reparations that Germany must pay.
    (D) creation of an international organization to preserve peace.

14. Throughout the 1930s, the United States responded to the aggressive actions of Germany, Italy, and Japan by

    (A) passing a series of neutrality acts.

(B)   providing economic aid to the targets of aggression.

(C)   recruiting soldiers and enacting a draft.

(D)   enacting an oil embargo against belligerent nations.

15. On the eve of Japan's attack on Pearl Harbor, most Americans

(A)   were preparing for war.

(B)   still wanted to keep the United States out of war.

(C)   were supportive of Japan's victories in the Pacific.

(D)   were ready to fight Germany but not Japan.

Questions 16-18 refer to the following excerpt.

It seems to me that God, with infinite wisdom and skill, is training the Anglo-Saxon race for an hour sure to come in the world's future…. The time is coming when the pressure of population on the means of subsistence will be felt here as it is now felt in Europe and Asia. Then will the world enter upon a new state of its history—the final competition of races, for which the Anglo-Saxon is being schooled…. Then this race of unequaled energy, with all the majesty of numbers and the might of wealth behind it—the representative, let us hope, of the largest liberty, the purest Christianity, the highest civilization—having developed peculiarly aggressive traits calculated to impress its institutions upon mankind, will spread itself over the earth….

— Josiah Strong, *Our Country*,1891

16. The views expressed by Josiah Strong represent the late 19th century debate over

(A)   the United States expanding westward to the Pacific.

(B)   the United States becoming a world power.

(C)   the acquisition of Hawaii and Alaska as US territories.

(D)   the building of a transcontinental railroad through unorganized territory.

17. The sentiments expressed in the excerpt above represent which of the following continuities in United States history?

(A)   Manifest Destiny.

(B)   Social Darwinism.

(C)   American Exceptionalism.

(D) All of the above.

18. The ideas expressed in the excerpt above were most directly challenged during the late nineteenth century by arguments that

   (A) the U.S. needed to first prove itself by winning the Spanish-American War.
   (B) the U.S. did not have the financial or military capacity for conquest.
   (C) the U.S. must focus on the reconstruction of the post-war South.
   (D) imperialism went against American ideals.

Questions 19-20 refer to the excerpt below

The Members of the League undertake to respect and preserve as against external aggression the territorial integrity and existing political independence of all Members of the League. In case of any such aggression or in case of any threat or danger of such aggression the Council shall advise upon the means by which this obligation shall be fulfilled.

— Article X, Covenant of the League of Nations, 1919

19. The excerpt above is best understood in the context of

   (A) the secret system of alliances that led to the outbreak of World War I.
   (B) the fear that Germany would remilitarize after World War I.
   (C) isolationist sentiment surrounding negotiations for the Treaty of Versailles.
   (D) the rejection of Woodrow Wilson's Fourteen Points.

20. Why did the United States public and Senate find the article above objectionable?

    (A) The US would have to allow Germany to pay reparations.

    (B) The Senate perceived that they would lose the power to declare war.

    (C) The American public would have to abandon its reliance on collective security.

    (D) Europe would default on all debts from World War I.

Questions 21-22 refer to the document below.

An African-American Military Policeman on a motorcycle in front of the "colored" MP entrance, Columbus, Georgia, 1942.
(*http://en.wikipedia.org/wiki/Racial_discrimination_against_African_Americans_in_the_U. S._Military#mediaviewer/File:African-americans-wwii-002.jpg*)

21. The photo above is best understood in the context of

    (A) Racial equality during World War II.

    (B) Segregation in the armed forces during World War II.

    (C) African Americans joining the Axis Power during Word War II.

    (D) African Americans refusing to report for the draft during World War II.

22. The situation depicted in the photo above contributed to which of the following movements?

(A) Bracero Program.

(B) Double-V Campaign.

(C) Nationwide boycotts of defense industries.

(D) Formation of the NAACP.

Questions 23-24 refer to the poster below.

"Join us in a victory job" poster, Department of National Service, 1943.

23. This poster was most likely intended to

(A) convince American women to enlist in the military.

(B) recruit women to fill jobs vacated by men during World War II.

(C) pass legislation which prohibited discrimination.

(D) generate support for Executive Order #8802.

24. The ideas expressed in the poster above could be used by policymakers to argue in favor of the

(A) Equal Rights Amendment.

(B) Civil Rights Act of 1964.

(C) Patriot Act.

(D) Voting Rights Act.

Questions 25-27 refer to the following document.

The President of the United States of America and the Prime Minister, Mr. Churchill, representing His Majesty's Government in the United Kingdom, being met together, deem it right to make known certain common principles in the national policies of their respective countries on which they base their hopes for a better future for the world....

Second, they desire to see no territorial changes that do not accord with the freely expressed wishes of the peoples concerned;

Third, they respect the right of all peoples to choose the form of government under which they will live; and they wish to see sovereign rights and self-government restored to those who have been forcibly deprived of them...

Eighth, they believe that all of the nations of the world, for realistic as well as spiritual reasons must come to the abandonment of the use of force...pending the establishment of a wider and permanent system of general security, that the disarmament of such nations is essential....

— The Atlantic Charter, 1941

25. The excerpt above most directly contradicts the United States commitment to

(A) Collective security.

(B) Non-intervention.

(C) Self-determination.

(D) The Lend-Lease program.

26. Which of the following actions of the mid-twentieth century most clearly reflects the perspective of this passage?

(A) Creation of the United Nations.
(B) Nuremburg Trials.
(C) Intervention in Korea.
(D) Creation of the Central Intelligence Agency.

27. The ideas expressed in the passage above most directly reflect which of the following continuities in American history?

(A) Challenges of maintaining liberty and national security.
(B) Pursuing international and domestic goals in acceptable ways.
(C) Policies of promoting and restricting international migration.
(D) Balancing technological advancement with environmental conservation.

DIFFICULTY LEVEL 3

28. What was the Root-Takahira agreement of 1908?

(A) It prohibited Japanese immigration to the United States.
(B) The United States and Japan agreed to respect each other's territorial holdings in the Pacific.
(C) The United States recognized Japan's takeover of mainland China.
(D) It marked the end of Japanese isolationism.

29. Which of the following was NOT an argument advanced by Anti-Imperialist League in the United States?

(A) Imperialism violated the "consent of the governed" philosophy of the Declaration of Independence.
(B) Despotism abroad might lead to despotism at home.
(C) Imperialism would diminish Anglo-Saxon superiority.
(D) Imperialism was inherently racist.

30. Why was President Woodrow Wilson forced to intervene in the affairs of Mexico in the early 1900s?

    (A) Venustiano Carranza became president of Mexico.

    (B) American business interests were in danger.

    (C) American sailors were arrested in Tampico, Mexico.

    (D) William Randolph Hearst used yellow journalism to campaign for involvement.

31. During World War II, the bracero program

    (A) promoted the integration of African Americans into white military units.

    (B) recruited women to work in factory jobs.

    (C) placed Japanese Americans into internment camps.

    (D) imported temporary contract laborers from Mexico.

32. The United States spent enormous sums of money on the Manhattan Project to develop the original atomic bomb because it believed

    (A) scientists like Albert Einstein might be recaptured by the Germans.

    (B) the Germans might acquire such a weapon first.

    (C) the Soviet Union was working on their own nuclear weapon.

    (D) the American public wanted the war to end quickly.

Period 1945-1980

PART A

DIFFICULTY LEVEL 1

1. United States ambassador George F. Kennan is perhaps best known for his proposed policy of

    (A) collective security.
    (B) appeasement.
    (C) containment.
    (D) détente.

DIFFICULTY LEVEL 2

2. Which of the following contributed to start of the Cold War following World War II?

    (A) Disagreements over postwar arrangements in Eastern Europe.
    (B) Soviet encroachment on Western Europe.
    (C) The proliferation of nuclear weapons in Soviet satellite nations.
    (D) Differences in postcolonial policies regarding African countries.

3. The Truman Doctrine originated as an announcement related to events in which of the following countries?

    (A) Yugoslavia.
    (B) Greece and Turkey.
    (C) Communist China.
    (D) Romania.

4. In what way did the Marshall Plan further the United States goal of containment?

(A) It provided military aid for Eastern Europe.

(B) It gave substantial financial assistance to rebuild Western Europe.

(C) It provided economic aid for Japan.

(D) It provided aid to developing countries to resist communism.

5. The North Atlantic Treaty Organization (NATO), formed in 1949, is an example of

   (A) popular sovereignty.

   (B) collective security.

   (C) secret alliances.

   (D) the domino theory.

6. Which of the following accounts for how Senator Joseph McCarthy first rose to national prominence in the 1950s?

   (A) He revealed that Communist spies were passing atomic secrets to the Soviet Union.

   (B) He charged that there was extensive Communist influence in Hollywood and elsewhere in the media.

   (C) He asserted that there was a Communist conspiracy within the U.S. Army.

   (D) He charged that dozens of known Communists were working within the U.S. State Department.

7. Why did President Harry Truman relieve General Douglas MacArthur from command of United Nations troops in Korea in 1951?

   (A) MacArthur openly mocked Truman's presidency.

   (B) MacArthur publicly disagreed with presidential policies.

   (C) MacArthur lost several crucial battles.

   (D) MacArthur started fighting in China.

8. The Gulf of Tonkin Resolution

   (A) Ended the war in Vietnam.
   (B) Reflected the bitter division in Congress over American involvement in Vietnam.
   (C) Was a policy statement about a general drawdown of troops in Vietnam.
   (D) Allowed the President to deploy combat troops in South Vietnam.

9. All of the following were actions taken by the Kennedy Administration during the Cuban Missile Crisis EXCEPT

   (A) sending economic aid to Cuba under the Alliance for Progress.
   (B) setting up a blockade preventing Soviet ships from entering Cuba.
   (C) reducing the number of United States missiles in Eastern Europe.
   (D) refraining from an airstrike of Cuba.

10. All of the following are examples of President Richard Nixon's foreign policy of détente EXCEPT

   (A) The strategic arms limitation talks (SALT).
   (B) Nixon's visit to the People's Republic of China.
   (C) Bombing the Ho Chi Minh trail in Cambodia.
   (D) Expanding trade with the Soviet Union.

11. In 1970, the Kent State University protests were an example of

   (A) The growing movement for women's equality.
   (B) The strength of the Black Power movement.
   (C) The public's growing dissatisfaction with the Vietnam War.
   (D) The beginning of an organized Gay Rights movement.

12. At the Camp David Accords, President Jimmy Carter brokered an agreement between the leaders of

   (A) Israel and Palestine.
   (B) Egypt and Israel.
   (C) Israel and Syria.
   (D) Syria and Egypt.

Questions 13-15 refer to the following map.

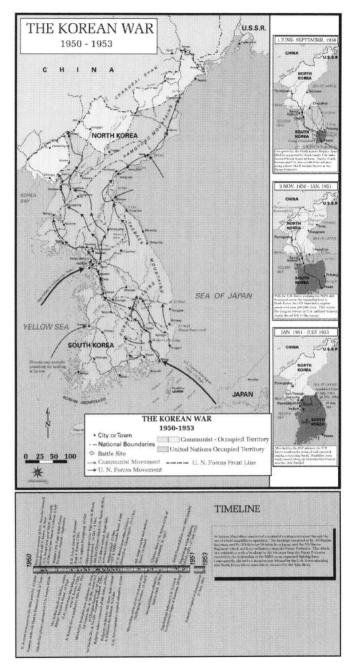

Map of Korean War, US Military Academy at West Point, 1953.
(*http://commons.wikimedia.org/wiki/File:Korea-overview.gif*)

13. The map above is best understood in the context of

    (A) Collective security.
    (B) Containment.
    (C) Brinksmanship.
    (D) The Potsdam Conference.

14. A constitutional issue that was frequently raised about United States involvement in the Korean conflict is

    (A) right to regulate commerce with foreign nations.
    (B) use of deficit spending to finance wars.
    (C) lack of a formal declaration of war by Congress.
    (D) Supreme Court's role in foreign policy decision-making.

15. After World War II, the United States departed most sharply from its traditional foreign policy when it

    (A) stopped foreign-aid programs.
    (B) sponsored disarmament treaties.
    (C) organized global systems of alliances.
    (D) recognized revolutionary governments.

Questions 16-17 refer to the excerpt below

"We began singing freedom songs and chanting, 'Resist! Resist!' and 'Burn Draft Cards, Not People'. . . . People in the audience were applauding us, shouting encouragement. Then some guys began to come out of the audience with draft cards in hand. They burned them. Alone, in pairs, by threes they came. Each flaming draft card brought renewed cheering and more people out of the crowd. . . . Some of the draft card burners were girls, wives, or girlfriends of male card burners. . . . It lasted this way for about half an hour."

— Martin Jezer, quoted in *The Vietnam War: Opposing Viewpoints*, April 16, 1967

16. The excerpt above is best understood in the context of

    (A) Richard Nixon's election as President.
    (B) growing opposition to the Vietnam War.
    (C) support for the conscription of young men to fight in war.
    (D) the repeal of the Selective Service Act.

17. The excerpt above represents which of the following continuities in United States history?

    (A) the popularity of socialism during wartime.
    (B) civil disobedience as a form of popular protest.
    (C) the balance of civil liberties and national security.
    (D) states' rights versus federal supremacy.

Questions 18-19 refer to the document below.

"We choose to go to the Moon in this decade and do the other things, not because they are easy, but because they are hard, because that goal will serve to organize and measure the best of our energies and skills, because that challenge is one that we are willing to accept, one we are unwilling to postpone, and one which we intend to win.... It is for these reasons that I regard the decision last year to shift our efforts in space from low to high gear as among the most important decisions that will be made during my incumbency in the office of the Presidency."

— John F. Kennedy, Speech at Rice University, Houston, September 12, 1962

18. The excerpt above is best understood in the context of

    (A) The end of détente.
    (B) The Soviet Union's successful launch of *Sputnik*.
    (C) The Soviet Union's development of the hydrogen bomb.
    (D) The signing of a nuclear test ban treaty.

19. Which challenge faced by the United States in the 1950s and 1960s is best exemplified in the excerpt above?

(A) The post-World War II economic downturn.

(B) The presence of proxy-wars in Southeast Asia.

(C) The U.S. struggle for global leadership.

(D) The process of decolonization and shifting alliances.

Questions 20-21 refer to the map below.

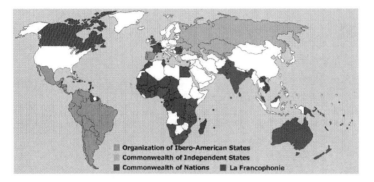

Four international organizations whose membership largely follows the pattern of previous colonial empires.

(http://en.wikipedia.org/wiki/Decolonization#mediaviewer/File:Postempire_Orgs_Map.png)

20. The map above is best understood in the context of post-1945

(A) imperialism.

(B) decolonization.

(C) mercantilism.

(D) international migration.

21. During the Cold War, post-colonial governments generally assumed a foreign policy of

    (A) containment.
    (B) nonalignment.
    (C) détente.
    (D) imperialism.

DIFFICULTY LEVEL 3

22. All of the following were attempts to detect communists in American government and society EXCEPT the

    (A) House Un-American Activities Committee (HUAC).
    (B) Central Intelligence Agency.
    (C) McCarran Internal Security Act.
    (D) Loyalty Review Board.

23. Why did many southern Democrats split from the party in 1948?

    (A) They accused President Truman of being weak on communism.
    (B) They opposed American membership in the United Nations.
    (C) President Truman signed an executive order desegregating the armed forces.
    (D) Truman converted to Catholicism.

24. In his 1961 farewell address, President Dwight D. Eisenhower warned Americans about the

    (A) rising levels of poverty in the United States.
    (B) military-industrial complex.
    (C) importance of the Civil Rights Movement.
    (D) need to strengthen Social Security.

PART B

DIFFICULTY LEVEL 1

1. Which of the following Supreme Court cases was overturned by the 1954 case of *Brown v. Board of Education of Topeka*?

   (A) *Dred Scott v. Sanford.*
   (B) *Schechter v. United States.*
   (C) *Plessy v. Ferguson.*
   (D) *Schenck v. United States.*

DIFFICULTY LEVEL 2

2. Which of the following civil rights groups is correctly paired with one of its leaders?

   (A) Student Nonviolent Coordinating Committee — Rosa Parks.
   (B) Black Panthers — Marcus Garvey.
   (C) NAACP — Malcolm X.
   (D) Southern Christian Leadership Conference — Martin Luther King, Jr.

3. Which of the following groups staged sit-ins to protest segregated facilities in the South?

   (A) Student Nonviolent Coordinating Committee.
   (B) Black Muslims.
   (C) Black Panthers.
   (D) Congress of Racial Equality.

4. Which of the following Civil Rights groups promoted Black separatism rather than racial integration?

   (A) NAACP.
   (B) Student Nonviolent Coordinating Committee.
   (C) Southern Christian Leadership Conference.
   (D) National of Islam.

5. Which of the following is true about the Black Power movement of the late 1960's?

   (A) Its actions were grounded in Christianity.
   (B) It advocated the violent overthrow of government.
   (C) It sought African American political and economic self-determination.
   (D) It promoted assimilation into white society.

6. Which of the following was NOT one of President Lyndon B. Johnson's Great Society programs?

   (A) Civil Rights Act.
   (B) Voting Rights Act.
   (C) Social Security Act.
   (D) Elementary and Secondary Education Act.

7. What was the principal goal of the National Organization of Women (NOW) when it was founded in 1966?

   (A) To fight for women's suffrage.
   (B) To challenge the Equal Rights Amendment.
   (C) To advance economic and social equality for women.
   (D) To advocate equal access for women to athletic facilities.

8. Cesar Chavez and Dolores Huerta co-founded the United Farm Workers (UFW) to

   (A) advocate for the free coining of silver.
   (B) push for government ownership of railroads.
   (C) unionize Mexican-American laborers.
   (D) nationalize the bracero movement.

9. Which of the following events is considered the beginning of an organized movement for gay rights?

(A) March on Washington.
(B) Stonewall Riots.
(C) Tet Offensive.
(D) Second Battle of Wounded Knee.

Questions 10-13 refer to the following excerpt.

"The problem lay buried, unspoken, for many years in the minds of American women. It was a strange stirring, a sense of dissatisfaction, a yearning that women suffered…Each suburban wife struggled with it alone. As she made the beds, shopped for groceries, matched slipcover material, ate peanut butter sandwiches with her children, chauffeured Cub Scouts and Brownies, lay beside her husband at night—she was afraid to even as of herself the silent question—'Is this all?'"

— Betty Friedan, *The Feminine Mystique*, 1963.

10. Which of the following was a major effect of the sentiment expressed in the excerpt above?

(A) The success of the Civil Rights Movement.
(B) The formation of the National Organization for Women.
(C) Passage of the Nineteenth Amendment.
(D) A return to the cultural conformity of the 1950s.

11. Which of the following developments in the 1960s and 1970s were LEAST similar to the ideas expressed in the excerpt?

(A) Equal Employment Opportunity Commission.
(B) Title IX of the United States Education Amendments.
(C) Supreme Court decision of *Swann v. Charlotte-Mecklenburg Schools*.
(D) Supreme Court Decision of *Roe v. Wade*.

12. Which of the following figures would disagree with the author of the statement above?

(A) Pauli Murray.
(B) Angela Davis.

(C) Phyllis Schlafly.

(D) Eleanor Roosevelt.

13. Which of the following documents demonstrates the strongest continuity with the ideas expressed in the passage?

(A) The Declaration of Sentiments.

(B) The Federalist Papers.

(C) Virginia and Kentucky Resolution.

(D) The Declaration of Independence.

Questions 14-16 refer to the excerpt below.

"It can hardly be argued that either students or teachers shed their constitutional rights to freedom of speech or expression at the schoolhouse gate.

In order for the State in the person of school officials to justify prohibition of a particular expression of opinion, it must be able to show that its action was caused by something more than a mere desire to avoid the discomfort and unpleasantness that always accompany an unpopular viewpoint. Certainly where there is no finding and no showing that engaging in the forbidden conduct would "materially and substantially interfere with the requirements of appropriate discipline in the operation of the school."

— Supreme Court decision in *Tinker v. Des Moines Independent Community School District*

14. Which of the following amendments to the U.S. Constitution is most closely associated with the excerpt above?

(A) First Amendment.

(B) Fourth Amendment.

(C) Fifth Amendment.

(D) Fourteenth Amendment.

15. The case of *Tinker v. Des Moines Independent Community School District* is best understood in the context of

(A) Continued segregation in the city school system.

(B) Censorship of the school's newspaper.

(C) The banning of prayer in public schools.

(D) Protest of the Vietnam War.

16. The rights expressed above would be most strongly defended today by which of the following special interest groups?
    (A) American Federation of Teachers.
    (B) American Civil Liberties Union.
    (C) National Rifle Association.
    (D) National Association of Elementary School Principals.

Questions 17-18 are based on the excerpt below.

"Each year more than 100,000 high school graduates with proved ability do not enter college because they cannot afford it. And if we cannot educate today's youth, what will we do in 1970 when elementary school enrollment will be five million greater than 1960? And high school enrollment will rise by five million. And college enrollment will increase by more than three million. In many places, classrooms are overcrowded and curricula are outdated. Most of our qualified teachers are underpaid, and many of our paid teachers are unqualified. So we must give every child a place to sit and a teacher to learn from. Poverty must not be a bar to learning, and learning must offer an escape from poverty. But more classrooms and more teachers are not enough. We must seek an educational system which grows in excellence as it grows in size. And this means better training for our teachers. It means exploring new techniques of teaching, to find new ways to stimulate the love of learning and the capacity for creation."

— Lyndon B. Johnson, *Great Society Speech,* 1964

17. Which of the following was a result of the ideas expressed in the speech above?

    (A) Peace Corps.

    (B) Head Start Program.

    (C) Civil Rights Act, 1964.

    (D) Voting Rights Act, 1965.

18. The speech above is best understood in the context of

    (A) The Vietnam War.

    (B) The Civil Rights Movement.

    (C) The War on Poverty.

    (D) The Anti-War Movement.

Questions 19-20 refer to the following article.

"Stop the Terror at Pine Ridge," *Osawatomie*, 1975
(*http://upload.wikimedia.org/wikipedia/commons/a/ab/Pine_Ridge_-_Osawatomie_2.JPG*)

19. The author of the article above is

    (A) calling on the federal government to advance desegregation.
    (B) requesting federal power to end racial discrimination.
    (C) raising awareness of the prevalence and persistence of poverty.
    (D) addressing issues of identity and social injustice.

20. The American Indian Movement of the 1960s and 1970s was most influenced by

    (A) the profound changes to the family structure in American society.
    (B) environmental problems and the abuse of natural resources.
    (C) Latinos and Asian Americans demanding greater equality.
    (D) the African American civil rights movement.

DIFFICULTY LEVEL 3

21. All of the following individuals are correctly paired with their social cause EXCEPT

    (A) Rachel Carson – environmentalism.
    (B) Michael Harrington – reduction of poverty in America.
    (C) Ralph Nader – consumer protection.
    (D) Barry Goldwater – affirmative action.

22. Which of the following organizations spearheaded the New Left movement in the 1960s?

    (A) Southern Christian Leadership Conference.
    (B) United Farm Workers.
    (C) Student Nonviolent Coordinating Committee.
    (D) Students for Democratic Society.

23. President Richard Nixon advocated a New Federalism political philosophy to

    (A) repeal New Deal and Great Society programs.
    (B) shift power from the federal government to state and local governments.

(C) enact an inflationary monetary policy.

(D) rejuvenate the African American Civil Rights Movement.

PART C

DIFFICULTY LEVEL 1

1. Which of the following represented mainstream 1950s cultural norms?

    (A) Middle-class consumerism.
    (B) Television shows depicting family life.
    (C) The popularity of comic books.
    (D) All of the above.

DIFFICULTY LEVEL 2

2. All of following were domestic developments in the United States during President Eisenhower's administration EXCEPT

    (A) the postwar baby boom.
    (B) a rise in the gross national product.
    (C) construction of the interstate highway system.
    (D) desegregation of the military.

3. During the 1950's, which of the following did NOT contribute to cultural conformity and homogeneity?

    (A) The growth of the suburbs.
    (B) The popularity of television.
    (C) the Beat Generation.
    (D) the second Red Scare.

4. Which president helped establish the Environmental Protection Agency and secured passage of the Clean Air Act?

    (A) Harry Truman.

    (B) John F. Kennedy.

    (C) Richard Nixon.

    (D) Jimmy Carter.

5. Between 1950 and 1980, women in the workplace

    (A) did not benefit from federal reforms for equal pay.

    (B) declined in numbers as a result of the baby boom.

    (C) were less educated than previous generations of women.

    (D) increased in numbers as social and cultural attitudes shifted.

6. All of the following limits on the authority of the president were results of the Watergate scandal EXCEPT

    (A) Presidential term limits.

    (B) Ethics in Government Act.

    (C) The Freedom of Information Act.

    (D) Campaign spending limits.

7. The demographic trend known as the "Graying of America" since the 1970s has ramifications for

    (A) consumer culture of American society.

    (B) the long-term viability of Social Security and Medicare.

    (C) rising premiums in the health care industry.

    (D) an increase in migrants from Latin America.

Questions 8-11 refer to the image below.

"Suburbia" by David Shankbone. (Licensed under CC BY-SA 3.0 via Wikimedia Commons -
*http://commons.wikimedia.org/wiki/File:Suburbia_by_David_Shankbone.jpg#mediaviewer/
File:Suburbia_by_David_Shankbone.jpg*)

8. The photo above is best understood in the context of

    (A) post-World War II economic growth.

    (B) the African-American Civil Rights movement of the 1950s.

    (C) Gilded Age advancements in steel construction.

    (D) mass internal migration due to the Great Depression.

9. Which of the following celebrated an idealized version of the life represented by the photograph above?

    (A) The Beat Generation.

    (B) The book *Catcher in the Rye*.

    (C) Films like *The Wild One* and *Rebel without a Cause*.

    (D) TV shows like *Leave it to Beaver* and *Father Knows Best*.

10. The photograph above shows what some social critics believed to be

(A) a sign that Americans were becoming more tolerant of cultural differences.

(B) evidence of the strength of the nation's largest cities.

(C) a representation of the conformity of postwar culture.

(D) the end of social and economic differentiation in housing.

11. During the 1950s, which group most directly challenged the portrayal of American life depicted in the photograph above?

(A) Artists and intellectuals.

(B) religious conservatives.

(C) internal migrants.

(D) business leaders.

Questions 12-13 are based on the graph below.

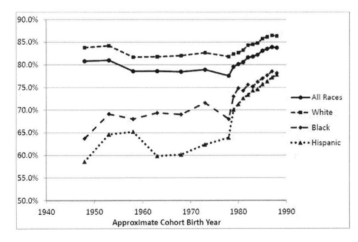

High School Graduation Rates, 1940-1990 (*http://profitofeducation.org/wp-content/uploads/2013/04/High-School-graduation-rates.png*)

12. Which of the following was a significant cause of the trend in high school graduation rates seen above?

(A) affirmative action programs.

(B) increase in federal funding for primary and secondary education.

(C) passage of the G.I. Bill.

(D) the end of the Vietnam War.

13. All of the following resulted in a greater emphasis on science and mathematics in secondary schools EXCEPT

(A) Cold War anxieties.

(B) The Soviet Union's successful launch of Sputnik.

(C) *Brown v. Board of Education.*

(D) The National Defense Education Act.

Questions 14-15 refer to the excerpt below.

In summary, it is evident that the Davis special admissions program involves the use of an explicit racial classification never before countenanced by this Court. It tells applicants who are not Negro, Asian, or Chicano that they are totally excluded from a specific percentage of the seats in an entering class…. But when a State's distribution of benefits or imposition of burdens hinges on ancestry or the color of a person's skin, that individual is entitled to a demonstration that the challenged classification is necessary to promote a substantial state interest. Petitioner has failed to carry this burden. For this reason, that portion of the California court's judgment holding petitioner's special admissions program invalid under the Fourteenth Amendment must be affirmed. I suspect that it would be impossible to arrange an affirmative-action program in a racially neutral way and have it successful. To ask that this be so is to demand the impossible. In order to get beyond racism, we must first take account of race. There is no other way. And in order to treat some persons equally, we must treat them differently. We cannot—we dare not—let the Equal Protection Clause perpetuate racial supremacy.

— Supreme Court decision in *Regents of the University of California v. Bakke* (1978)

14. The Supreme Court decision above is best understood in the context of the federal government's efforts to

(A) Increase educational and employment opportunities for women and minorities.

(B) Improve the American economy by guaranteeing that employees will be highly skilled.

(C) Decrease social welfare costs by requiring recipients of public assistance to work.

(D) Reduce the Federal deficit by increasing government efficiency.

15. The 1978 ruling of the Supreme Court in *Regents of the University of California v. Bakke* represents which of the following continuities in United States history?

(A) Federal enforcement the First Amendment's Establishment Clause.

(B) Federal and state abandonment of Civil Rights legislation.

(C) The right of states to nullify federal mandates.

(D) The challenges of enforcing the Fourteenth Amendment's Equal Protection Clause.

Questions 16-17 refer to the excerpt below.

"….During the war years the role of government was vastly expanded. After that came the reaction. Most of it, unquestionably, was motivated by a desire to rehabilitate the prestige of private production and therewith of producers…. A community decision to have a new school means that the individual surrenders the necessary amount, willy-nilly, in his taxes. But if he is left with that income, he is a free man. He can decide between a better car or a television set…. The difficulty is that this argument leaves the community with no way of preferring the school…. The final problem of the productive society is what it produces…. The line which divides our area of wealth from our area of poverty is roughly that which divides privately produced and marketed goods and services from publicly rendered services. For we have failed to see the importance, indeed the urgent need, of maintaining a balance…."

— John Kenneth Galbraith: *The Affluent Society* (1958)

16. The ideas expressed in the excerpt above are most likely a response to

(A) The spread of communism and American involvement abroad.

(B) post-World War II economic prosperity.

(C) Women leaving the workforce and going back to the role of homemakers following World War II.

(D) Government taking on a more extensive role in the American economy following World War II.

17. According to the excerpt above, which of the following has become a measurement for the economic success of a nation?

(A) Public works projects.

(B) National healthcare and welfare.

(C) Gross domestic product.

(D) Average educational attainment.

Questions 18-19 refer to the following image.

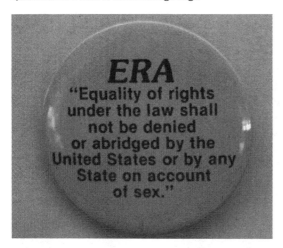

Campaign button in support of the Equal Rights Amendment, 1970s.
(*https://farm4.staticflickr.com/3250/3054041911_0a68c394e6.jpg*)

18. The image above was most likely a response to

(A) the counterculture's assault the status quo in American society.

(B) the impact of the 14th Amendment on the women's rights movement.

(C) the debate between liberals and conservatives over the women's rights movement.

(D) Supreme Court decisions expanding individual freedoms.

19. Which of the following groups from an earlier era in United States history would most likely support the sentiments expressed in the image above?

(A) Antifederalists opposed to the ratification of the Constitution.

(B) Revivalist preachers during the Second Great Awakening.

(C) States' rights advocates during the antebellum era.

(D) Middle-class social reformers during the Gilded Age.

DIFFICULTY LEVEL 3

20. Influential intellectual and cultural critics of the 1950s were most concerned with

(A) the availability of free higher education.

(B) alienation and conformity in modern society.

(C) the domino effect and the spread of communism.

(D) political apathy in the post-war era.

21. Former Alabama governor George Wallace's popularity in the 1968 presidential campaign illustrates the

(A) decline of the two-party system.

(B) exploitation of race as a national political issue.

(C) growing power of the New Left in American politics.

(D) persistence of anticommunism as a political force.

22. Which of the following was NOT a characteristic of the American economy during President Carter's term in office?

    (A) energy crisis.

    (B) rampant inflation.

    (C) rising unemployment.

    (D) increased union membership.

23. The 1970's saw an increase in all of the following EXCEPT

    (A) the number of women holding political office.

    (B) the influence of Christian fundamentalism on politics.

    (C) the average age of Americans.

    (D) the percentage of two-parent households.

24. The 1979 nuclear accident at Three Mile Island resulted in

    (A) the American Indian Movement.

    (B) the proliferation of nuclear weapons in North and South America.

    (C) public pressure to free the United States from dependence on foreign energy sources.

    (D) support for the movement against nuclear power.

Period 1980-present

PART A

DIFFICULTY LEVEL 2

1. Despite their many differences, what was one similarity between Jimmy Carter and Ronald Reagan as presidential candidates?

   (A) They capitalized on their status as Washington outsiders.

   (B) They pledged less American involvement in foreign affairs.

   (C) The promised to cut taxes for the upper class.

   (D) They both had successful careers in private business.

2. As a result of the Iran-Contra Affair in 1986,

   (A) hostages were freed from the United States embassy in Iran.

   (B) Ronald Reagan was reelected president.

   (C) members of Reagan's administration were indicted.

   (D) Congress authorized the training of counterinsurgents in South America.

3. Why was President Bill Clinton impeached in 1998?

   (A) He admitted to having a sexual affair with a White House intern.

   (B) He allegedly committed perjury and obstruction of justice.

   (C) He illegally conducted military airstrikes in Kosovo.

   (D) He was not impeached.

Use the following passage to answer questions 4 and 9.

"We must reverse the trend America finds herself in today. Young people between the ages of twenty-five and forty have been born and reared in a different world than Americans of years past. The television set has been their primary baby-sitter. From the television set they have learned situation ethics and immorality—they have learned a loss of respect for human life. They have learned to disrespect the family as God has established it. They have been educated in a public-school system that is permeated with secular humanism…."

— *Listen, America* (1980), Jerry Falwell

4. The speech above is best understood in the context of

    (A) the expansion of liberal social policies during the 1980s.
    (B) the growth of Christian fundamentalism in concert with the resurgence of conservative values.
    (C) the banning of abortion rights throughout the United States.
    (D) an increase in federal funding for public education.

Questions 5-6 refer to the following excerpt.

"As Republican Members of the House of Representatives and as citizens seeking to join that body we propose not just to change its policies, but even more important, to restore the bonds of trust between the people and their elected representatives.

That is why, in this era of official evasion and posturing, we offer instead a detailed agenda for national renewal, a written commitment with no fine print.

This year's election offers the chance, after four decades of one-party control, to bring to the House a new majority that will transform the way Congress works. That historic change would be the end of government that is too big, too intrusive, and too easy with the public's money. It can be the beginning of a Congress that respects the values and shares the faith of the American family.

Like Lincoln, our first Republican president, we intend to act "with firmness in the right, as God gives us to see the right." To restore accountability to Congress. To end its cycle of scandal and disgrace. To make us all proud again of the way free people govern themselves."

— *Contract with America,* Newt Gingrich and Dick Armey, 1994

5. The excerpt above most directly challenges which of the following 20th century developments?

(A) The belief the government can solve many social and economic problems in American.

(B) The growth of evangelical and fundamentalist Christian churches opposed to liberal social policies.

(C) The end of the Cold War and new challenges to American power.

(D) The women's rights movement that began to achieve success for women in the work force.

6. Which of the following groups would have been mostly likely to support the *Contract with America?*

(A) Feminists.

(B) Union members.

(C) Southern evangelical Christians.

(D) Civil Rights leaders.

Question 7 refers to the graph below.

Total Deficits vs. National Debt Increases ($ Billions)

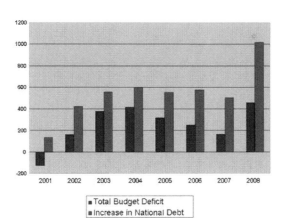

7. All of the following actions during George W. Bush's presidency contributed to the data shown in the graph above EXCEPT

   (A) the Wars in Iraq and Afghanistan.
   (B) the tax cuts of 2001 and 2003.
   (C) No Child Left Behind.
   (D) the expansion of Medicare.

DIFFICULTY LEVEL 3

8. During the 1980s, "Reaganomics," or supply-side economics, led to

   (A) increased spending on federal programs.
   (B) greater tax revenues for the federal government.
   (C) a large increase in the public debt.
   (D) lower military expenditures than during the Carter administration.

9. Based on the excerpt above, Jerry Falwell would have agreed with all of the following Supreme Court decisions EXCEPT

   (A) *U.S. v. Lopez* (1995).
   (B) *Clinton v. Jones* (1997).
   (C) *Planned Parenthood of Southeastern PA v. Casey* (1992).
   (D) *Bush v. Gore* (2000).

PART B

DIFFICULTY LEVEL 1

1. Ronald Reagan's improved relationship with Mikhail Gorbachev during the president's second term resulted in

   (A) an eventual end to the Cold War.

   (B) increased tensions between NATO and Warsaw Pact nations.

   (C) expansion of containment to include South American nations.

   (D) attempts to recolonize African nations.

2. Which of the following events caused the other three?

   (A) The U.S. War in Afghanistan.

   (B) Passage of the Patriot Act.

   (C) The U.S. invasion of Iraq.

   (D) The 9/11 attacks.

DIFFICULTY LEVEL 2

3. The 1991 invasion of Iraq by the United States under President George H. W. Bush was prompted by

   (A) A communist takeover in Iraq.

   (B) The use of weapons of mass destruction by Iraq.

   (C) Iraq's invasion of Kuwait.

   (D) An Islamic fundamentalist coup in Iraq.

4. During the post-Cold War era, the most challenging foreign policy development has been

    (A) genocide in sub-Saharan Africa.

    (B) Radical Islamist movements.

    (C) peacekeeping efforts in Latin America.

    (D) ethnic conflict in the Balkans.

5. Which of the following groups has been most critical of the USA PATRIOT Act since its passage in 2001?

    (A) Joint Chiefs of Staff.

    (B) African Americans.

    (C) Civil libertarians.

    (D) United Nations.

Questions 6-7 refer to the following excerpt.

"The only force capable of getting this job done is NATO, the powerful military alliance of democracies that has guaranteed our security for half a century now. And as NATO's leader and the primary broker of the peace agreement, the United States must be an essential part of the mission. If we're not there, NATO will not be there. The peace will collapse; the war will reignite; the slaughter of innocents will begin again. A conflict that already has claimed so many victims could spread like poison throughout the region, eat away at Europe's stability and erode our partnership with our European allies. And America's commitment to leadership will be questioned if we refuse to participate in implementing a peace agreement we brokered right here in the United States, especially since the presidents of Bosnia, Croatia and Serbia all asked us to participate, and all pledged their best efforts to the security of our troops."

— "Presidential Address: Clinton Asks Nation to Back U.S. Role in Bosnian Peace," Bill Clinton, November 27, 1995

6. The excerpt above represents which of the following continuities in the post-World War II era?

(A) preemptive attacks on foreign nations.

(B) reliance on international organization and alliances in times of conflict.

(C) containment of communism.

(D) isolation from foreign wars.

7. During the 1990s, the United States took part in peacekeeping missions in all of the following countries EXCEPT:

(A) Haiti.

(B) Bosnia.

(C) Somalia.

(D) Rwanda.

Questions 8-10 refer to the graph below.

U.S. Defense Spending Trends – 2001 to 2014 ($ Billion)

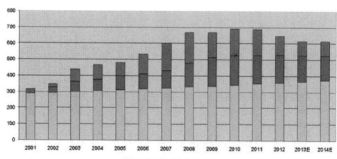

*Note: Amounts are discretionary budget authority
Source: Overview-U.S. Department of Defense FY2014 Budget Request

8. The graph above is best understood in the context of

   (A) rising defense spending during the 1980s as part of "Reaganomics."
   (B) isolationism of the 1990s.
   (C) the end of the Cold War.
   (D) the expansion of domestic programs in the 2000s.

9. Which of the following contributed to the rise in defense spending during the 2000s?

   (A) War in Irag.
   (B) War in Afghanistan.
   (C) War on Terror.
   (D) All of the above.

10. The overall trend in the graph best supports the concern raised by

    (A) Eisenhower's Farewell Address regarding the "military industrial complex".
    (B) Kennedy's pledge to "pay any price" in his Inaugural Address.
    (C) Johnson's development of the Great Society.
    (D) Reagan's Inaugural Address regarding the role of government.

DIFFICULTY LEVEL 3

11. As part of the "Reagan Doctrine," the United States invaded the small Caribbean island of Grenada in 1983 to

    (A) Help the United Kingdom recover the island from Argentina.
    (B) Remove a newly installed Marxist government.
    (C) Prevent a planned attach of the US Virgin Islands.
    (D) Capture the Island's president, a suspected drug trafficker.

PART C

DIFFICULTY LEVEL 2

1. As a result of the 21st-century concerns about reliance on foreign energy sources, the United States has

   (A) reduced its dependence on imported oil.
   (B) created a comprehensive plan for alternative fuel sources, such as wind and solar energy.
   (C) increased domestic oil and gas drilling.
   (D) implemented a drastic reduction in carbon emissions.

2. Since the 1960s, new migrants from which region most significantly increased the populations of the American South and West?

   (A) Eastern Europe.
   (B) Africa.
   (C) Latin America.
   (D) Middle East.

Question 3 refers to the excerpt below.

U.S. Healthcare Costs as a Percentage of GDP

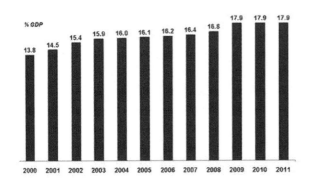

Source: Centers for Medicare and Medicaid Services

http://en.wikipedia.org/wiki/Patient_Protection_and_Affordable_Care_Act#mediaviewer/Fil e:U.S._Healthcare_Costs_as_a_Percentage_of_GDP.png

3. To address the issue depicted in the graph above, President Obama signed the

   (A) Lilly Ledbetter Fair Pay Act.
   (B) Affordable Care Act.
   (C) American Recovery and Reinvestment Act.
   (D) Children's Health Insurance Program Reauthorization Act.

Question 4 refers to the document below.

"The institution of civil marriage confers a social status and important legal benefits, rights, and privileges. ... The same-sex couples are denied equal access to civil marriage. ... Same-sex couples who enter into a civil union are denied equal access to all the benefits, rights, and privileges provided by federal law to those of married couples ... The benefits, rights, and privileges associated with domestic partnerships are not universally available, are not equal to those associated with marriage, and are rarely portable ... Denial of access to marriage to same-sex couples may especially harm people who also experience discrimination based on age, race, ethnicity, disability, gender and gender identity, religion, socioeconomic status and so on ... The APA believes that it is unfair to deny same-sex couples legal access to civil marriage and to all its attendant benefits, rights, and privileges."

— American Psychological Association, "Resolution on Sexual Orientation and Marriage," (2004)

4. The excerpt above is best understood in the context of

   (A) growing hostility toward gender equality in the United States.

   (B) increasing traction of the gay rights movement in the United States.

   (C) a backlash against conservative family values in the 21st century.

   (D) a decline in the number of voters who identify as "Independents."

DIFFICULTY LEVEL 3

5. Which of the following has NOT contributed to growing income inequality over the last generation?

   (A) outsourcing jobs to non-American workers.

   (B) a decline in the strength of unions.

   (C) a decrease in the number of mechanized jobs.

   (D) stagnant middle-class wages.

6. Demographic changes in the late 20th and early 21st centuries have been centered on all of the following EXCEPT

   (A) Family structure.

   (B) National identity.

   (C) Gender roles.

   (D) Media conglomerates.

ANSWERS

Period 1491-1607

PART A

DIFFICULTY LEVEL 1

1. ANSWER: B

Archaeologists estimate that the first humans came to the Americas between 10,000 and 40,000 years ago. They believe migrants crossed a land bridge connecting modern-day Siberia and Alaska. This land bridge was exposed by retreating sea levels during the Ice Age but is now submerged beneath the Bering Sea.

2. ANSWER: C

Unlike indigenous peoples in Central and South America, the Indians in the Great Basin and Western Plains did not develop permanent communities prior to 1492. Instead, they adapted to environmental challenges and lack of natural resources by adopting a mobile, nomadic lifestyle.

DIFFICULTY LEVEL 2

3. ANSWER: A

Before the arrival of Columbus, the Maya in Central America, the Aztecs in what is now Mexico, and the Incas in what is now Peru developed highly-organized societies and cultivated crops for a stable food supply. The Maya and Aztecs both cultivated corn (maize) and the Incas cultivated potatoes. It was only after the discovery of the New World that potatoes became a staple crop in much of Europe.

4. ANSWER: A

(chronological reasoning; comparison/contextualization)

Large buildings atop the main mounds of Kincaid indicate temples or council houses, which in turn demonstrate the Indians advanced political economy and belief system.

Carved figurines in coal and fluorite characterize the local iconography, with images showing connections to the Southeastern Ceremonial Complex (SECC).

5. **ANSWER: B**

(comparison/contextualization)

The Mississippian culture was a mound-building Native American culture that flourished in what is now the Midwestern, Eastern, and Southeastern United States from approximately 800 to 1600 CE, varying regionally.

6. **ANSWER: A**

(chronological reasoning)

In most places, the development of Mississippian culture coincided with adoption of comparatively large-scale, intensive maize agriculture, which supported larger populations and craft specialization. Craft specialization allowed other members of the community to focus on other work, such as architecture, warfare, and artistic endeavors.

7. **ANSWER: B**

(chronological reasoning)

After the Native Americans arrived, they gradually began to migrate throughout North and South America. As they spread out across the Americas, the Indians adapted to the varied geographical conditions, resulting in hundreds of tribes with varied languages and cultures.

8. **ANSWER: C**

(chronological reasoning; comparison/contextualization)

Although Native Americans were able to establish widespread trade and communication networks to obtain necessary food and commodities, they were unable to use such networks to unite against a common European enemy following the arrival of Columbus.

PART B

DIFFICULTY LEVEL 1

1. ANSWER: A

As a result of the European encounter with the New World, approximately 90 percent of the Native American population died from diseases to which they had no immunity. This trend was part of the broader Columbian Exchange: the transatlantic exchange of plants, animals, and diseases between Europe and the Americas.

2. ANSWER: C

European contact with Native Americans had a devastating impact on the native populations of the Caribbean and North and South America. Europeans drove Native Americans from their land and, in many cases, killed them through armed conflicts and disease.

DIFFICULTY LEVEL 2

3. ANSWER: A

(comparison/contextualization)

Columbus's mention of the Native Americans' interest and amazement with weapons and iron demonstrates the very different worldviews of the two cultures. Not only were the Indians "ignorant" of such advanced weaponry, but they had not seen such physical manmade objects as glass beads before 1492. One must keep in mind, however, that this excerpt represents Columbus' point of view to an audience of European readers.

4. ANSWER: D

(chronological reasoning)

During the 15th and 16th centuries, Spanish conquistadores used Christianity as a way to justify the oppression of Native Americans. Although some missionaries, such as Bartolomé de las Casas, spoke out against mistreatment of the Indians, most Europeans believed that their Christian faith permitted them to conquer and convert non-Christians.

5. **ANSWER: B**

(use of evidence)

When Columbus comments on the Native Americans' religion, he writes, "they would easily become Christians." This demonstrates that he saw religion as important, and thus supports the argument that religious conversion was one of Spain's principal objectives.

PART C

DIFFICULTY LEVEL 1

1. ANSWER: D

After Spanish *conquistadores* conquered parts of Central and South America, they were granted land and natives by the Spanish king. Native Americans were forced to farm or mine the land while their Spanish masters reaped the benefits. Eventually, after violence and disease decimated the Indian population, the Spanish looked to West Africa for slaves to replace the lost source of labor.

DIFFICULTY LEVEL 2

2. ANSWER: C

Although Spain's power and wealth diminished once the English, Dutch, and French colonized North America, Christianity, and especially Catholicism, has endured in Central and South America.

3. ANSWER: A

(comparison/contextualization)

Unlike Europeans, Native Americans did not believe land ownership was exclusive or permanent. Instead, Indian tribes might defend their use of the land, but once they left or lost control of the land, they did not retain ownership.

4. ANSWER: D

(chronological reasoning)

Prior to European contact, Native Americans frequently warred with other tribes. As a result, Europeans were often able to exploit this hostility among tribes when they arrived by playing one tribe against another, and easily conquered tribes with whom they came in contact.

5. ANSWER: D

(chronological reasoning; comparison/contextualization)

The Treaty of Tordesillas was signed in 1494, dividing the newly discovered lands outside Europe between the Portuguese Empire and Spanish Empire. This line of demarcation was about halfway between the Cape Verde Islands (already Portuguese) and the islands entered by Christopher Columbus on his first voyage (claimed for Spain). The lands to the east would belong to Portugal and the lands to the west to Spain. The Portuguese King John II was not pleased with that arrangement, feeling that it gave him far too little land, but also gave the Portuguese rights to Brazil, which is still influenced by Portuguese language and culture.

6. **ANSWER: D**

(comparison/contextualization; interpretation/synthesis)

Because England did not begin colonizing the New World until the late 16th Century, Queen Elizabeth I would have likely opposed the Treaty of Tordesillas, which divided the New World between Spain and Portugal. However, it should be noted that many countries considered it a hollow document and failed to heed it. Nevertheless, The Treaty of Tordesillas has been invoked by Chile in the 20th century to defend the principle of an Antarctic sector extending along a meridian to the South Pole, as well as the assertion that the treaty made Spanish (or Portuguese) all undiscovered land south to the Pole. It was also invoked by Argentina in the 20th century as part of its claim to the Falkland Islands/Malvinas Islands.

DIFFICULTY LEVEL 3

7. **ANSWER: C**

England's defeat of the Spanish Armada, the most powerful naval force in the world, helped to ensure England's naval dominance in the North Atlantic. This superiority gave them confidence and determination to establish their own colonies in the Western Hemisphere.

Period 1607-1754

PART A

DIFFICULTY LEVEL 1

1. ANSWER: A

A joint-stock company is a business entity in which different stakes can be bought and owned by shareholders. Each shareholder owns company stock in proportion, limiting the liability of any one person. The first joint-stock companies to be implemented in the Americas were The London Company and The Plymouth Company. In modern *corporate law*, the existence of a joint-stock company is often synonymous with *incorporation* (i.e. possession of *legal personality* separate from shareholders) and limited liability (meaning that the shareholders are only liable for the company's debts to the value of the money they invested in the company). And as a consequence joint-stock companies are commonly known as *corporations* or *limited companies*.

2. ANSWER: D

The Mayflower Compact, written by leaders of The Plymouth Company/Colony aboard the Mayflower, was an agreement among male colonists to create and abide by a just set of laws. This was one of many early examples of democracy in Colonial America. Other examples included the Virginia House of Burgesses and the Fundamental Orders of Connecticut.

3. ANSWER: C

For geographic reasons, New England did not rely on cash crops for its economy, which was very diverse. Instead, the region relied on subsistence farming, trade, fishing, shipbuilding, and manufacturing products within the household (sometimes referred to as "homespun").

4. ANSWER: C

While slavery began for economic reasons—first to supplement and then to replace indentured servitude—it was justified on the basis of race and perpetuated by heredity. This was made possible, among other reasons, by legalized Slave Codes. For example, the Virginia Slave Code of 1662 states, "all children born in this country shall be held bond or free only according to the condition of the mother."

DIFFICULTY LEVEL 2

5. **ANSWER: C**

After Henry Hudson explored the region in 1609, the Dutch claimed the area for themselves, establishing the colony of New Netherland and its capital, New Amsterdam. The Netherlands granted the Dutch East India Company economic control of the region.

6. **ANSWER: A**

Ethnically, the Middle Colonies were more diverse than the other British colonial regions in North America and tended to be more socially tolerant. For example, they were settled by Germans, Scotch-Irish, and English, and represented a wide range of religions, including Quakers, Mennonites, and Lutherans. The Middle Colonies were also economically diverse. They became known as the Breadbasket Colonies for their grain exports, but also had thriving lumber and shipbuilding industries.

7. **ANSWER: C**

Roger Williams' promotion of Liberty of Conscience, which argued for separation of church and state and tolerance of the Native Americans, resulted in his expulsion from Massachusetts Bay colony. His ideas were considered dangerous to Puritan orthodoxy, which did not tolerate dissenting religious views.

8. **ANSWER: D**

By the early 1700s, Black slavery existed in every colony. Although the Northern colonies were not as economically dependent on slavery, they also participated in the transatlantic slave trade. While the South relied on indentured servitude for much of the 1600s, by the late 17th century colonies had passed Slave Codes establishing a labor system of permanent slavery based on race and heredity.

9. **ANSWER: B**

(comparison/contextualization)

When the Puritans arrived in New England in the early 17th century, they were seeking to establish colonies free from the religious persecutions that they had experienced in

England. Puritans were not, however, interested in extending religious tolerance. Believing they were God's "elect," or "visible saints," they sought to establish a "City upon a Hill" to serve as a model for mankind.

10. ANSWER: D

(chronological reasoning; use of evidence)

Because the Puritans were hostile to practices and views that challenged Puritan orthodoxy, they banished Roger Williams for his belief in Liberty of Conscience, or separation of church and state. Anne Hutchinson was exiled for antinomianism, In Christianity, an **antinomian** is one who denies the fixed meaning and applicability of moral law and believes that salvation is attained solely through faith and divine grace. Williams established the colony of Rhode Island in the 1630s, which allowed freedom of religion, and Hutchinson followed him shortly thereafter.

11. ANSWER: C

(use of evidence)

The Puritans who settled in New England wanted the freedom to practice their religion, which was based on Calvinist views of predestination. According to Winthrop, the community had to keeps its covenant with God to ensure prosperity.

12. ANSWER: C

(interpretation/synthesis)

American exceptionalism is the theory that the United States is qualitatively different from other countries. This exceptionalism is based on a unique American ideology that emphasizes liberty, egalitarianism, individualism, republicanism, democracy, and laissez-faire economics. By declaring Massachusetts Bay a "City upon a Hill," Winthrop begins a long trend highlighting America's exceptionalism in the world.

13. ANSWER: B

(chronological reasoning)

Bacon's Rebellion was an armed rebellion in 1676 by Virginia settlers led by Nathaniel Bacon against the rule of Governor William Berkeley. The colony's disorganized frontier political structure, combined with accumulating grievances (including frequent Indian attacks and the Governor's refusal to allow Bacon to be a part of his fur trade with the

Native Americans) helped to motivate a popular uprising against Berkeley, who had failed to address the demands of the colonists regarding their safety.

14. ANSWER: B

(chronological reasoning)

Following Bacon's Rebellion, the Planter Class began looking for less troublesome laborers. Because the availability of indentured servants was already declining, they looked to African slaves as a permanent labor force. According to the historian Edmund S. Morgan, Bacon's rebellion, namely the potential for lower class revolt in the colony, led to the transition over to slavery. He wrote, "...But for those with eyes to see, there was an obvious lesson in the rebellion. Resentment of an alien race might be more powerful than resentment of an upper class. Virginians did not immediately grasp it. It would sink in as time went on...."

15. ANSWER: D

(interpretation/synthesis)

Each of these Colonial-Era rebellions reflected colonists' discontent with a distant authority figure, just as Nathanial Bacon was targeting Governor Berkeley's policies. Leisler's Rebellion, 1689 to 1691, was an uprising in lower New York against the policies of King James II of England. The Paxton Boys were frontiersmen of Scots-Irish origin who formed a vigilante group to retaliate in 1763 against local American Indians. Following attacks on the Conestoga, they marched to Philadelphia to present their grievances to the legislature. The Regulator Movement was an uprising in the British North America's Carolina colonies, lasting from about 1765 to 1771, in which citizens took up arms against colonial officials. Though the rebellion did not change the power structure, some historians consider it a catalyst to the American Revolutionary War.

PART B

DIFFICULTY LEVEL 1

1. ANSWER: A

Most Europeans believed that Native Americans were their inferiors. They sought to exploit them for economic gain, convert them to Christianity, and use them as military allies. For example, the Spanish developed the *encomienda* system to enslave the Native Americans, and although the Natives taught the English much about the land, the English viewed them as savages. The French were one of the few European powers who viewed the natives as economic and military allies.

2. ANSWER: A

When they arrived in the New World, the French sought to control the fur trade and built trading posts throughout the St. Lawrence Valley and around the Great Lakes region, in what is present-day Canada. Generally speaking, they had genial relations with the Native Americans, trading fur pelts with them and helping the Huron people fight the Iroquois.

3. ANSWER: C

After the "Starving Time," John Rolfe introduced the cultivation of tobacco, which he successfully harvested in 1614 and which became a highly profitable cash crop for the colony. Rolfe is also famous for marrying Pocahontas, daughter of the chief of the Powhatan Confederacy.

DIFFICULTY LEVEL 2

4. ANSWER: A

When the English arrived in Jamestown in 1607, the natives initially welcomed and provided crucial provisions and support for the colonists, who were not agriculturally inclined. Relations with the newcomers soured early on, but it was the Native American population that suffered because of warfare, not the colonists. Mortality at Jamestown itself was very high due to disease and starvation, with over 80% of the colonists perishing in 1609-1610 in what became known as the "Starving Time."

5. **ANSWER: D**

The British colony of Georgia was founded by James Oglethorpe. The last of the original 13 Colonies, Georgia would provide a defensive buffer between South Carolina and Spanish Florida. In addition, the colony housed thousands of imprisoned debtors from England's overcrowded prisons.

6. **ANSWER: A**

(arguments/ evidence)

The "Huron Carol" is a Canadian Christmas hymn written in 1642 by Jean de Brébeuf, a French Jesuit missionary living among the Hurons in Canada. Brébeuf wrote the lyrics in the native language of the Huron people. It demonstrates the mostly positive relationship the French had with Native Americans, as well as their interest in Catholic conversion and the fur trade.

7. **ANSWER: B**

(chronological reasoning)

Although the French had better relationships with the Native Americans than the Spanish and English, they still sought the power, wealth, glory, and Christian conversions that all European settlers desired at this time.

8. **ANSWER: C**

(comparison/contextualization)

Although the Pueblos had long been divided, in 1680 they united under Popé, whose dwelling is shown above, against the Spanish. The Pueblo killed 400 Spanish and drove the remaining 2,000 settlers out of the province of Santa Fe de Nuevo México. Twelve years later, the Spanish returned and were able to reoccupy New Mexico with little opposition.

9. **ANSWER: B**

(chronological reasoning

The Pueblo Revolt of 1680 — also known as Popé's Rebellion — was an uprising of most of the Pueblo Indians against the Spanish colonizers in the province of Santa Fe de Nuevo México, present day New Mexico. The Pueblo killed 400 Spanish and drove the remaining 2,000 settlers out of the province. It was uncommon for Native Americans to unite and defeat a European foe.

Period 1607-1754

10. ANSWER: B

King Philip's War, sometimes called Metacom's War, was an armed conflict between Native American inhabitants of present-day New England and English colonists and their Native American allies in 1675–Over 600 colonists and 3,000 Native Americans died. The military defeat of the Native Americans meant that most of Massachusetts, Connecticut and Rhode Island land was nearly completely open to colonial settlement.

PART C

DIFFICULTY LEVEL 1

1. ANSWER: C

The Maryland Toleration Act was a law mandating religious tolerance for all Christians, but it sentenced to death anyone denying the divinity of Jesus (including Jews and atheists). As the first law on religious tolerance in British North America, it influenced related laws in other colonies. In addition, portions of it were echoed in the writing of the First Amendment to the United States Constitution, which enshrined religious freedom in American law.

2. ANSWER: A

In search of economic opportunities and a more tolerant environment in which to build communities of "holy conversation," some Quakers (also known as the Society of Friends) emigrated to what is now the Northeastern region of the United States in the early 1680s. While in some areas like New England they continued to experience persecution, they were able to establish thriving communities in the Delaware Valley. The only two colonies that tolerated Quakers in this time period were Rhode Island and Pennsylvania, where Quakers established themselves politically. In Rhode Island, 36 governors in the first 100 years were Quakers. Pennsylvania was established by affluent Quaker William Penn in 1682, and as an American state run under Quaker principles.

DIFFICULTY LEVEL 2

3. ANSWER: C

The first colleges in Colonial New England were established to ensure an adequate supply of ministers, which was considered the most prestigious profession at the time. Harvard was established in 1636 and Yale was founded in 1701, making these Ivy League schools two of the oldest in the United States.

4. ANSWER: C

Because of the unequal gender ratio in the South (i.e., men outnumbered women) and the high mortality rate among young men, women were generally allowed to retain a separate title to their property. This was atypical for the time period, since most women forfeited property rights after marriage.

5. **ANSWER: D**

The Dominion of New England in America (1686–1689) was an administrative union of English colonies in the New England region of North America. Its political structure represented centralized control more akin to the model used by the Spanish monarchy in New Spain. Most colonists opposed it because they deeply resented being stripped of their traditional rights. Under Governor Sir Edmund Andros, the Dominion tried to make legal and structural changes, but most of these were undone, and the Dominion was overthrown as soon as word was received that King James had left the throne in England. One notable success was the introduction of the Church of England into Massachusetts, whose Puritan leaders had previously refused to allow it any sort of foothold.

6. **ANSWER: C**

The First Great Awakening took place in British North America during the 1730s and 1740s. The leaders of the Great Awakening, such as Jonathan Edwards and George Whitefield, sought a strong emotional response from their congregations. The evangelical movement of the 1740s also played a key role in the development of democratic thought, which ushered in the period of the American Revolution and created demand for religious freedom.

7. **ANSWER: B**

(comparison/contextualixzation)

Edwards was among the most prominent ministers during the First Great Awakening, which took place during the 1730s and 1740s in the British North American colonies. Edwards' emotional, evangelical sermons typically juxtaposed images of Hell and damnation with God's salvation.

8. **ANSWER: B**

(chronological reasoning)

In response to the Enlightenment's emphasis on reason and scientific inquiry, Protestant ministers feared that colonists were becoming less religious. As a result, ministers sought to place a renewed emphasis on religion for existing church members. Therefore, the First Great Awakening focused on converting people who were already church members with a new style of preaching that was evangelical and emotional.

9. **ANSWER: C**

(chronological reasoning)

The new style of sermons and the way people practiced their faith breathed new life into religion in America. Participants became passionately and emotionally involved in their religion, rather than passively listening to intellectual discourse in a detached manner. Ministers who used this new style of preaching were generally called "new lights," while the preachers who remained unemotional were referred to as "old lights." People affected by the revival began to study the Bible at home. This effectively decentralized the means of informing the public on religious matters and was akin to the individualistic trends present in Europe during the Protestant Reformation. The Awakening played a major role in the lives of women, especially, though rarely were they allowed to preach or take public roles.

10. **ANSWER: D**

(comparison/contextualization)

The *Zenger Trial* is considered a landmark case in American jurisprudence. In late 1733, John Peter Zenger began printing *The New York Weekly Journal*, in which he voiced opinions critical of the colonial governor, William Cosby. On Governor Cosby's orders, the sheriff arrested Zenger. After a grand jury refused to indict him, the attorney general Richard Bradley charged him with libel, or publishing false statements damaging a person's reputation. In defending Zenger in this landmark case, his lawyers attempted to establish the precedent that a statement, even if defamatory, is not libelous if it can be proven, thus affirming freedom of the press in America.

11. **ANSWER: A**

(chronological reasoning)

Both Zenger and Hutchinson were subject to arbitrary rules in which they had no say. Hutchinson was convicted of antinomianism, one who broke the moral codes and legal statutes of the colony, and was eventually banished. Zenger, who was ultimately acquitted, was charged with libel for speaking out against the royal governor.

12. **ANSWER: B**

(chronological reasoning; crafting historical arguments from historical evidence)

Although slavery was integral to the development of the Triangle Trade, the question is asking specifically about the exchange of raw materials. Mercantilism was an economic system in which a country, such as Great Britain, acquired raw materials from its colonies and sold them back to the colonies as manufactured goods.

13. ANSWER: B

(comparison and contextualization)

Navigation Acts were a series of laws that restricted the use of foreign ships for trade between Britain and its colonies. They began in 1651 and ended 200 years later. They reflected the policy of mercantilism, which sought to keep all the benefits of trade inside the Empire, and minimize the loss of gold and silver to foreigners. On the whole, the Acts of Trade and Navigation were obeyed, except for the Molasses Act of 1733, which led to extensive smuggling because no effective means of enforcement was provided until the 1750s. Irritation because of stricter enforcement under the Sugar Act of 1764 became one source of resentment by merchants in the American colonies against Great Britain. This in turn helped push the colonies to start the American Revolution.

DIFFICULTY LEVEL 3

14. ANSWER: C

Jefferson, a student of the Enlightenment and a proponent of democracy, believed New England town meetings were quintessentially democratic. A town meeting is a form of direct democratic rule that has been used in New England since the 17th century, in which most or all the members of a community come together to legislate policy and budgets for local government.

15. ANSWER: A

The Half-Way Covenant was a form of partial church membership created by New England in 1662. Colonial leaders felt that the people of the English colonies were drifting away from their original religious purpose. First-generation settlers were beginning to die out, while their children and grandchildren often expressed less religious piety, and more desire for material wealth. In response, the Half-Way Covenant provided a partial church membership for the children and grandchildren of church members. Those who accepted the Covenant and agreed to follow the creed within the church could participate in the Lord's supper. Crucially, the Half-Way covenant provided that the children of holders of the covenant could be baptized in the church. These partial members, however, couldn't accept communion or vote.

16. ANSWER: D

The Salem witch trials were a series of hearings and prosecutions of people accused of witchcraft in colonial Massachusetts between February 1692 and May 1693. The trials resulted in the executions of twenty people, most of them women. In at least two important respects—quality of land and access to market—those farmers on the eastern (or Town) side of the Village had a significant advantage. Historians Paul Boyer and Stephen Nissenbaum have shown that resentment against those living in the eastern part of Salem caused many of the accusations. They write, "Modern topographical maps show what any Salem Village farmer knew from first-hand experience: the best lands in the Village were the broad, flat meadows of the eastern part, nearest the coast, while the western part was increasingly broken up by sharp little hills and marshy depressions. The eastern side of the Village, too, was significantly closer to the network of roads and waterways which gave access to Salem Town and her markets."

Period 1754-1800

PART A

DIFFICULTY LEVEL 1

1. ANSWER: A

The costs associated with the French and Indian war left Great Britain looking for revenue. After Great Britain's Parliament passed the Stamp Act without consulting the colonists, their rallying cry became, "No Taxation without Representation." Parliament insisted that they had the colonists' best interests at heart, because all colonists had "virtual representation" in Parliament. In protest, the elected leaders from several colonies organized the Stamp Act Congress, because the tax marked the first time Great Britain taxed the colonists for the purpose of raising revenue and not for regulating trade. Although the tax was ultimately repealed, the colonists' distrust of Great Britain persisted.

2. ANSWER: D

The Age of Enlightenment was an era in which cultural and intellectual forces in Western Europe emphasized reason, analysis and individualism rather than traditional lines of authority. American revolutionaries were indebted to Enlightenment thinkers for their ideas about natural rights, liberty, and government. The Americans closely followed English and Scottish political ideas, as well as some French thinkers such as Rousseau and Montesquieu. During the Enlightenment there was a great emphasis upon liberty, democracy, republicanism and religious tolerance. John Locke's ideas had perhaps the greatest influence on American notions of the inherent natural rights of the individual and the government's responsibility for protecting those rights.

3. ANSWER: B

The Proclamation of Neutrality was a formal announcement issued by President George Washington in May 1793 declaring the nation neutral in the conflict between France and Great Britain. Washington's cabinet members agreed that neutrality was essential; the nation was too young and its military was too small to risk any sort of engagement with either France or Britain.

4. ANSWER: C

Convened by Benjamin Franklin in 1754, The Albany Congress was a meeting of representatives sent by the legislatures of the northern seven of the thirteen British North American colonies (specifically Connecticut, Maryland, Massachusetts, New Hampshire, New York, Pennsylvania, and Rhode Island). Representatives discussed better relations with the Native American tribes and common defensive measures against the French threat from Canada in the opening stage of the French and Indian War. Franklin had hope to reach agreement on a Plan of Union, modeled after the Iroquois Confederacy; the colonies rejected the union. The meeting, however, was the first time colonists met together and it provided a model that came in handy when setting up the Stamp Act Congress in 1765 as well as the First Continental Congress in 1774, both of which were preludes to the American Revolution.

5. ANSWER: B

The war changed economic, political, governmental and social relations between three European powers (Britain, France, and Spain), their colonies and colonists, and the natives that inhabited the territories they claimed. As a result of the war, Britain became the dominant power in North America, but both France and Britain suffered financially. For many native populations, the elimination of French power in North America meant the disappearance of a strong ally and counterweight to British expansion, leading ultimately to dispossession of their native lands.

6. ANSWER: A

Following the French and Indian War, Great Britain became the dominant power in North America and gained territory that had belonged previously to the French. To organize Great Britain's new North American Empire and to stabilize relations with Native Americans, King George III forbade colonists from settling west of the Appalachian Mountains. Some historians have argued that colonial resentment of the proclamation contributed to the growing divide between the colonies and the mother country.

7. ANSWER: C

The committees of correspondence were organized by the Patriot leaders of the Thirteen Colonies on the eve of the American Revolution. They coordinated responses to Britain and shared their plans. For example, the Maryland Committee of Correspondence was instrumental in setting up the First Continental Congress. The committees of correspondence rallied opposition on common causes and established plans for collective action–the group of committees was the beginning of what later became a formal political union among the colonies. The committees became the leaders of the American resistance to British actions.

8. **ANSWER: A**

(chronological reasoning)

Following the French and Indian War, the Treaty of Paris was signed on February 10, 1763, by Great Britain, France and Spain, with Portugal in agreement, after Britain's victory over France and Spain during the Seven Years' War. The signing of the treaty formally ended the French and Indian War in North American and marked the beginning of an era of British dominance outside Europe. Britain gained much of France's possessions in North America.

9. **ANSWER: B**

(comparison and contextualization)

Before the Treaty of Paris (1763), North America east of the Mississippi River was largely claimed by either Great Britain or France, but large areas had no settlements by Europeans.

The French population numbered about 75,000 and was heavily concentrated along the St. Lawrence River valley. British colonies had a population of about 1.5 million and ranged along the eastern coast of the continent, from Nova Scotia and Newfoundland in the north, to Georgia in the south. In between the French and the British, large areas were dominated by native tribes. After the French and Indian War, of course, Great Britain became the dominant force in North America.

10. **ANSWER: B**

(chronological reasoning; interpretation and synthesis)

After the Treaty of Paris (1763) was signed, England passed the Proclamation of 1763, which prohibited colonial settlement west of Appalachia. The colonists saw this as a threat to their sovereignty. In addition, England left behind a standing peacetime army in the colonies. Colonists were responsible for funding the military presences through various taxes, and housing the soldiers through the Quartering Act. Interestingly, residual irritation over the Quartering Act would later lead to the inclusion of the Third Amendment in the Bill of Rights, which places restrictions on quartering soldiers in private homes without the owner's consent.

11. **ANSWER: C**

(comparison and contextualization)

The Boston Tea Party was a political protest by the Sons of Liberty in Boston and took place on December 16, 1773. The demonstrators, some disguised as American Indians, destroyed an entire shipment of tea sent by the East India Company, in defiance of the Tea Act of 1773. The Boston Tea Party was a key event in the growth of the American Revolution. Parliament responded in 1774 with the Coercive Acts, or Intolerable Acts, which, among other provisions, ended local self-government in Massachusetts and closed Boston's ports. Colonists up and down the Thirteen Colonies in turn responded to the Coercive Acts with additional acts of protest and by convening the First Continental Congress, which petitioned the British monarch for repeal of the acts and coordinated colonial resistance to them.

12. **ANSWER: D**

(historical arguments from historical evidence)

As the founder of the Sons of Liberty and an ardent Patriot—somebody who supported separating from England—Samuel Adams would have supported the publication of Paine's *Common Sense*, which inspired people in the Thirteen Colonies to declare and fight for independence from Great Britain in the summer of 1776. It was sold and distributed widely and read aloud at taverns and meeting places. In proportion to the population of the colonies at that time (2.5 million), it had the largest sale and circulation of any book published in American history.

13. **ANSWER: D**

(chronological reasoning)

In his Farewell Address, George Washington gives a number of pieces of advice to the American people for maintaining a strong republic. Among them, he reinforces his reasoning behind the Proclamation of Neutrality he made during the French Revolutionary Wars. Despite the 1778 Treaty of Alliance with France, Washington argues that from what he, and his advisors, understood and continue to believe, the United States had a right to remain neutral in the conflict and furthermore that all nations, besides France and Britain of course, have agreed with his stance. Along with stating his belief that justice and humanity required him to remain neutral during the conflict, he also argues that the stance of neutrality was necessary to allow the new government a chance to mature and gain enough strength to control its own affairs.

14. **ANSWER: A**

(chronological reasoning)

To this day, Washington's Farewell Address is considered to be one of the most important documents in American history. Despite his refusal to recognize the obligations of the Treaty of Alliance with France, Washington's hope that the United States would end permanent alliances with foreign nations would not be fully realized until 1800 with the signing of Convention of 1800 (Treaty of Mortefontaine). The treaty officially ended the 1778 Treaty of Alliance in exchange for ending the Quasi-War with France and establishment of most favored nation trade relations with Napoleonic France. In 1823, Washington's foreign policy goals would be further realized with the issuing of the Monroe Doctrine, which promised non-interference in European affairs so long as the nations of Europe did not seek to re-colonize or interfere with the newly independent Latin American nations of Central and South America. It would not be until the foundation of the 1949 North Atlantic Treaty Organization (NATO) that the United States would again enter into a permanent military alliance with any foreign nation.

DIFFICULTY LEVEL 3

15. ANSWER: D

The French and Indian War (1754–1763) was the North American theater of the worldwide Seven Years' War. The war was fought between the colonies of British America and New France, with both sides supported by military units from their parent countries of Great Britain and France, as well as Native American allies. The war was fought primarily along the frontiers between New France and the British colonies, from Virginia in the South to Nova Scotia in the North. It began with a dispute over control of the Ohio River Valley at confluence of the Allegheny and Monongahela rivers. The dispute erupted into violence in the Battle of Jumonville Glen in May 1754, during which Virginia militiamen under the command of 22-year-old George Washington ambushed a French patrol.

16. ANSWER: A

Letters from a Farmer in Pennsylvania is a series of essays written by the Pennsylvania lawyer and legislator John Dickinson from 1767 to 1768. The twelve letters were widely read and reprinted throughout the thirteen colonies and were important in uniting the colonists against the Townshend Acts, which levied taxes on essential goods. While acknowledging the power of Parliament in matters concerning the whole British Empire, Dickinson argued that the colonies were sovereign in their internal affairs. He argued that taxes laid upon the colonies by Parliament for the purpose of raising revenue, rather than regulating trade, were unlawful.

PART B

DIFFICULTY LEVEL 1

1. ANSWER: A

Drafted by John Dickinson, a moderate, the Olive Branch Petition was adopted by the Second Continental Congress on July 5, 1775, in a final attempt to avoid a full-on war between the Thirteen Colonies the Congress represented and Great Britain. The petition affirmed American loyalty to Great Britain and entreated the king to prevent further conflict.

2. ANSWER: C

The Declaration of Independence was adopted by the Continental Congress on July 4, 1776. The document announced that the thirteen American colonies, then at war with Great Britain, regarded themselves as thirteen newly independent sovereign states that were no longer a part of the British Empire. The Declaration justified the independence of the United States by listing colonial grievances against King George III and by asserting certain natural and legal rights—rights that John Locke and other Enlightenment thinkers had expounded upon—including a right of revolution against a government that did not have the consent of the governed or protect people's rights.

3. ANSWER: D

Abigail Adams was an advocate of married women's property rights and more opportunities for women, particularly in the field of education. Women, she believed, should not submit to laws not made in their interest, nor should they be content with the simple role of being companions to their husbands. They should educate themselves and be recognized for their intellectual capabilities, so they could guide and influence the lives of their children and husbands.

She is known for her March 1776 letter to John Adams and the Continental Congress, requesting that they, "...remember the ladies, and be more generous and favorable to them than your ancestors. Do not put such unlimited power into the hands of the Husbands. Remember all Men would be tyrants if they could. If particular care and attention is not paid to the Ladies we are determined to foment a Rebellion, and will not hold ourselves bound by any Laws in which we have no voice, or Representation."

4. ANSWER: C

At the Constitutional Convention of 1787, the document that was adopted looked quite different from what exists now, since 27 changes, or amendments, have been added since its ratification. For instance, the Bill of Rights, the first ten amendments that detail our rights in a limited government, was not added until 1791. The U.S. Constitution was built on a series of compromises, many having to do with representation in the legislative branch. The Great Compromise, or the Connecticut Compromise, established a bicameral legislature comprised of a Senate with fixed representation and a House of Representatives with proportional representation. The issue of representation for slave states was addressed with the Three-Fifths Compromise, which allowed 3/5 of a state's slave population to count for purposes of taxation and congressional representation.

5. **ANSWER: C**

The Bill of Rights is the collective name for the first ten amendments to the United States Constitution. Proposed to assuage the fears of Anti-Federalists who had opposed Constitutional ratification, these amendments guarantee a number of personal freedoms, limit the government's power in judicial and other proceedings, and reserve some powers to the states and the public.

6. **ANSWER: C**

The Alien and Sedition Acts were signed into law by President John Adams in 1798 during an undeclared naval war with France, later known as the Quasi-War. Authored by the Federalists, the laws were purported to strengthen national security, but critics argued that they were primarily an attempt to suppress voters who disagreed with the Federalist party. The acts were denounced by Democratic-Republicans and ultimately helped them to victory in the 1800 election, when Thomas Jefferson defeated the incumbent President Adams.

DIFFICULTY LEVEL 2

7. **ANSWER: B**

Salutary neglect refers to an unofficial and long-term 17th- and 18th-century British policy of avoiding strict enforcement of parliamentary laws, meant to keep the American colonies obedient to England. Salutary neglect was a large contributing factor that led to the American Revolutionary War. Since the imperial authority did not assert the power that it had, the colonists were left to govern themselves. These essentially sovereign colonies soon became accustomed to the idea of self-government. They also realized that they were powerful enough to defeat the British (with help from France) and decided to revolt. Such prolonged isolation eventually resulted in the emergence of a collective identity that considered itself separate from Great Britain.

8. **ANSWER: C**

The Articles of Confederation established the United States of America as a confederation of sovereign states and served as its first constitution. It was formally ratified by all 13 states in early 1781 and provided domestic and international legitimacy for the Continental Congress to direct the American Revolutionary War, conduct diplomacy with Europe, and deal with territorial issues and Native American relations. Nevertheless, the weakness of the government created by the Articles became a matter of concern for key nationalists. Fearful of creating a strong central government that might become tyrannical, the Articles of Confederation denied the national government the ability to tax, coin money, or raise a military.

9. **ANSWER: D**

Despite its many weaknesses, the government under the Articles of Confederation had several successes, including the Treaty of Paris (1783), which ended the Revolutionary War, and the Northwest Ordnance of 1787, which created the Northwest Territory, the first organized territory of the United States, from lands beyond the Appalachian Mountains, between British Canada and the Great Lakes to the north and the Ohio River to the south. The upper Mississippi River formed the Territory's western boundary. The most significant intended purpose of this legislation was its mandate for the creation of new states from the region. It provided that at least three but not more than five states would be established in the territory, and that once such a state achieved a population of 60,000 it would be admitted into representation in Congress on an equal footing with the original thirteen states.

10. **ANSWER: B**

The Federalist (later known as *The Federalist Papers*) is a collection of 85 articles and essays written by Alexander Hamilton, James Madison, and John Jay promoting the ratification of the United States Constitution. There are many highlights among the essays of *The Federalist*. *Federalist* No. 10, in which Madison discusses the means of preventing rule by majority faction and advocates a large, commercial republic, is generally regarded as the most important of the 85 articles from a philosophical perspective; it is complemented by *Federalist* No. 14, in which Madison takes the measure of the United States and declares it appropriate for an extended republic.

11. **ANSWER: A**

The Whiskey Rebellion was a tax protest in the United States beginning in 1791, during the presidency of George Washington. The rebellion was provoked by the imposition of an excise tax on distilled spirits. Although the tax applied to all distilled spirits, whiskey was by far the most popular distilled beverage in 18th-century America, so the excise became widely known as a "whiskey tax." The new excise was a part of treasury secretary Alexander Hamilton's program to fund war debt incurred during the Revolutionary War.

12. ANSWER: A

The Kentucky and Virginia Resolutions were political statements drafted in 1798 and 1799, in which the Kentucky and Virginia legislatures took the position that the federal Alien and Sedition Acts were unconstitutional. Introducing the doctrine of nullification, the resolutions argued that the states had the right and the duty to declare unconstitutional any acts of Congress that were not explicitly authorized by the Constitution. In doing so, they argued for states' rights and strict constructionism of the Constitution. The Kentucky and Virginia Resolutions of 1798 were written secretly by Vice President Thomas Jefferson and James Madison, respectively.

13. ANSWER: D

(comparison and contextualization)

John Locke's political theory was founded on social contract theory. Locke believed that human nature is characterized by reason and tolerance. In a natural state, all people were equal and independent. In addition, everyone had a natural right to defend his "Life, health, Liberty, or Possessions." Most scholars trace the phrase "life, liberty, and the pursuit of happiness," in the American Declaration of Independence, to Locke's theory of rights.

Locke also advocated governmental separation of powers and believed that revolution is not only a right but an obligation in some circumstances, especially when the government has failed to protect people's natural rights. These ideas would come to have profound influence on the Declaration of Independence and the Constitution of the United States.

14. ANSWER: A

(chronological reasoning)

Even after fighting in the American Revolutionary War began at Lexington and Concord in April 1775, many colonists still hoped for reconciliation with Great Britain.

When the Second Continental Congress convened in May 1775, some delegates hoped for eventual independence, but no one yet advocated declaring it. Although many colonists no longer believed that Parliament had any sovereignty over them, they still professed loyalty to King George, whom they hoped would intercede on their behalf. They were to be disappointed after the King rejected the Olive Branch Petition, a final attempt at reconciliation. The following year, delegates to the Continental Congress authorized the Declaration of Independence.

15. ANSWER: D

(chronological reasoning; interpretation and sythesis)

The enduring legacy of the Declaration of Independence is evident both in United States history and in its influence on other countries. It was referenced by advocates for women's suffrage in the 19th and 20th centuries, by Abraham Lincoln in his opposition to slavery, and by civil rights leaders in their push for equal protection under the law. In addition, the inspiration and content of the French "Declaration of the Rights of Man and Citizen" (1789) emerged largely from the ideals of the American Revolution. Finally, independence movements in Central and South America have drawn on the ideas of the Declaration of Independence.

16. ANSWER: D

(comparison and contextualization)

The debate over how best to interpret the Constitution began during George Washington's presidency. Thomas Jefferson, Washington's Secretary of State who became the leader of the Democratic-Republican party, was a strict constructionist who believed that the Constitution was to be read literally and that the federal government could only assume powers delegated by the Constitution. Alexander Hamilton, Secretary of Treasury and leader of the Federalist party, was a loose constructionist who believed that the Constitution's implied powers gave the federal government greater authority to take actions, such as the creation of a National Bank, that were not explicitly stated in the Constitution.

17. ANSWER: C

(chronological reasoning)

During Washington's presidency, political factions soon formed around dominant personalities such as Alexander Hamilton, the Secretary of the Treasury, and Thomas Jefferson, the Secretary of State, who opposed Hamilton's broad vision of a powerful federal government. Jefferson especially objected to Hamilton's flexible view of the Constitution, which stretched to include a national bank.

18. ANSWER: B

(comparison and contextualization)

In his famous Farewell Address of 1796, George Washington warned about the dangers of political parties to the government and the country as a whole. His warnings took on added significance with the recent creation of the Democratic-Republican Party by Jefferson, to oppose Hamilton's Federalist Party, created a year earlier in 1791, which in many ways promoted the interest of certain regions and groups of Americans over others. While Washington accepted the fact that it is natural for people to organize and operate within groups like political parties, he also sought to repress them lest they weaken and divide the newly formed republic.

DIFFICULTY LEVEL 3

19. ANSWER: A

After the Constitution was drafted, many farmers in rural areas feared that the new government would give too much power to the central government at the expense of state and local governments and personal liberties. Although these Anti-Federalists were composed of diverse elements, they tended to represent poorer, rural communities who feared wealthy interests consolidating their power. Some of the opposition believed that the central government under the Articles of Confederation was sufficient. Still others believed that while the national government under the Articles was too weak, the national government under the Constitution would be too strong.

20. ANSWER: D

Alexander Hamilton's *First Report on the Public Credit*, delivered to Congress on January 9, 1790, called for payment in full on all government debts as the foundation for establishing government credit. This, argued Hamilton, was required to create a favorable climate for investment in government securities, and to transform the public debt into a source of capital. When Hamilton's Report was made public in January 1790, speculators in Philadelphia and New York sent buyers by ship to southern states to buy up securities before that section of the country became aware of the plan. The fact that devalued certificates were relinquished by holders at low rates reflected the widely held conviction in the South that the credit and assumption measures would be defeated in Congress.

The value of government certificates continued to fall months after Hamilton's scheme was published, and "the sellers speculated upon the purchasers." Representative James Madison vigorously led the opposition to Hamilton's plan. He characterized Secretary Hamilton's "redemption" as a formula to defraud "battle-worn veterans of the war for independence" and a handout to well-to-do speculators, mostly rich northerners, including some members of Congress.

PART C

DIFFICULTY LEVEL 1

1. ANSWER: D

In his first inaugural address, Thomas Jefferson tried to stem the partisan rivalries that began during the 1790s, and asked his fellow Americans to rise above party politics. In the election of 1800, sometimes referred to as the "Revolution of 1800," Thomas Jefferson defeated John Adams after a long, bitter re-match of the 1796 election. While the Democratic-Republicans were well organized at the state and local levels, the Federalists were disorganized, and suffered a bitter split between their two major leaders, President Adams and Alexander Hamilton. The jockeying for electoral votes, regional divisions, and the propaganda smear campaigns created by both parties made the election recognizably modern.

DIFFICULTY LEVEL 2

2. ANSWER: A

When the Revolutionary War ended in 1783, the rural farming population in western Massachusetts was generally unable to meet the demands being made of them by merchants or the civil authorities, and individuals began to lose their land and other possessions when they could not fulfill their debt and tax obligations. This led to strong resentments against tax collectors and the courts, where creditors obtained and enforced judgments against debtors, and where tax collectors obtained judgments authorizing property seizures. Overlaid upon these financial issues was the fact that veterans had received little pay during the war and faced difficulty paying their debts. Some of the soldiers, Daniel Shays among them, began to organize protests against these oppressive economic conditions.

3. ANSWER: D

Jay's Treaty was a 1795 treaty between the United States and Great Britain that is credited with averting war, resolving issues remaining since the Treaty of Paris of 1783 (which ended the American Revolution), and facilitating ten years of peaceful trade between the United States and Britain in the midst of the French Revolutionary Wars, which began in 1792. The terms of the treaty were designed primarily by Secretary of the Treasury Alexander Hamilton, strongly supported by the chief negotiator John Jay, and supported by President George Washington. The treaty gained the primary American goals, which included the withdrawal of British Army units from pre-Revolutionary forts that it had failed to relinquish in the Northwest Territory of the United States (the area west of Pennsylvania and north of the Ohio River). The treaty was hotly contested by the Jeffersonians in each state, who feared that closer economic ties with Britain would strengthen Hamilton's Federalist Party, promote aristocracy, and undercut republicanism.

4. ANSWER: B

By terms of Pinckney's Treaty of 1795, Spain and the United States agreed that the southern boundary of the United States with the Spanish Colonies of East Florida and West Florida was a line beginning on the Mississippi River, or the current boundary between the present states of Florida and Georgia and the line from the northern boundary of the Florida panhandle to the northern boundary of that portion of Louisiana east of the Mississippi. More importantly, this treaty allowed the United States to navigate the Mississippi River and access the important port of New Orleans. The agreement also put the lands of the Chickasaw and Choctaw Nations of American Indians within the new boundaries of the United States, a fact that contributed to further conflict with the native populations.

5. ANSWER: C

(historical arguments/evidence)

In the late 18th and early 19th centuries, with the growing emphasis being placed on republicanism, women were expected to help promote these values; they had a special role in raising the next generation. In Linda K. Kerber's article "The Republican Mother: Women and the Enlightenment—An American Perspective," she compares republican motherhood to the "Spartan model" of childhood, where children are raised to value patriotism and sacrifice of their own needs for the greater good of the country. By doing so, the mothers would encourage their sons to pursue liberty and roles in the government, while their daughters would perpetuate the domestic sphere with the next generation. In addition, women were permitted to receive more of an education than they previously had been allowed. Abigail Adams advocated women's education, as demonstrated in many of her letters to her husband, John Adams.

6. ANSWER: B

(comparison/contextualization; interpretation/synthesis)

During the Colonial Era, women were expected to maintain the domestic sphere and were denied full legal, political, and social equality. In that respect, not much had changed by the late 18th century. After the American Revolution, many Christian ministers, promoted the ideals of republican motherhood. They believed this was the appropriate path for women. Traditionally, women had been viewed as morally inferior to men, especially in the areas of sexuality and religion. This stemmed from Eve's "Original Sin" in the Bible. However, as the nineteenth century drew closer, many Protestant ministers and moralists argued that modesty and purity were inherent in women's nature, giving them a unique ability to promote Christian values with their children.

7. ANSWER: D

(chronological reasoning)

The Cult of Domesticity, or Cult of True Womanhood, which grew out of Republican Motherhood in America, was a prevailing value system among the upper and middle classes during the nineteenth century in the United States. This value system emphasized new ideas of femininity, the woman's role within the home and the dynamics of work and family. "True women" were supposed to possess four cardinal virtues: piety, purity, domesticity, and submissiveness. The women and men who most actively promoted these standards were generally white, Protestant, and lived in New England and the Northeastern United States. The Cult of Domesticity revolved around the women being the center of the family. Although all women were supposed to emulate this ideal of femininity, black, working class, and immigrant women did not fit the definition of "true women" because of social prejudice.

8. ANSWER: B

(chronological reasoning)

In the excerpt above, Secretary of War Henry Knox is responding to the Constitution's neglect of questions about the relationship between Native American tribes and the federal government. The original United States Constitution specifically mentions the relationship between the United States federal government and Native American tribes only twice:

- Article I, Section 2, Clause 3 states that "Representatives and direct Taxes shall be apportioned among the several States ... excluding Indians not taxed."
- Article I, Section 8 of the Constitution states that "Congress shall have the power to regulate Commerce with foreign nations and among the several states, and with the

Indian tribes," determining that Indian tribes were separate from the federal government, the states, and foreign nations.

Knox's proposals were an effort to rectify that neglect and to establish a foundation for the nation's future relations with Native Americans.

9. **ANSWER: C**

(comparison/contextualization)

At the end of the 18th century, the consolidation of the United States government posed new and difficult challenges for American Indians. Their most difficult challenges were related to treaty disputes and Americans' efforts to seize their lands. The United States, under both the Articles of Confederation and the Constitution, negotiated with Indian groups to try and secure access for white settlement in the west. Numerous treaties from the mid and late 1780s created favorable terms for new settlement, but they were usually achieved through liquor, bribes, or physical threats. These challenges would persist through the 19th century.

DIFFICULTY LEVEL 3

10. **ANSWER: C**

Shays' Rebellion was similar to previous rebellions in American history in its targeting of a distant authority. Shays' Rebellion was an armed uprising that took place in Massachusetts during 1786 and 1787, which some historians believe "fundamentally altered the course of United States' history." Fueled by economic inequality, regressive tax policies, and growing disaffection with State and Federal governments, Revolutionary War veteran Daniel Shays led a group of rebels (called Shaysites) in rising up first against Massachusetts' courts, and later in marching on the United States' Federal Armory at Springfield in an unsuccessful attempt to seize its weaponry and overthrow the government. Although Shays' Rebellion met with defeat militarily, it bore fruit in forcing the Federal government to reconsider the extent of its own powers at the U.S. Constitutional Convention, and by drawing General George Washington out of retirement en route to his Presidency, among influencing other changes to America's young democracy.

11. **ANSWER: D**

The Haitian Revolution provoked mixed reactions in the United States. Southern Slaveholders feared that the slave revolution might spread from the island of Hispaniola to the slave plantations of the Southern United States. They believed that the African people whom they enslaved would be inspired by the Haitian Revolution. But there were anti-slavery advocates in northern cities who believed that consistency with the principles of the American Revolution—life, liberty, and equality for all—demanded that the U.S. support the slave insurgents.

12. ANSWER: B

The Battle of Fallen Timbers (August 20, 1794) is considered the final battle of the Northwest Indian War, a struggle between American Indian tribes affiliated with the Western Confederacy, including minor support from the British, against the United States for control of the Northwest Territory (an area north of the Ohio River, east of the Mississippi River, and southwest of the Great Lakes). The battle, which was a decisive victory for the United States, ended major hostilities in the region until Tecumseh's War and the Battle of Tippecanoe in 1811. The defeat of the Indians led to the signing of the Treaty of Greenville in 1795, which ceded much of present-day Ohio to the United States. It is the location of the present-day Indiana city of Fort Wayne. Behind this line of forts, white settlers moved into the Ohio country, leading to the admission of the state of Ohio in 1803. Tecumseh, a young Shawnee veteran of Fallen Timbers who did not sign the Greenville Treaty, would renew American Indian resistance in the years ahead.

Period 1800-1848

PART A

DIFFICULTY LEVEL 1

1. ANSWER: A

Marbury v. Madison was a landmark United States Supreme Court case in which the Court formed the basis for the exercise of judicial review in the United States under Article III of the Constitution. Judicial review allows the federal courts to declare acts of Congress or actions by the Executive Branch to be unconstitutional. The case resulted from a petition to the Supreme Court by William Marbury, who had been appointed Justice of the Peace in the District of Columbia by President John Adams but whose commission was not subsequently delivered. Marbury petitioned the Supreme Court to force the new Secretary of State James Madison to deliver the documents. The Court, with John Marshall as Chief Justice, found that Madison's refusal to deliver the commission was both illegal and remediable. Nonetheless, the Court stopped short of compelling Madison (by writ of mandamus) to hand over Marbury's commission, instead holding that the provision of the Judiciary Act of 1789 that enabled Marbury to bring his claim to the Supreme Court was itself unconstitutional, since it purported to extend the Court's original jurisdiction beyond that which Article III established. The petition was therefore denied.

2. ANSWER: A

In 1830, a group of Native Americans collectively referred to as the Five Civilized Tribes: the Cherokee, Chickasaw, Choctaw, Muscogee, and Seminole, were living as autonomous nations in what would be called the American Deep South. Andrew Jackson helped gain Congressional passage of the Indian Removal Act of 1830, which authorized the government to extinguish Native American title to lands in the Southeast. By the end of the decade in 1840, tens of thousands of Native Americans were driven off their land east of the Mississippi River. Oklahoma was the new home for the Cherokee, which was promised by the federal government to last for an eternity, but that never happened. When Oklahoma became an official state of the United States in the first decade of the 20th century, Indian land there became lost forever and the Cherokee were then again forced to move farther westward.

3. **ANSWER: D**

The Seneca Falls Convention was the first women's rights convention "to discuss the social, civil, and religious condition and rights of woman." The principal organizers were

Elizabeth Cady Stanton and Lucretia Mott, who proposed the Declaration of Sentiments to address grievances against the United States government. Their demands included the a woman's right to an education, to suffrage, and to property. The convention was seen by some of its contemporaries, including featured speaker Mott, as one important step among many others in the continuing effort by women to gain for themselves a greater proportion of social, civil and moral rights, while it was viewed by others as a revolutionary beginning to the struggle by women for complete equality with men. Stanton considered the Seneca Falls Convention to be the beginning of the women's rights movement.

4. **ANSWER: B**

The Whig Party was a political party active in the middle of the 19th century. Considered integral to the Second Party System and operating from the early 1830s to the mid-1850s, the party was formed in opposition to the policies of President Andrew Jackson and his Democratic Party. In particular, the Whigs supported the supremacy of Congress over the Presidency and favored a program of modernization and economic protectionism. This name was chosen to echo the American Whigs of 1776, who fought for independence, and because "Whig" was then a widely recognized label of choice for people who identified as opposing tyranny. The Whig Party counted among its members such national political luminaries as Daniel Webster, William Henry Harrison, and their preeminent leader, Henry Clay of Kentucky.

DIFFICULTY LEVEL 2

5. **ANSWER: B**

The longest-serving Chief Justice and the fourth longest-serving justice in U.S. Supreme Court history, John Marshall dominated the Court for over three decades and played a significant role in the development of the American legal system. Most notably, he reinforced the principle that federal courts are obligated to exercise judicial review, by disregarding purported laws if they violate the constitution. Thus, Marshall cemented the position of the American judiciary as an independent and influential branch of government. Furthermore, Marshall's court made several important decisions relating to federalism, affecting the balance of power between the federal government and the states during the early years of the republic. In particular, he repeatedly affirmed the supremacy of federal law over state law, and supported an expansive reading of the enumerated powers, or a loose construction of the Constitution.

6. ANSWER: B

As a Democratic-Republican, Thomas Jefferson believed that most government power should reside with the states, and that the size and scope of the federal government should be limited by a strict construction of the U.S. Constitution. In office, he demonstrated a commitment to these principles by allowing the Alien and Sedition Acts to expire and by reducing the size of the military. He did, however, contradict his strict interpretation of the Constitution when he approved the Louisiana Purchase in 1803.

7. ANSWER: C

During the Napoleonic Wars, Britain did not recognize the right of a British subject to relinquish his status as a British subject, emigrate and transfer his national allegiance as a naturalized citizen to any other country. Thus while the United States recognized British-born sailors on American ships as Americans, Britain did not. The Royal Navy went after them by intercepting and searching U.S. merchant ships for deserters. Impressment actions such as the Chesapeake–Leopard Affair outraged Americans, because they infringed on national sovereignty and denied America's ability to naturalize foreigners.[16] Moreover, in addition to recovering deserters, Britain considered United States citizens born British liable for impressment. American anger at impressment grew when British frigates were stationed just outside U.S. harbors in view of U.S. shores and searched ships for contraband and impressed men while in U.S. territorial waters. "Free trade and sailors' rights" was a rallying cry for the United States throughout the conflict. Other causes of the War of 1812 included British support for American Indian raids, America's desire to expand its territory, and heightened nationalism due to the election of "War Hawk" Republicans to Congress in 1810.

8. ANSWER: D

The American System was an economic plan that played a prominent role in American policy during the first half of the 19th century. Rooted in the "American School" ideas of Alexander Hamilton, the plan consisted of three mutually reinforcing parts: a tariff to protect and promote American industry; a national bank to foster commerce; and federal subsidies for roads, canals, and other 'internal improvements' to develop profitable markets for agriculture. Congressman Henry Clay was the plan's foremost proponent and the first to refer to it as the "American System".

9. **ANSWER: C**

The Tariff of 1828 was passed by Congress to protect industry in the northern United States. It was labeled the Tariff of Abominations by its southern detractors because of the negative effects it had on the antebellum Southern economy. The major goal of the tariff was to protect industries in the northern United States. The South, however, was harmed directly by having to pay higher prices on goods the region did not produce, and indirectly because reducing the exportation of British goods to the U.S. made it difficult for the British to pay for the cotton they imported from the South. The reaction in the South, particularly in South Carolina, would lead to the Nullification Crisis that began in late 1832. The Nullification Crisis was a sectional crisis during the presidency of Andrew Jackson created by South Carolina's 1832 Ordinance of Nullification. This ordinance declared by the power of the State that the federal Tariffs of 1828 and 1832 were unconstitutional and therefore null and void within the sovereign boundaries of South Carolina. In late February both a Force Bill, authorizing the President to use military forces against South Carolina, and a new negotiated tariff, the Compromise Tariff of 1833, were passed by Congress. The South Carolina convention reconvened and repealed its Nullification Ordinance on March 11, 1833.

10. **ANSWER: B**

The Cult of Domesticity or Cult of True Womanhood was a prevailing value system among the upper and middle classes during the nineteenth century in the United States and Great Britain. This value system emphasized new ideas of femininity, the woman's role within the home and the dynamics of work and family. "True women" were supposed to possess four cardinal virtues: piety, purity, domesticity, and submissiveness. The women and men who most actively promoted these standards were generally white, Protestant, and lived in New England and the Northeastern United States. The cult of domesticity revolved around the women being the center of the family; they were considered "The light of the home." Although all women were supposed to emulate this ideal of femininity, black, working class, and immigrant women did not fit the definition of "true women" because of social prejudice.

11. **ANSWER: A**

Transcendentalism was a religious, philosophical, and intellectual movement that developed during the late 1820s and '30s in the Eastern region of the United States as a protest against the general state of spirituality and, in particular, the state of intellectualism at Harvard University. Among the transcendentalists' core beliefs was the inherent goodness of both people and nature. They believe that society and its institutions—particularly organized religion and political parties—ultimately corrupt the purity of the individual. They have faith that people are at their best when truly "self-reliant" and independent. It is only from such real individuals that true community could be formed. Leaders associated with this movement include Ralph Waldo Emerson, Henry David Thoreau, and Margaret Fuller.

12. ANSWER: C

The Second Great Awakening was a Protestant revival movement during the early 19th century in the United States. The movement began around 1790, gained momentum by 1800, and after 1820 membership rose rapidly among Baptist and Methodist congregations whose preachers led the movement. It has been described as a reaction against skepticism, deism, and rationalism. Leaders of the movement believed in the perfectibility of people and were highly moralistic in their endeavors. Converts were taught that to achieve salvation they needed not just to repent personal sin but also work for the moral perfection of society, which meant eradicating sin in all its forms. Thus, evangelical converts were leading figures in a variety of 19th century reform movements.

13. ANSWER: B

(chronological reasoning)

A cotton gin is a machine that quickly and easily separates cotton fibers from their seeds, allowing for much greater productivity than manual cotton separation. The first modern mechanical cotton gin was created by American inventor Eli Whitney in 1793, and patented in 1794. It used a combination of a wire screen and small wire hooks to pull the cotton through, while brushes continuously removed the loose cotton lint to prevent jams. Whitney's gin revolutionized the cotton industry in the United States, but also led to the growth of slavery in the American South as the demand for cotton workers rapidly increased. The invention has thus been identified as an inadvertent contributing factor to the outbreak of the American Civil War.

14. ANSWER: B

(historical argumentation/evidence)

The historian James M. McPherson defines an abolitionist "as one who before the Civil War had agitated for the immediate, unconditional, and total abolition of slavery in the United States." He does not include antislavery activists such as Abraham Lincoln or the Republican Party, which called for the gradual ending of slavery. The white abolitionist movement in the North was led by social reformers, especially William Lloyd Garrison, founder of the American Anti-Slavery Society; writers such as John

Greenleaf Whittier and Harriet Beecher Stowe. Black activists included former slaves such as Frederick Douglass; and free blacks such as the brothers Charles Henry Langston and John Mercer Langston, who helped found the Ohio Anti-Slavery Society. Some abolitionists said that slavery was criminal and a sin; they also criticized slave owners of using black women as concubines and taking sexual advantage of them. Despite their ability to raise awareness about the horrors of slavery, and to persuade more people to take a stance against it, slavery continued to grow in the United States until its abolition after the Civil War.

15. ANSWER: C

(chronological reasoning)

Although issues of federalism and states' rights surrounded debates over slavery's legality and expansion throughout the nineteenth century, the growth of slavery until 1860 best represents an internal struggle over the meanings of equality and freedom. By the 1850s, many Northerners, especially those in the newly formed Republican Party, had come to see slavery as a violation of the democratic principles spelled out in the Declaration of Independence. Not until after the Civil War would the United States experience what Abraham Lincoln labeled "a new birth of freedom," in which slavery would no longer exist.

16. ANSWER: B

(comparison/contextualization)

During the 1820s and 1830s, the United States was expanding democracy in ways that allowed ordinary Americans to participate in the political process. By 1840, many states had eliminating the landowning requirement for voting, but this new access to the franchise did not include African Americans, women, Native Americans, or immigrants. State electors for president also began basing their electoral votes on their state's popular vote. Finally, national nominating conventions replaced the caucus system for choosing nominees for major parties. All of the reforms ushered in the "Age of Jackson," or the era during which common white men played a deciding role in politics and government.

17. ANSWER: A

(comparison/contextualization)

During the early 1800s until the start of the Civil War, religion was renewed through a Second Great Awakening. Evangelists on a "divine mission" believed that churches were the proper agents of change, not violence or political movements. Ardent believers in the perfectibility of society tried communal living with distinctly utopian goals, convinced that ultimately their small fellowships would grow into larger, more influential gatherings for the common good of all. Women began to explore the possibility of individual rights and equality with men. Their agenda was quite vast and included not only the right to vote but also such diverse problems as prohibition and world peace. Reformers, sure that the dire human conditions in prisons, workhouses and asylums were the result of bad institutions and not bad people, made gallant efforts to alleviate pain and suffering. Hopes were high that cures for social disorders in America caused by rapid expansion, population growth, and industrialization would work (*http://www.ushistory.org/us/26.asp*).

18. ANSWER: A

(historical argument/evidence)

While Tocqueville lauds American for its general condition of equality, one must keep in mind that he is viewing the United States from the prospective of his European background. In Europe, monarchs still reigned and democracy was very limited. Therefore, despite the existence of slavery, the treatment of Native Americans, and discrimination against immigrants, Tocqueville believed American to be far more democratic than its European counterparts.

19. ANSWER: C

(contextualization)

John C. Calhoun's Speech to the US Senate (1837) articulated the pro-slavery political argument during the period at which the ideology was at its most mature (late 1830s - early 1860s). Calloun and other pro-slavery theorists championed a class-sensitive view of American antebellum society. They felt that the bane of many past societies was the existence of the class of the landless poor. Southern pro-slavery theorists felt that this class of landless poor was inherently transient and easily manipulated, and as such often destabilized society as a whole. Thus, the greatest threat to democracy was seen as coming from class warfare that destabilized a nation's economy, society, government, and threatened the peaceful and harmonious implementation of laws. They believed that slavery stabilized southern society.

20. ANSWER: B

(historical argument/evidence)

In the early 19th century abolitionist movements gathered momentum in the Unites States, and many European countries had abolished slavery in the first half of the 19th century. The increasing rarity of slavery, combined with an increase in the number of slaves caused by a boom in the cotton trade, drew attention and criticism to the Southern states' continuation of slavery. Faced with this growing "antislavery" movement, slaveholders and their sympathizers began to articulate an explicit defense of slavery.

21. ANSWER: A

(contextualization, use of evidence)

The abolition of slavery was the cause of free African-Americans. The best known African American abolitionist was Frederick Douglass. Douglass escaped from slavery when he was 21 and moved to Massachusetts. As a former house servant, Douglass was able to read and write. In 1841, he began to speak to crowds about what it was like to be enslaved. His talents as an orator and writer led people to question whether or not he had actually been born a slave. All this attention put him at great risk. Fearful that his master would claim him and return him to bondage, Douglass went to England, where he continued to fight for the cause. A group of abolitionists eventually bought his freedom and he was allowed to return to the United States. He began publishing an anti-slavery newspaper known as the *North Star*. Douglass served as an example to all who doubted the ability of African Americans to function as free citizens (*http://www.ushistory.org/us/28b.asp*).

22. ANSWER: A

(comparison, use of evidence)

Although they were not slaves, Native Americans experienced oppression at the hands of the American government during the antebellum era. After the passage of the Indian Removal Act of 1830, President Andrew Jackson forced Native Americans to cede their territory east of the Mississippi River. The United States government forced them on a 1,200 mile "Trail of Tears," during which thousands of natives died, to settle in Oklahoma.

23. ANSWER: B

(historical causation)

The cartoon above is depicting American reactions to the Embargo Act, which was highly unpopular. The Embargo Act made illegal any and all exports from the United

States. It was sponsored by President Thomas Jefferson and enacted by Congress. The goal was to force Britain and France to respect American rights during the Napoleonic Wars. They were engaged in a major war; the U.S. wanted to remain neutral and trade with both sides, but neither side wanted the other to have the American supplies. The American goal was to use economic coercion to avoid war, punish Britain, and force it to respect American rights. Thus, the embargo was imposed in response to violations of U.S. neutrality.

24. ANSWER: C

(historical causation)

The Embargo was in fact hurting the United States as much as Britain or France. Britain, expecting to suffer most from the American regulations, built up a new South American market for its exports, and the British shipowners were pleased that American competition had been removed by the action of the U.S. government. Jefferson placed himself in a strange position with his Embargo policy. Though he had so frequently and eloquently argued for as little government intervention as possible, he now found himself assuming extraordinary powers in an attempt to enforce his policy. The presidential election of 1808, in which James Madison defeated Charles Pinckney, showed that the Federalists were regaining strength, and helped to convince Jefferson and Madison that the Embargo would have to be removed. Shortly before leaving office, in March 1809, Jefferson signed the repeal of the failed Embargo. Despite its unpopular nature, the Embargo Act did have some limited, unintended benefits, especially as entrepreneurs and workers responded by bringing in fresh capital and labor into New England textile and other manufacturing industries, lessening America's reliance on the British merchants.

DIFFICULTY LEVEL 3

25. ANSWER: A

The Hartford Convention was a series of meetings from December 15, 1814 – January 5, 1815 in Hartford, Connecticut, in which New England Federalists met to discuss their grievances concerning the ongoing War of 1812 and the political problems arising from the federal government's increasing power. Despite radical outcries among Federalists for New England secession and a separate peace with Great Britain, moderates outnumbered them and extreme proposals were not a major focus of the debate. The convention discussed removing the three-fifths compromise, which gave slave states more power in Congress, and requiring a two-thirds supermajority in Congress for the admission of new states, declarations of war, and laws restricting trade. However, weeks after the convention's end, news of Major General Andrew Jackson's overwhelming victory in New Orleans swept over the Northeast, discrediting and disgracing the Federalists, resulting in their decline as a major national political force.

PART B

DIFFICULTY LEVEL 1

1. ANSWER: D

Andrew Jackson was elected as a symbol of the "common man," and in some cases, such as the National Bank veto, he stood up to moneyed interests to defend ordinary Americans. But he was also a strong proponent of executive authority over states' rights, rejecting South Carolina's proclamation of nullification of the Tariff of 1828. Likewise, he eschewed Texas's efforts to enter the United States for fear that it would fan the flames of regionalism and highlight sectional differences between slave states and free states. The correct answers, Indian removal, is a reference to his approval of the Indian Removal Act, which dispossessed Native Americans of their land east of the Mississippi River.

2. ANSWER: D

Perhaps no one had as great an impact on the development of the industrial north as Eli Whitney. Whitney raised eyebrows when he walked into the US Patent office, took apart ten guns, and reassembled them mixing the parts of each gun. Whitney lived in an age where an artisan would handcraft each part of every gun. No two products were quite the same. Whitney's milling machine allowed workers to cut metal objects in an identical fashion, making interchangeable parts. It was the start of the concept of mass production. Over the course of time, the device and Whitney's techniques were used to make many others products.

DIFFICULTY LEVEL 2

3. ANSWER: C

During the early industrial age in New England, textile mills, such as the one in Lowell, Massachusetts, employed daughters of propertied New England farmers, between the ages of 15 and (There also could be "little girls" who worked there about the age of 13.) By 1840, at the height of the Industrial Revolution, the textile mills had recruited over 8,000 women, who came to make up nearly seventy-five percent of the mill workforce. As the New England textile industry rapidly expanded in the 1850s and 1860s, textile managers turned to survivors of the Great Irish Famine who had recently immigrated to the United States in large numbers.

4. **ANSWER: D**

The Erie Canal originally ran about 363 miles from Albany, New York, on the Hudson River to Buffalo, New York, at Lake Erie. Built to create a navigable water route from New York City and the Atlantic Ocean to the Great Lakes, the canal helped New York eclipse Philadelphia as the largest city and port on the Eastern Seaboard of the United States. The canal was the first transportation system between the eastern seaboard (New York City) and the western interior (Great Lakes) of the United States that did not require portage. The canal fostered a population surge in western New York, opened regions farther west to settlement, and helped New York City become the chief U.S. port.

5. **ANSWER: A**

(historical causation)

For over a hundred years, people had dreamed of building a canal across New York that would connect the Great Lakes to the Hudson River to New York City and the Atlantic Ocean. After unsuccessfully seeking federal government assistance, DeWitt Clinton successfully petitioned the New York State legislature to build the canal and bring that dream to reality. The canal spanned 350 miles between the Great Lakes and the Hudson River and was an immediate success. Between its completion and its closure in 1882, it returned over $121 million in revenues on an original cost of $7 million. Its success led to the great Canal Age. By bringing the Great Lakes within reach of a metropolitan market, the Erie Canal opened up the unsettled northern regions of Ohio, Indiana and Illinois. It also fostered the development of many small industrial companies, whose products were used in the construction and operation of the canal (*ushistory.org*).

6. **ANSWER: C**

(historical causation, use of evidence)

The invention of the steam engine was critically important for the expansion of the U.S. transportation network by 1853. Steam engines provided the power needed to build parts of the nation's transportation infrastructure and also powered the steamships that traveled along the canals at this time.

7. **ANSWER: B**

(historical contextualization, causation)

During the antebellum period, the South was still an agrarian economy. The development of the cotton gin in the 1790s served to expand cotton plantations and slavery. The wealth that plantation owners generated from cotton exports made the

American South one of the richest regions in the world. As a result, there was little incentive for the South to industrialize, urbanize, and expand its transportation network.

8. **ANSWER: A**

(causation)

Immigrants traveling to the United States during the antebellum era crossed the oceans on large ships. Once they arrived in the United States, they tended to settle along the coasts, the Irish on the east coast and the Chinese along the west coast.

9. **ANSWER: C**

(use of evidence)

During the first 30 years of the 1800s, American industry was truly born. Household manufacturing was almost universal in colonial days, with local craftsmen providing for their communities. This new era introduced factories, with machines and predetermined tasks, producing items to be shipped and sold elsewhere. New England, where the first American factories appeared, was well suited for industry because of their abundant natural resources, including the system of river that provided power for the early factories.

10. **ANSWER: B**

Southern states opposed high tariffs because it made foreign goods more expensive. The South had leveraged their abundant King Cotton crops to work out favorable trade arrangements with Great Britain, from which they purchased manufactured goods. With the tariff, these goods became more costly than products manufactured in the North. Since the South had no industrial base, the region was forced to enter into a neo-mercantilist economic relationship with Northern manufacturers.

11. **ANSWER: C**

(causation, contextualization)

Samuel F. B. Morse invented the telegraph and Morse Code. Morse was an artist having a great deal of difficulty making enough money to make ends meet. He started pursuing a number of business opportunities which would allow him to continue his work as an artist. Out of these efforts came the telegraph. The first telegram in the United States was sent by Morse in 1838, across two miles of wire at Speedwell Ironworks near Morristown, New Jersey, although it was only later, in 1844, that he sent the message "WHAT HATH GOD WROUGHT" from the Capitol in Washington to the old Mt. Clare

Depot in Baltimore. From then on, commercial telegraphy took off in America with lines linking all the major metropolitan centers on the East Coast within the next decade. The overland telegraph connected the west coast of the continent to the east coast by October 1861, bringing an end to the Pony Express.

DIFFICULTY LEVEL 3

12. ANSWER: A

The Louisiana Purchase of 1803 intensified American Migration to the west that was already well underway. Anglo-American settlement in the 18th century had largely been confined to the eastern seaboard. By 1820, however, the total U.S. population had already reached 9.6 million and fully 25 percent of them lived west of the Appalachians in nine new states and three territories. Westward expansion and national trade required improved transportation. States responded by giving charters to private companies to build roads (called turnpikes since they charged a fee), bridges, canals, or to operate ferry services. The state gave these companies special legal privileges because they provided a service that could benefit a wide segment of the population.

13. ANSWER: B

The Maysville Road veto occurred on May 27, 1830, when President Andrew Jackson vetoed a bill which would allow the Federal government to purchase stock in the Maysville, Washington, Paris, and Lexington Turnpike Road Company, which had been organized to construct a road linking Lexington and Maysville on the Ohio River, the entirety of which would be in the state of Kentucky. Its advocates regarded it as a part of the national Cumberland Road system. Congress passed a bill in 1830 providing federal funds to complete the project. Jackson vetoed the bill on the grounds that federal funding of intrastate projects of this nature was unconstitutional. He declared that such bills violated the principle that the federal government should not be involved in local economic affairs. Jackson also pointed out that funding for these kinds of projects interfered with paying off of the national debt.

14. ANSWER: B

While the Indian Removal Act of 1830 made the move of the tribes voluntary, it was often abused by government officials. The best-known example is the Treaty of New Echota, which was negotiated and signed by a small faction of Cherokee tribal members, not the tribal leadership, on December 29, 1835. It resulted in the forced relocation of the tribe in 1838. An estimated 4,000 Cherokee died in the march, now known as the Trail of Tears. Missionary organizer Jeremiah Evarts urged the Cherokee Nation to take their case to the U.S. Supreme Court. Under Chief Justice John Marshall, the Court ruled that Native American tribes were sovereign nations (*Cherokee Nation v. Georgia*, 1831), and state laws had no force on tribal lands (*Worcester v. Georgia*, 1832).

PART C

DIFFICULTY LEVEL 1

1. **ANSWER: A**

The purchase of the Louisiana Territory took place during the Presidency of Thomas Jefferson. It removed France's presence in the region and protected both U.S. trade access to the port of New Orleans and free passage on the Mississippi River. The Louisiana territory encompassed all or part of 15 present U.S. states and two Canadian provinces. The land purchased contained all of present-day Arkansas, Missouri, Iowa, Oklahoma, Kansas, and Nebraska; parts of Minnesota that were west of the Mississippi River; most of North Dakota; most of South Dakota; northeastern New Mexico; northern Texas; the portions of Montana, Wyoming, and Colorado east of the Continental Divide; Louisiana west of the Mississippi River, including the city of New Orleans; and small portions of land that would eventually become part of the Canadian provinces of Alberta and Saskatchewan.

2. **ANSWER: C**

The Monroe Doctrine was a US foreign policy regarding Latin American countries in 1823. It stated that further efforts by European nations to colonize land or interfere with states in North or South America would be viewed as acts of aggression, requiring U.S. intervention. At the same time, the doctrine noted that the United States would neither interfere with existing European colonies nor meddle in the internal concerns of European countries. The Doctrine was issued in 1823 at a time when nearly all Latin American colonies of Spain and Portugal had achieved or were at the point of gaining independence from the Portuguese and Spanish Empires; Peru consolidated its independence in 1824, and Bolivia would become independent in 1825, leaving only Cuba and Puerto Rico under Spanish rule. The United States, working in agreement with Britain, wanted to guarantee that no European power would move in.

3. **ANSWER: C**

In the 19th century, Manifest Destiny was the widely held belief in the United States that American settlers were destined to expand throughout the continent. Historians have for the most part agreed that there are three basic themes to Manifest Destiny: The special virtues of the American people and their institutions; America's mission to redeem and remake the west in the image of agrarian America; An irresistible destiny to accomplish this essential duty.

DIFFICULTY LEVEL 2

4. ANSWER: B

The Adams–Onís Treaty of 1819, also known as the Purchase of Florida, was a treaty between the United States and Spain that gave Florida to the U.S. and set out a boundary between the U.S. and New Spain (now Mexico). Spain had long rejected repeated American efforts to purchase Florida. But by 1818, Spain was facing a troubling colonial situation where the cession of Florida made sense. Spain had been exhausted by the Peninsular War in Europe and needed to rebuild its credibility and presence in its colonies. Revolutionaries in Central and South America were beginning to demand independence. Spain was unwilling to invest further in Florida, encroached on by American settlers, and it worried about the border between New Spain and the United States. With minor military presence in Florida, Spain was not able to restrain the Seminole warriors who routinely crossed the border and raided American villages and farms, as well as protected southern slave refugees from slave owners and traders of the southern United States. By 1819 Spain was forced to negotiate, as it was losing its hold on its American empire, with its western territories primed to revolt. Madrid decided to cede the territory to the United States through the Adams–Onís Treaty in exchange for settling the boundary dispute along the Sabine River in Spanish Texas. The treaty established the boundary of U.S. territory and claims through the Rocky Mountains and west to the Pacific Ocean, in exchange for the U.S. paying residents' claims against the Spanish government up to a total of $5,000,000 and relinquishing the US claims on parts of Spanish Texas west of the Sabine River and other Spanish areas, under the terms of the Louisiana Purchase.

5. ANSWER: A

The Monroe Doctrine is long and couched in diplomatic language, but its essence is expressed in two key passages; the first is the introductory statement, which asserts that the New World is no longer subject to colonization by the European countries. The second key passage, a fuller statement of the Doctrine, is addressed to the "allied powers" of Europe. It clarifies that the United States remains neutral on existing European colonies in the Americas but is opposed to "interpositions" that would create new colonies among the newly independent Spanish American republics.

6. **ANSWER: D**

Originally inhabited by Native Americans, the region that became the Oregon Territory was explored by Europeans first by sea. The first documented exploration came in 1776 by the Spanish, with British and American vessels visiting the region within a few years. Later, land based exploration by Alexander Mackenzie and the Lewis and Clark Expedition along with the establishment of the fur trade in the region set up a variety of conflicting territorial claims by European powers and the United States. These conflicts led to several treaties, including the Treaty of 1818 that set up a "joint occupation" between the United States and the British over the region that included parts of the current U.S. states of Idaho, Oregon, Washington, Wyoming, and Montana as well as the Canadian province of British Columbia. In 1846, the Oregon boundary dispute between the U.S. and Britain was settled with the signing of the Oregon Treaty. The British gained sole possession of the land north of the 49th parallel and all of Vancouver Island, with the United States receiving the territory south of that line.

7. **ANSWER: C**

(historical argument/evidence)

By 1850, the issue of slavery was growing more contentious. As each new territory and state entered the union, the vexing question became whether or not to allow slavery. The Missouri Compromise of 1820 attempted to solve the problem by permitted Missouri to enter as a slave state and Maine would enter as a free state, maintaining the delicate free-state/slave-state balance in the Senate. However, once Mexico ceded the entire Southwest to the United States following the Mexican War (1846-1848), the issue resurfaced, resulted in the Compromise of 1850, and delaying the onset of civil war for another decade.

8. **ANSWER: C**

(chronological reasoning)

The Missouri Compromise was a federal statute in the United States that regulated slavery in the country's western territories. The compromise, devised by Henry Clay, was agreed to by the pro-slavery and anti-slavery factions in the United States Congress and passed as a law in 1820. It prohibited slavery in the former Louisiana Territory north of the parallel 36°30′ north, except within the boundaries of the proposed state of Missouri. The passage of the Missouri Compromise took place during the presidency of James Monroe.

9. **ANSWER: D**

(chronological reasoning; comparison/contextualization)

Even with the profitability of King Cotton, the North outpaced the South in terms of population growth and wealth. By 1860, the Northern population was at 21 million compared to the South's 9 million. Moreover, the North controlled 97% of the country's manufacturing sector, leading to a disparity in wealth between North and South.

10. ANSWER: B

(causation; use of evidence)

The Missouri Compromise was a federal statute in the United States that regulated slavery in the country's western territories. The compromise, devised by Henry Clay, was agreed to by the pro-slavery and anti-slavery factions in the United States Congress and passed as a law in 1820. It prohibited slavery in the former Louisiana Territory north of the parallel 36°30′ north, except within the boundaries of the proposed state of Missouri. The passage of the Missouri Compromise took place during the presidency of James Monroe. In an April 22 letter to John Holmes, Thomas Jefferson wrote that the division of the country created by the Compromise Line would eventually lead to the destruction of the Union. Congress's consideration of Missouri's admission also raised the issue of sectional balance, for the country was equally divided between slave and free states with eleven each. To admit Missouri as a slave state would tip the balance in the Senate (made up of two senators per state) in favor of the slave states. For this reason, northern states wanted Maine admitted as a free state.

11. ANSWER: C

(contextualization; use of evidence)

Congress' consideration of Missouri's admission raised the issue of sectional balance, for the country was equally divided between slave and free states with eleven each. To admit Missouri as a slave state would tip the balance in the Senate (made up of two senators per state) in favor of the slave states. For this reason, northern states wanted Maine admitted as a free state. On the constitutional side, the Compromise of 1820 was important as the example of Congressional exclusion of slavery from U.S. territory acquired since the Northwest Ordinance. Following Maine's 1820 and Missouri's 1821 admissions to the Union, no other states were admitted until 1836, when Arkansas was admitted.

12. ANSWER: D

(comparison/contextualization)

In the 19th century, Manifest Destiny was the widely held belief in the United States that American settlers were destined to expand throughout the continent. Historians have for the most part agreed that there are three basic themes to Manifest Destiny: The special virtues of the American people and their institutions; America's mission to redeem and remake the west in the image of agrarian America; An irresistible destiny to accomplish this essential duty. Coined by John O'Sullivan in the 1840s, the term Manifest Destiny was defended on notions of liberty and self-government found in the Declaration of Independence. Ironically, opponents of Manifest Destiny and, later, imperialism would use the same arguments to fight for self-determination of native peoples.

13. ANSWER: A

(contextualization)

This map shows the boundaries of the United States and neighboring nations as they appeared in 1845. The Webster–Ashburton Treaty had formalized the border of Maine in the northeast, while the Republic of Texas in the southwest had a disputed border with Mexico. President John Tyler shared the Texans' desire for annexation, but it took several years of political wrangling to achieve. The Oregon Border issue also remained unresolved, as the territory was shared by the United States and Great Britain until 1846.

DIFFICULTY LEVEL 3

14. ANSWER: C

Henry Adams and other historians argue that Jefferson was hypocritical in purchasing the Louisiana Territory, pointing to the fact that Jefferson was a strict constructionist in his views on the Constitution, yet allegedly took a loose constructionist view of the Constitution regarding the Louisiana Purchase. The American purchase of the Louisiana territory was not accomplished without domestic opposition. Many people believed he, and other Jeffersonians such as James Madison, were being hypocritical by doing something they surely would have argued against with Alexander Hamilton. The Federalists strongly opposed the purchase, favoring close relations with Britain over closer ties to Napoleon. Both Federalists and Jeffersonians were concerned about whether the purchase was constitutional. Many members of the House of Representatives opposed the purchase. Majority Leader John Randolph led the opposition. The House called for a vote to deny the request for the purchase, but it failed by two votes, 59–The Federalists even tried to prove the land belonged to Spain, not France, but available records proved otherwise.

15. ANSWER: C

Abolitionists and their supporters were wary of Manifest Destiny because of its tendency to rekindle debates over slavery. The annexation of new territories and admission of new states pitted "free soilers," those who opposed the expansion of slavery, against slaveholders. Slaveholders were interested in moving farther west to expand their cotton empire, and abolitionists wanted to halt the spread, and ultimately eliminate, the "peculiar institution" of slavery.

Period 1844-1877

PART A

DIFFICULTY LEVEL 1

1. ANSWER: D

The Homestead Act of 1862 was signed into law by President Abraham Lincoln on May 20, 1862. Anyone who had never taken up arms against the U.S. government (including freed slaves and women), was 21 years or older, or the head of a family, could file an application to claim a federal land grant. There was also a five-year residency requirement. Settlers found land and staked their claims, usually in individual family units, although others formed closer knit communities. Often, the homestead consisted of several buildings or structures besides the main house. The Homestead Act of 1862 gave rise later to a new phenomenon, large land rushes, such as the Oklahoma Land Runs of the 1880s and 90s.

2. ANSWER: B

Thousands of optimistic Americans and even a few foreigners dreamed of finding a bonanza and retiring at a very young age. Ten years after the 1849 California Gold Rush, new deposits were gradually found throughout the West. Colorado yielded gold and silver at Pikes Peak in 1859 and Leadville IN 1873. Nevada claimed Comstock Lode, the largest of American silver strikes. From Idaho to Arizona, boom towns flowered across the American West. They produced not only gold and silver, but zinc, copper, and lead, all essential for the eastern Industrial Revolution. Soon the West was filled with ne'er-do-wells hoping to strike it rich (*http://www.ushistory.org/us/41a.asp*)

DIFFICULTY LEVEL 2

3. ANSWER: B

The war between Mexico and the United States began in 1846 over a Texas boundary dispute. President James K. Polk ordered General Zachary Taylor and his troops into the disputed territory, which provoked a violent response from Mexico. In July of that same year, transcendentalist writer Henry David Thoreau refused to pay his taxes because of his opposition to the Mexican-American War and slavery, and he spent a night in jail because of this refusal. The experience had a strong impact on Thoreau. Thoreau published an essay entitled "Resistance to Civil Government" (also known as "Civil Disobedience"), espousing a radical new form of social resistance. Thoreau's writings went on to influence many public figures, like Mohandas Gandhi, U.S. President John F. Kennedy, and American civil rights activist Martin Luther King, Jr.

4. ANSWER: D

The Treaty of Guadalupe Hidalgo is the peace treaty signed on February 2, 1848, in the Villa de Guadalupe Hidalgo (now a neighborhood of Mexico City) between the United States and Mexico that ended the Mexican–American War (1846–48). With the defeat of its army and the fall of its capital, Mexico entered into negotiations to end the war. The treaty called for the US to pay $15 million to Mexico and to pay off the claims of American citizens against Mexico up to $3.25 million. It gave the United States the Rio Grande as a boundary for Texas, and gave the United States ownership of California and a large area comprising New Mexico, Arizona, Nevada, Utah, and parts of Wyoming and Colorado. Mexicans in those annexed areas had the choice of relocating to within Mexico's new boundaries or receiving American citizenship with full civil rights. Over 90% chose to become US citizens. The US Senate ratified the treaty by a vote of 38–The opponents of this treaty were led by the Whigs, who had opposed the war and rejected Manifest Destiny in general.

5. ANSWER: A

The Know Nothing movement was an American political movement that operated on a national basis during the mid-1850s. It promised to purify American politics by limiting or ending the influence of Irish Catholics and other immigrants, thus reflecting nativism and anti-Catholic sentiment. It was empowered by popular fears that the country was being overwhelmed by German and Irish Catholic immigrants, whom they saw as hostile to republican values and controlled by the Pope in Rome. Mainly active from 1854 to 1856, it strove to curb immigration and naturalization, but met with little success. Membership was limited to Protestant men. There were few prominent leaders, and the largely middle-class membership fragmented over the issue of slavery. The most prominent leaders were former President Millard Fillmore (the party's presidential nominee in 1856), U.S. Representative Nathaniel P. Banks, and former U.S. Representative Lewis C. Levin.

6. ANSWER: B

The immigration of large numbers of Irish and German Catholics to the United States in the period between 1830 and 1860 made religious differences between Catholics and Protestants a political issue. Violence occasionally erupted at the polls. Protestants alleged that Pope Pius IX had put down the failed liberal Revolutions of 1848 and that he was an opponent of liberty, democracy, and Republicanism. One Boston minister described Catholicism as "the ally of tyranny, the opponent of material prosperity, the foe of thrift, the enemy of the railroad, the caucus, and the school." These fears encouraged conspiracy theories regarding papal intentions of subjugating the United States through a continuing influx of Catholics controlled by Irish bishops obedient to and personally selected by the Pope. In 1849, an oath-bound secret society, the Order of the Star Spangled Banner, was created by Charles B. Allen in New York City. Fear of Catholic immigration led to a dissatisfaction with the Democratic Party, whose leadership in many cities included Catholics of Irish descent. Activists formed secret groups, coordinating their votes and throwing their weight behind candidates sympathetic to their cause. When asked about these secret organizations, members were to reply, "I know nothing," which led to their popularly being called Know Nothings.

7. ANSWER: C

During the mid to late 1800s, the United States government provided assistance to railroad companies as they expanded out west. In addition to commissioning the Transcontinental Railroad in 1862—which was to be completed in 1869 and marked the connection of the Atlantic and Pacific Oceans by rail—the United States government provided private companies with land grants. The federal government operated a land grant system between 1855 and 1871, through which new railway companies in the uninhabited West were given millions of acres they could sell or pledge to bondholders. A total of 129 million acres were granted to the railroads before the program ended, supplemented by a further 51 million acres granted by the states, and by various government subsidies. This program enabled the opening of numerous western lines, especially the Union Pacific-Central Pacific with fast service from San Francisco to Omaha and east to Chicago. West of Chicago, many cities grew up as rail centers, with repair shops and a base of technically literate workers.

8. ANSWER: B

The Homestead Act was passed in 1862 and granted 160 acres of land to settlers who agreed to farm it for at least five years. The Transcontinental Railroad was commissioned in 1862 and completed in 1869; it connected the Atlantic and Pacific oceans by rail. The Morrill Land Grant Act provided land for agricultural colleges. The

Dawes Act did not promote westward settlement. Instead, it divided Native American reservations into private plots of land to encourage assimilation.

9. **ANSWER: C**

(contextualization)

The Pacific Railroad Acts were a series of acts of Congress that promoted the construction of the transcontinental railroad in the United States through authorizing the issuance of government bonds and the grants of land to railroad companies. Although the War Department was authorized by the Congress in 1853 to conduct surveys of five different potential transcontinental routes from the Mississippi ranging from north to south and submitted a massive twelve volume report to Congress with the results in early 1855, no route or bill could be agreed upon and passed authorizing the Government's financial support and land grants until the secession of the Southern states removed their opposition to a central route. The Pacific Railroad Act of 1862 was the original act. The Pacific Railroad Act of 1862 began federal government grant of lands directly to corporations; before that act, the land grants were made to the states, for the benefit of corporations.

10. **ANSWER: B**

(historical causation; synthesis)

The Native Americans saw the addition of the railroad as a violation of their treaties with the United States. Natives began to raid the moving labor camps that followed the progress of the line. Railroad companies responded by increasing security and hiring marksmen to kill American Bison, which were both a physical threat to trains and the primary food source for many of the Plains Indians. The Native Americans then began killing laborers when they realized that the so-called "Iron Horse" threatened their existence. Security measures were further strengthened, and progress on the railroad continued. Native Americans continued to fight for control of their land over the next 30 years but would ultimately become dispossessed of their land.

11. **ANSWER: D**

(contextualization)

This song was written on the eve of the United States war with Mexico. It makes reference to the border dispute near the Rio Grande, which prompted President James K. Polk to send troops to the disputed territory, thus beginning the war. The song also mentions "murdering...men in Texas," a reference to the Alamo battle, in which

Mexican troops killed American revolutionaries in the Texas war for independence. Finally, the entire song is couched in the language of Manifest Destiny, which claimed that most North American territory belonged to the United States.

12. ANSWER: D

(historical causation)

A month before the end of the war, Polk was criticized in a United States House of Representatives amendment to a bill praising Major General Zachary Taylor for "a war unnecessarily and unconstitutionally begun by the President of the United States." This criticism, in which Congressman Abraham Lincoln played an important role with his Spot Resolutions, followed congressional scrutiny of the war's beginnings, including factual challenges to claims made by President Polk. The vote followed party lines, with all Whigs supporting the amendment. Lincoln's attack won lukewarm support from fellow Whigs in Illinois but was harshly attacked by Democrats, who rallied pro-war sentiments in Illinois; Lincoln's Spot resolutions haunted his future campaigns in the heavily Democratic state of Illinois, and were cited by enemies well into his presidency.

13. ANSWER: D

(patterns of continuity and change over time)

The excerpt above discusses the conflicts between white settlers and the Native Americans, writing that "Many were attacked by Indians just before and after us.... A few persons were killed, and other wounded and much stock run off." This trend of fighting for land rights has been common throughout United States history, beginning during the original encounter with Europeans in the fifteenth century and continuing throughout the nineteenth century.

14. ANSWER: A

(use of evidence)

Dunlap discusses "stores, hotels and shops" quartz and gold mines. Each mining bonanza required a town. Many towns had as high as a 9-to-1 male-to-female ratio. The ethnic diversity was great. Mexican immigrants were common. Native Americans avoided the mining industry, but mestizos, the offspring of Mexican and Native American parents, often participated. Many African Americans aspired to the same get-rich-quick idea as whites. Until excluded by federal law in 1882, Chinese Americans were numerous in mining towns. It is these mining towns that often conjure images of the mythical American Wild West. Most did have a saloon (or several) with swinging doors and a player piano. But miners and prospectors worked all day; few had the luxury of spending it at the bar. By nighttime, most were too tired to carouse. Weekends might bring folks out to the saloon for gambling or drinking, to engage in the occasional bar fight, or even to hire a prostitute. Law enforcement was crude. Many towns could not afford a sheriff, so vigilante justice prevailed. Occasionally a posse, or hunting party, would be raised to capture a particularly nettlesome miscreant. When the bonanza was at its zenith, the town prospered. But eventually the mines were exhausted or proved fruitless. Slowly its inhabitants would leave, leaving behind nothing but a ghost town (*http://www.ushistory.org/us/41a.asp*).

15. ANSWER: D

(contextualization; continuity over time)

The Sand Creek Massacre can best be understood as a part of a larger pattern of interaction between Americans and American Indians that was shaped by whites' assumptions about their cultural and racial superiority. It was an atrocity in the American Indian Wars that occurred on November 29, 1864, when a 700-man force of Colorado Territory militia attacked and destroyed a peaceful village of Cheyenne and Arapaho inhabited in southeastern Colorado Territory, killing and mutilating an estimated 70–163 Indians, about two-thirds of whom were women and children.

16. ANSWER: A

(historical argument/evidence)

The editorial above allows historians to understand contemporary responds to the Sand Creek Massacre. For instance, the editors of the *Rocky Mountain News* express skepticism of the United States government's response and hold the Native Americans accountable. Recent accounts hold the United States government culpable for the senseless murders. The site, on Big Sandy Creek in Kiowa County, is now preserved by the National Park Service. The Sand Creek Massacre National Historic Site was dedicated on April 28, 2007, almost 142 years after the massacre.

The Sand Creek Massacre Trail in Wyoming follows the paths of the Northern Arapaho and Cheyenne in the years after the massacre. Alexa Roberts, superintendent of the Sand Creek Massacre National Historic Site, has said that the trail represents a living portion of the history of the two tribes. An exhibit about Sand Creek, titled Collision: The Sand Creek Massacre 1860s-Today, opened in 2012 with the new History Colorado Center in Denver. The exhibit immediately drew criticism from members of the Northern Cheyenne tribe. In April 2013, History Colorado agreed to close the exhibit to public view while consultations were made with the Northern Cheyenne. On December

3, 2014, Colorado Governor John Hickenlooper formally apologized to descendants of Sand Creek massacre victims gathered in Denver to commemorate the 150th anniversary of the event. Hickenlooper stated, "We should not be afraid to criticize and condemn that which is inexcusable. ... On behalf of the state of Colorado, I want to apologize. We will not run from this history."

DIFFICULTY LEVEL 3

17. ANSWER: C

The Mexican War of Independence (1810–1821) severed control that Spain had exercised on its North American territories, and the new country of Mexico was formed from much of the individual territory that had comprised New Spain. The new country emerged essentially bankrupt from the war against Spain, and Mexico encouraged settlers to create their own militias for protection against hostile Indian tribes. Texas was very sparsely populated and in the hope that an influx of settlers could control the Indian raids, the government liberalized immigration policies for the region. By the 1830s, the Tejanos in Texas were vastly outnumbered by people born in the United States. To address this situation, President Anastasio Bustamante implemented a prohibition against further immigration to Texas from the United States, although American citizens would be allowed to settle in other parts of Mexico. Furthermore, the property tax law, intended to exempt immigrants from paying taxes for ten years, was rescinded, and tariffs were increased on goods shipped from the United States. Bustamante also ordered all Tejas settlers to comply with the federal prohibition against slavery or face military intervention. American settlers, however, simply circumvented or ignored the laws, and eventually fought for Texas independence from Mexico.

PART B

DIFFICULTY LEVEL 1

1. ANSWER: B

John Brown's raid on Harpers Ferry was an attempt by the white abolitionist John Brown to start an armed slave revolt in 1859 by seizing a United States arsenal at Harpers Ferry, Virginia. Brown's raid, accompanied by 20 men in his party, was defeated by a detachment of U.S. Marines led by Col. Robert E. Lee. John Brown had originally asked Harriet Tubman and Frederick Douglass, both of whom he had met in his formative years as an abolitionist in Springfield, Massachusetts, to join him in his raid, but Tubman was prevented by illness, and Douglass declined, as he believed, correctly, Brown's plan would fail.

DIFFICULTY LEVEL 2

2. ANSWER: A

The Compromise of 1850 defused a four-year political confrontation between slave and free states regarding the status of territories acquired during the Mexican-American War (1846–1848). The compromise, drafted by Whig Senator Henry Clay of Kentucky and brokered by Clay and Democratic Senator Stephen Douglas, reduced sectional conflict. The Compromise was greeted with relief, although each side disliked specific provisions which included the following:

- Texas surrendered its claim to New Mexico, over which it had threatened war, as well as its claims north of the Missouri Compromise Line. It retained the Texas Panhandle and the federal government took over the state's public debt.
- California was admitted as a free state with its current boundaries.
- The South prevented adoption of the Wilmot Proviso that would have outlawed slavery in the new territories, and the new Utah Territory and New Mexico Territory were allowed, under the principle of popular sovereignty, to decide whether to allow slavery within their borders. In practice, these lands were generally unsuited to plantation agriculture and their settlers were uninterested in slavery.
- The slave trade (but not slavery altogether) was banned in Washington D.C.

3. **ANSWER: B**

The new version of the Fugitive Slave Law required federal judicial officials in all states and federal territories, including in those states and territories in which slavery was prohibited, to actively assist with the return of escaped slaves to their masters in the states and territories permitting slavery. Any federal marshal or other official who did not arrest an alleged runaway slave was liable to a fine of $1,000. Law-enforcement officials everywhere in the United States had a duty to arrest anyone suspected of being a fugitive slave on no more evidence than a claimant's sworn testimony of ownership. The suspected slave could not ask for a jury trial or testify on his or her own behalf. In addition, any person aiding a runaway slave by providing food or shelter was to be subject to six months' imprisonment and a $1,000 fine. The Fugitive Slave Act was essential to meet Southern demands. In terms of public opinion in the North the critical provision was that ordinary citizens were required to aid slave catchers. Many northerners deeply resented this requirement that they personally aid and abet slavery. Resentment towards this act continued to heighten tensions between the North and South, as inflamed by abolitionists such as Harriet Beecher Stowe. Her book *Uncle Tom's Cabin* stressed the horrors of recapturing escaped slaves, and outraged Southerners

4. **ANSWER: C**

Uncle Tom's Cabin was the best-selling novel of the 19th century and the second best-selling book of that century, following the Bible. It is credited with helping fuel the abolitionist cause in the 1850s and stoking Northern opposition to the Fugitive Slave Law. The impact attributed to the book is great, reinforced by a story that when Abraham Lincoln met Stowe at the start of the Civil War, Lincoln declared, "So this is the little lady who started this great war." The quote is apocryphal; it did not appear in print until 1896. Literary scholar Daniel Vollaro has argued that, "The long-term durability of Lincoln's greeting as an anecdote in literary studies and Stowe scholarship can perhaps be explained in part by the desire among many contemporary intellectuals...to affirm the role of literature as an agent of social change."

5. **ANSWER: B**

Founded in the Northern states in 1854 by anti-slavery activists, modernizers, ex-Whigs, and ex-Free Soilers, the Republican Party quickly became the principal opposition to the dominant Democratic Party and the briefly popular Know Nothing Party. The main cause was opposition to the Kansas–Nebraska Act, which repealed the Missouri Compromise by which slavery was kept out of Kansas. The Northern Republicans saw the expansion of slavery as a great evil. The first public meeting where the name

"Republican" was suggested for a new anti-slavery party was held on March 20, 1854 in a schoolhouse in Ripon, Wisconsin. The Republicans' initial base was in the Northeast and the upper Midwest. With the realignment of parties and voters in the Third Party System, the strong run of John C. Fremont in the 1856 Presidential election demonstrated it dominated most northern states. Early Republican ideology was reflected in the 1856 slogan "free labor, free land, free men", which had been coined by Salmon P. Chase, a Senator from Ohio (and future Secretary of the Treasury and Chief Justice of the United States). "Free labor" referred to the Republican opposition to slave labor and belief in independent artisans and businessmen. "Free land" referred to Republican opposition to plantation system whereby slave owners could buy up all the good farmland, leaving the yeoman independent farmers the leftovers. The Party strived to contain the expansion of slavery, which would cause the collapse of the slave power and the expansion of freedom.

6. **ANSWER: D**

The *Dred Scott* decision was applauded by proslavery southerners. *Dred Scott v. Sandford* was a landmark decision by the U.S. Supreme Court in which the Court held that African Americans, whether enslaved or free, could not be American citizens and therefore had no standing to sue in federal court, and that the federal government had no power to regulate slavery in the federal territories acquired after the creation of the United States. This meant slaveowners could bring slaves wherever they settled. Dred Scott, an enslaved African American man who had been taken by his owners to free states and territories, attempted to sue for his freedom. In a 7–2 decision written by Chief Justice Roger B. Taney, the Court denied Scott's request. For only the second time in its history the Supreme Court ruled an Act of Congress to be unconstitutional.

7. **ANSWER: B**

The main theme of the Lincoln–Douglas debates was slavery, particularly the issue of slavery's expansion into the territories. It was Douglas's Kansas-Nebraska Act that repealed the Missouri Compromise's ban on slavery in the territories of Kansas and Nebraska, and replaced it with the doctrine of popular sovereignty, which meant that the people of a territory could decide for themselves whether to allow slavery. Lincoln said that popular sovereignty would nationalize and perpetuate slavery. Douglas argued that both Whigs and Democrats believed in popular sovereignty and that the Compromise of 1850 was an example of this. Lincoln said that the national policy was to limit the spread of slavery, and mentioned the Northwest Ordinance of 1787, which banned slavery from a large part of the modern-day Midwest, as an example of this policy. The Compromise of 1850 allowed the territories of Utah and New Mexico to decide for or against slavery, but it also allowed the admission of California as a free state, reduced the size of the slave state of Texas by adjusting the boundary, and ended the slave trade (but not slavery itself) in the District of Columbia. In return, the South got a stronger fugitive slave law than the version mentioned in the Constitution. Whereas Douglas said that the Compromise of 1850 replaced the Missouri Compromise ban on slavery in the Louisiana Purchase territory north and west of the state of Missouri, Lincoln said that this was false, and that Popular Sovereignty and the *Dred Scott* decision were a departure from the policies of the past that would nationalize slavery.

8. ANSWER: B

The Freeport Doctrine was articulated by Stephen A. Douglas at the second of the Lincoln-Douglas debates on August 27, 1858, in Freeport, Illinois. Abraham Lincoln was campaigning to take Douglas' U.S. Senate seat by strongly opposing all attempts to expand the geographic area in which slavery was practiced. Lincoln tried to force Douglas to choose between the principle of popular sovereignty proposed by the Kansas-Nebraska Act (which left the fate of slavery in a U.S. territory up to its inhabitants), and the majority decision of the United States Supreme Court in the case of *Dred Scott v. Sandford*, which stated that slavery could not legally be excluded from U.S. territories (since Douglas professed great respect for Supreme Court decisions, and accused the Republicans of disrespecting the court, yet this aspect of the *Dred Scott* decision was contrary to Douglas' views and politically unpopular in Illinois). Instead of making a direct choice, Douglas' response stated that despite the court's ruling, slavery could be prevented from any territory by the refusal of the people living in that territory to pass laws favorable to slavery (i.e., Slave Codes). Likewise, if the people of the territory supported slavery, legislation would provide for its continued existence.

9. ANSWER: A

(contextualization; historical causation)

The House Divided Speech was an address given by Abraham Lincoln on June 16, 1858, at what was then the Illinois State Capitol in Springfield, upon accepting the Illinois Republican Party's nomination as that state's United States senator. The speech became the launching point for his unsuccessful campaign for the Senate seat held by Stephen A. Douglas; this campaign would climax with the Lincoln-Douglas debates of 1858. After the *Dred Scott* decision, many northerners and members of the newly-formed Republican Party feared that slavery would spread throughout the country, since the Supreme Court forbade congress from passing laws banning slavery in the territories.

10. ANSWER: D

(use of evidence; synthesis)

In his speech, Abraham Lincoln warns that the United States will cease to be divided, and that slavery will either be permitted everywhere or be abolished. The Thirteenth Amendment formally abolished slavery everywhere in the United States, whereas the other choices served only to further divide the nation.

11. ANSWER: B

(historical causation)

The United States presidential election of 1860 was the 19th quadrennial presidential election. The election was held on Tuesday, November 6, 1860, and served as the immediate impetus for the outbreak of the American Civil War. The United States had been divided during the 1850s on questions surrounding the expansion of slavery and the rights of slave owners. In 1860, these issues broke the Democratic Party into Northern and Southern factions, and a new Constitutional Union Party appeared. In the face of a divided opposition, the Republican Party, dominant in the North, secured a majority of the electoral votes, putting Abraham Lincoln in the White House with almost no support from the South. Southerners believed that the Republican Party was hostile to slavery and their way of life.

12. ANSWER: B

(historical causation)

Before Lincoln's inauguration, South Carolina and six additional Southern states declared their secession and later formed the Confederacy. Secessionists from four additional Border states joined them when Lincoln's call to restore federal property in the South forced them to take sides, and two states, Kentucky and Missouri, attempted to remain neutral. At the 1864 election, the Union had admitted Kansas, West Virginia, and Nevada as free-soil states, while the Civil War disrupted the entire electoral process in the South, as no electoral votes were cast by any of the eleven states that had joined the Confederacy. Following South Carolina's unanimous 1860 secession vote, no other Southern states considered the question until 1861, and when they did none were unanimous. All had populations which cast significant numbers of Unionist votes in either the legislature, conventions, popular referendums, or in all three. However, voting to remain in the Union did not necessarily translate into being a northern sympathizer and, once hostilities actually commenced, many of these who voted to remain, particularly in the Lower South, accepted the majority decision, and supported the Confederacy.

13. ANSWER: C

(historical causation; contextualization)

Lincoln refused to recognize the Confederacy, declaring secession illegal. His main goal was to preserve the Union. There were attempts at compromise. For example, the Crittenden Compromise would have extended the Missouri Compromise line of 1820, dividing the territories into slave and free, contrary to the Republican Party's free-soil platform. Lincoln rejected the idea, saying, "I will suffer death before I consent ... to any concession or compromise which looks like buying the privilege to take possession of this government to which we have a constitutional right." Lincoln, however, did tacitly support the proposed Corwin Amendment to the Constitution, which passed Congress before Lincoln came into office and was then awaiting ratification by the states. That proposed amendment would have protected slavery in states where it already existed and would have guaranteed that Congress would not interfere with slavery without Southern consent. A few weeks before the war, Lincoln sent a letter to every governor informing them Congress had passed a joint resolution to amend the Constitution. Lincoln was open to the possibility of a constitutional convention to make further amendments to the Constitution. En route to his inauguration by train, Lincoln addressed crowds and legislatures across the North. The president-elect then evaded possible assassins in Baltimore, who were uncovered by Lincoln's head of security, Allan Pinkerton. On February 23, 1861, he arrived in disguise in Washington, D.C., which was placed under substantial military guard. Lincoln directed his inaugural address to the South, proclaiming once again that he had no intention, or inclination, to abolish slavery in the Southern states, and that every effort should be made to reunite the country.

14. ANSWER: C

(use of evidence; historical argumentation)

This excerpt from President James Buchanan's memoirs discusses the heightened sectionalism of the 1850s, which he blames partly on Hinton Helper's book *The Impending Crisis of the South*. Buchanan also discusses Helper's stirring up class warfare between poor whites and slave-owners, and the unfathomable proposition of compensating slaves for their work.

15. ANSWER: B

(contextualization)

Hinton Helper's book *The Impending Crisis of the South,* which Buchanan cites, focused on the regional economic and demographics differences between the North and the South. According to Helper, the differences between the two societies, and the South's disadvantages, could be explained by their divergent economies.

16. ANSWER: B

(historical argument/evidence)

It is likely that James Buchanan was trying to burnish his poor legacy with the publication of his memoirs. The day before his own death, Buchanan predicted that "history will vindicate my memory." Nevertheless, historians criticize Buchanan for his unwillingness or inability to act in the face of secession. Historical rankings of United States Presidents, considering presidential achievements, leadership qualities, failures and faults, consistently place Buchanan among the least successful presidents. In an academic poll of 47 British academics specializing in American history and politics in 2011, it was reported that he came last (40th). They were asked to evaluate the performance of every president from 1789 to 2009 (excluding William Henry Harrison and James Garfield, both of whom died shortly after taking office) in five categories: vision/agenda-setting, domestic leadership, foreign policy leadership, moral authority and positive historical significance of their legacy.

DIFFICULTY LEVEL 3

17. ANSWER: D

The Kansas–Nebraska Act of 1854 created the territories of Kansas and Nebraska, opening new lands for settlement, and had the effect of repealing the Missouri Compromise of 1820 by allowing white male settlers in those territories to determine through popular sovereignty whether they would allow slavery within each territory. The act was designed by Democratic Senator Stephen A. Douglas of Illinois, whose initial purpose of the Kansas–Nebraska Act was to open up many thousands of new farms and make feasible a Midwestern Transcontinental Railroad. It became a problem when popular sovereignty was written into the proposal so that the voters of the moment would decide whether slavery would be allowed or not. The result was that pro- and anti-slavery elements flooded into Kansas with the goal of voting slavery up or down, leading to Bleeding Kansas.

18. ANSWER: B

William Lloyd Garrison (December 12, 1805 – May 24, 1879) was a prominent American abolitionist, journalist, suffragist, and social reformer. He is best known as the editor of the abolitionist newspaper The Liberator, which he founded in 1831 and published in Massachusetts until slavery was abolished by Constitutional amendment after the American Civil War. He was one of the founders of the American Anti-Slavery Society. He promoted "immediate emancipation" of slaves in the United States. Garrison became famous as one of the most articulate, as well as most radical, opponents of slavery. His approach to emancipation stressed "moral suasion," non-violence, and passive resistance.

19. ANSWER: A

As a result of the Panic of 1857, the southern economy suffered little whereas the northern economy took a significant hit and made a slow recovery. The area affected the most by the Panic was the Great Lakes region and the troubles of that region were "quickly passed to those enterprises in the East that depended upon western sales." In about a year, much of the economy in the north and the entire south recovered from the Panic. Near the end of the Panic, in about 1859, tensions between the North and South regarding the issue of slavery in the United States were increasing. The Panic of 1857 encouraged those in the South who believed the idea that the north needed the south to keep a stabilized economy and southern threats of secession were temporarily quelled. Southerners believed the Panic of 1857 made the north "more amenable to southern demands" and would help to keep slavery alive in the United States.

PART C

1. ANSWER: C

After the Civil War, African Americans were still economically disadvantaged. Most had skills best suited to the plantation. By the early 1870s sharecropping became the dominant way for the poor to earn a living. Wealthy whites allowed poor whites and blacks to work land in exchange for a share of the harvest. The landlord would sometimes provide food, seed, tools, and shelter. Sharecroppers often found themselves in debt, for they had to borrow on bad terms and had to pay excessively for basic supplies. When the harvest came, if the debt exceeded harvest revenues, the sharecropper remained bound to the owner. In many ways, this system resembled slavery.

DIFFICULTY LEVEL 2

2. ANSWER: B

The Civil War was precipitated by a Confederate attack on the United States military base at Fort Sumter, which was in the process of being resupplied by the North. Lincoln had said the North would not attack the South first, despite his non-recognition of the Confederacy as a legitimate state. After the attack on Fort Sumter, however, Lincoln committed the United States military to achieving his goal of preserving the union.

3. ANSWER: A

On paper, the Union outweighed the Confederacy in almost every way. Nearly 21 million people lived in 23 Northern states. The South claimed just 9 million people — including 3.5 million slaves — in 11 Confederate Sates. Despite the North's greater population, however, the South had an army almost equal in size during the first year of the war. The North had an enormous industrial advantage as well. At the beginning of the war, the Confederacy had only one-ninth the industrial capacity of the Union. But that statistic was misleading. In 1860, the North manufactured 97 percent of the country's firearms, 96 percent of its railroad locomotives, 94 percent of its cloth, 93 percent of its pig iron, and over 90 percent of its boots and shoes. The North had twice the density of railroads per square mile. Since the North controlled the navy, the seas were in the hands of the Union. A blockade could suffocate the South. Still, the Confederacy was not without resources and willpower. The South could produce all the food it needed, though transporting it to soldiers and civilians was a major problem. The South also had a great nucleus of trained officers. Seven of the eight military colleges in the country were in the South (*http://www.ushistory.org/us/33b.asp*)

4. **ANSWER: B**

When the North enthusiastically rallied behind the Union after the Confederate attack on Fort Sumter on April 12, 1861, Lincoln concentrated on the military and political dimensions of the war effort. His primary goal was to reunite the nation. He unilaterally suspended habeas corpus, arresting and temporarily detaining thousands holding secessionist or anti-war views in the Border States without trial, ignoring the *Ex parte Merryman* ruling that such suspension is permitted only to Congress.

5. **ANSWER: D**

The Emancipation Proclamation, issued on September 22, 1862, and put into effect on January 1, 1863, declared free the slaves in 10 states not then under Union control, with exemptions specified for areas already under Union control in two states. Once the abolition of slavery in the rebel states became a military objective, as Union armies advanced south, more slaves were liberated until all three million of them in Confederate territory were freed. Lincoln's comment on the signing of the Proclamation was: "I never, in my life, felt more certain that I was doing right, than I do in signing this paper." Enlisting former slaves in the military was official government policy after the issuance of the Emancipation Proclamation.

6. **ANSWER: D**

Before his Assassination, President Lincoln proposed the Ten Percent Plan, which promised readmission to rebellious states if 10% of eligible voters pledged loyalty to the Union. When Andrew Johnson became president, he followed much of Lincoln's plan. Johnson believed the Southern states should decide the course that was best for them. He also felt that African-Americans were unable to manage their own lives and did not think that African-Americans deserved to vote. He also gave amnesty and pardon to many former Confederates. He returned all property, except, of course, their slaves, to former Confederates who pledged loyalty to the Union and agreed to support the 13th Amendment, which ended slavery. Confederate officials and owners of large taxable estates were required to apply individually for a Presidential pardon. Many former Confederate leaders were soon returned to power. and some even sought to regain their Congressional seniority. Johnson's vision of Reconstruction had proved remarkably lenient. Very few Confederate leaders were persecuted. By 1866, 7,000 Presidential pardons had been granted (*http://www.ushistory.org/us/35a.asp*).

7. ANSWER: A

Although it was proposed and temporarily implemented in Georgia by General William T. Sherman, the plan for land distribution for former slaves was never realized. Radical Republicans wanted to punish the South, and to prevent the ruling class from continuing in power. They successfully passed the Military Reconstruction Act of 1867, which divided the South into five military districts and outlined how the new governments would be designed. Under federal bayonets, African Americans, including those who had recently been freed, received the right to vote, hold political offices, and become judges and police chiefs. They held positions that formerly belonged to Southern Democrats. Many in the South were aghast. President Johnson vetoed all the Radical initiatives, but Congress overrode him each time. It was the Radical Republicans who impeached President Johnson in 1868. The Senate, by a single vote, failed to convict him, but his power to hinder radical reform was diminished.

8. ANSWER: D

During Reconstruction, many Southern whites resented and rejected the changes taking place all about them. Taxes were high. The economy was stagnant. Corruption ran rampant. Carpetbaggers and scalawags made matters worse. Carpetbaggers were Northerners who saw the shattered South as a chance to get rich quickly by seizing political office now barred from the old order. After the war these Yankees hastily packed old-fashioned traveling bags, called carpetbags, and rushed south. "Scalawags" were southern whites who allied themselves with the Republican Party, and also took advantage of the political openings.

9. ANSWER: B

The Compromise of 1877 was a purported informal, unwritten deal that settled the intensely disputed 1876 U.S. presidential election, pulled federal troops out of state politics in the South, and ended the Reconstruction Era. Through the Compromise, Republican Rutherford B. Hayes was awarded the White House over Democrat Samuel J. Tilden on the understanding that Hayes would remove the federal troops whose support was essential for the survival of Republican state governments in South Carolina, Florida, and Louisiana. The compromise involved Democrats who controlled the House of Representatives allowing the decision of the Electoral Commission (United States) to take effect. The outgoing president, Republican Ulysses S. Grant, removed the soldiers from Florida. As president, Hayes removed the remaining troops in South

Carolina and Louisiana. As soon as the troops left, many white Republicans also left and the "Redeemer" Democrats took control. What exactly happened is somewhat contested as the documentation is scanty. Black Republicans felt betrayed as they lost power.

10. ANSWER: B

(use of evidence; contextualization)

At the end of the Civil War, Lincoln's initial goal of preserving the Union had not wavered, and his Second Inaugural Address makes clear that Lincoln wants to reunite the country without punishing the South. Lincoln offered a model for reinstatement of Southern states called the Ten Percent Reconstruction plan. It decreed that a state could be reintegrated into the Union when 10% of the 1860 vote count from that state had taken an oath of allegiance to the U.S. and pledged to abide by Emancipation. Voters could then elect delegates to draft revised state constitutions and establish new state governments. All southerners except for high-ranking Confederate army officers and government officials would be granted a full pardon. Lincoln guaranteed southerners that he would protect their private property, though not their slaves. By 1864, Louisiana, Tennessee, and Arkansas had established fully functioning Unionist governments.

11. ANSWER: C

(comparison)

Johnson was initially left to devise a Reconstruction policy without legislative intervention, as Congress was not due to meet again until December 1865. Radical Republicans told the President that the Southern states were economically in a state of chaos and urged him to use his leverage to insist on rights for freedmen as a condition of restoration to the Union. But Johnson, with the support of other officials including Seward, insisted that the franchise was a state, not a federal matter. The Cabinet was divided on the issue. Johnson's first Reconstruction actions were two proclamations, with the unanimous backing of his Cabinet, on May One recognized the Virginia government led by provisional Governor Francis Pierpont. The second provided amnesty for all ex-rebels except those holding property valued at $20,000 or more; it also appointed a temporary governor for North Carolina and authorized elections. Neither of these proclamations included provisions regarding black suffrage or freedmen's rights. The President ordered constitutional conventions in other former rebel states.

12. ANSWER: B

(historical causation; interpretation)

During Reconstruction, Republicans took control of all Southern state governorships and state legislatures, except for Virginia. As a result of Reconstruction-Era Amendments, the Republican coalition elected numerous African Americans to local, state, and national offices. Though they did not dominate any electoral offices, black men as representatives voting in state and federal legislatures marked a drastic social change. At the beginning of 1867, no African American in the South held political office, but within three or four years about 15 percent of the officeholders in the South were black—a larger proportion than in 1990. Other African-American men who served were already leaders in their communities, including a number of preachers. As happened in white communities, not all leadership depended upon wealth and literacy.

13. ANSWER: D

(contextualization; interpretation; synthesis)

One source of opposition to the Fifteenth Amendment was the women's suffrage movement, which before and during the Civil War had made common cause with the abolitionist movement. However, with the passage of the Fourteenth Amendment, which had explicitly protected only male citizens in its second section, activists found the civil rights of women divorced from those of blacks. Matters came to a head with the proposal of the Fifteenth Amendment, which barred race discrimination but not gender discrimination in voter laws. After an acrimonious debate, the American Equal Rights Association, the nation's leading suffragist group, split into two rival organizations: the National Woman Suffrage Association of Susan B. Anthony and Elizabeth Cady Stanton, who opposed the amendment, and the American Woman Suffrage Association of Lucy Stone and Henry Browne Blackwell, who supported it. The two groups remained divided until the 1890s.

14. ANSWER: B

(interpretation; contextualization)

The Fourteenth Amendment was designed to protect the rights of freedmen and to put the key provisions of the Civil Rights Act into the Constitution, but it went much further. It extended citizenship to everyone born in the United States (except visitors and Indians on reservations), penalized states that did not give the vote to freedmen, and most importantly, created new federal civil rights that could be protected by federal courts. Johnson used his influence to block the amendment in the states since three-fourths of the states were required for ratification (the amendment was later ratified.). The moderate effort to compromise with Johnson had failed, and a political fight broke out between the Republicans on one side, and on the other side, Johnson and his allies in the Democratic Party in the North, and the conservative groupings in each Southern state.

15. ANSWER: D

(causation)

The first Ku Klux Klan was founded in 1865 in Pulaski, Tennessee, by six veterans of the Confederate Army. The name is probably derived from the Greek word kuklos, which means circle. Although there was little organizational structure above the local level, similar terrorist groups rose across the South and adopted the same name and methods. Klan groups spread throughout the South as an insurgent movement during the Reconstruction era in the United States. As a secret vigilante group, the Klan targeted freedmen and their allies; it sought to restore white supremacy by threats and violence, including murder, against black and white Republicans. In 1870 and 1871, the federal government passed the Force Acts, which were used to prosecute Klan crimes. Prosecution of Klan crimes and enforcement of the Force Acts suppressed Klan activity. In 1874 and later, newly organized and openly active paramilitary organizations, such as the White League and the Red Shirts, started a fresh round of violence aimed at suppressing blacks' voting and running Republicans out of office. These contributed to segregationist white Democrats regaining political power in all the Southern states by 1877.

16. ANSWER: B

(comparison; contextualization)

Although Congress, run by the Radical Republicans, and President Andrew Johnson, a southern Democrat, had markedly different approaches to reconstructing the Union after the Civil War, they shared the goal of reuniting the nation. Republicans in Congress wanted to punish the South and ensure civil rights for African Americans as part of their Reconstruction plan, while Johnson wanted to offer amnesty to most Southerners for a rapid readmission of states.

17. ANSWER: C

(continuity and change; comparison)

In *The Spirit of the Laws* (1748), Montesquieu described the separation of political power among a legislature, an executive, and a judiciary. Montesquieu's approach was to present and defend a form of government which was not excessively centralized in all its powers to a single monarch or similar ruler. He based this model on the Constitution of the Roman Republic and the British constitutional system. Montesquieu took the view that the Roman Republic had powers separated so that no one could usurp complete power. In the British constitutional system, Montesquieu discerned a separation of powers among the monarch, Parliament, and the courts of law.

18. ANSWER: A

(contextualization; use of evidence)

According to white Southerners, passage of the Fifteenth Amendment, which extended suffrage to black men, would result in political chaos. Popular perception of freedmen included racist stereotypes about their inability to handle freedom and the pressures of elected office.

19. ANSWER: C

(use of evidence)

While Republican whites supported measures for black civil rights, the conservative whites typically opposed these measures. Some supported armed attacks to suppress black power. They self-consciously defended their own actions within the framework of an Anglo-American discourse of resistance against tyrannical government, and they broadly succeeded in convincing many fellow white citizens. The opponents of Reconstruction formed state political parties, affiliated with the national Democratic Party, and often named the "Conservative party." They supported or tolerated violent paramilitary groups, such as the White League in Louisiana and the Red Shirts in Mississippi and the Carolinas that assassinated and intimidated both black and white Republican leaders at election time. Historian George C. Rable called such groups the "military arm of the Democratic Party." Historian Walter Lynwood Fleming describes mounting anger of Southern whites: "The Negro troops, even at their best, were everywhere considered offensive by the native whites ... The Negro soldier, impudent by reason of his new freedom, his new uniform, and his new gun, was more than Southern temper could tranquilly bear, and race conflicts were frequent."

20. ANSWER: A

(argumentation; interpretation)

After Reconstruction ended in 1877 and Northern troops were withdrawn from the former Confederacy, southern states began passing laws to restrict the rights of African Americans. The Jim Crow laws were racial segregation laws enacted after the Reconstruction period in Southern United States, at state and local levels, and which continued in force until 1965, which mandated *de jure* racial segregation in all public facilities in Southern states of the former Confederacy, with, starting in 1890, a "separate but equal" status for African Americans. The separation in practice led to conditions for African Americans that were inferior to those provided for white Americans, systematizing a number of economic, educational and social disadvantages. *De jure* segregation mainly applied to the Southern United States, while Northern segregation was generally *de facto* — patterns of segregation in housing enforced by covenants, bank lending practices and job discrimination, including discriminatory union practices for decades.

Jim Crow laws mandated the segregation of public schools, public places and public transportation, and the segregation of restrooms, restaurants and drinking fountains for whites and blacks. The U.S. military was also segregated, as were federal workplaces, initiated in 1913 under President Woodrow Wilson, the first Southern president since 1856. His administration practiced overt racial discrimination in hiring, requiring candidates to submit photos.

21. ANSWER: C

(use of evidence; synthesis; interpretation)

Southern Democrats passed laws to make voter registration and electoral rules more restrictive, with the result that political participation by most blacks and many poor whites began to decrease. Between 1890 and 1910, ten of the eleven former Confederate states, starting with Mississippi, passed new constitutions or amendments that effectively disfranchised most blacks and tens of thousands of poor whites through a combination of poll taxes, literacy and comprehension tests, and residency and record-keeping requirements. Grandfather clauses temporarily permitted some illiterate whites to vote but using the same law prevented most blacks from voting. Voter turnout dropped drastically through the South as a result of such measures.

22. ANSWER: A

(use of evidence; contextualization)

The Black Codes were laws passed by Southern states in 1865 and 1866, after the Civil War. These laws had the intent and the effect of restricting African Americans' freedom, and of compelling them to work in a labor economy based on low wages or debt. Republicans—and especially Radical Republicans—would have opposed the regulations in the legislation above. In general, Republicans sought greater equality for African Americans and hoped to see them participate in a free-labor system. For this reason, Republicans in Congress passed the Civil Rights Act and the Fourteenth

Amendment to the Constitution, protecting the rights of African Americans as full citizens.

23. ANSWER: D

(contextualization)

Since the early 1800s, many laws in both North and South discriminated systematically against free Blacks. In the South, "slave codes" placed significant restrictions on Black Americans who were not themselves slaves. A major purpose of these laws was maintenance of the system of white supremacy that made slavery possible. With legal prohibitions of slavery ordered by the Emancipation Proclamation, acts of state legislature, and eventually the Thirteenth Amendment, Southern states adopted new laws to regulate Black life. Although these laws had different official titles, they were (and are) commonly known as Black Codes. The defining feature of the Black Codes was vagrancy law which allowed local authorities to arrest the freed people and commit them to involuntary labor.

DIFFICULTY LEVEL 3

24. ANSWER: B

King Cotton diplomacy refers to the diplomatic methods employed by the Confederacy during the American Civil War to coerce the United Kingdom and France to support the Confederate war effort by implementing a cotton trade embargo against the United Kingdom and the rest of Europe. The Confederacy believed that both the United Kingdom and France, who before the war depended heavily on southern cotton for textile manufacturing, would support the Confederate war effort if the cotton trade were restricted. Ultimately, cotton diplomacy did not work in favor of the Confederacy. In fact, the cotton embargo transformed into a self-embargo which restricted the Confederate economy. Ultimately, the growth in the demand for cotton that fueled the antebellum economy did not continue.

25. ANSWER: B

At the beginning of the Civil War, Lincoln believed that the fighting would be over within three months. After several Union defeats, however, it became clear that waging and winning the war would prove difficult. As a result, there was a genuine fear within the Lincoln Administration that Great Britain and France would recognize the Confederate States of America as a legitimate, independent. After the Union's victory at

Antietam and Lincoln's issuance of the Emancipation Proclamation, European countries openly supported the Union.

26. ANSWER: C

The Impeachment of Andrew Johnson, who became the 17th President of the United States after Abraham Lincoln was assassinated, was one of the most dramatic events in the political life of the United States during Reconstruction. The first impeachment of a sitting United States president, it was the culmination of a lengthy political battle between the Southern Democrat Johnson and the "Radical Republican" movement that dominated Congress and sought control of the South through Reconstruction policies. Johnson was impeached on February 24, 1868, in the U.S. House of Representatives on eleven articles of impeachment detailing his "high crimes and misdemeanors,' in accordance with Article Two of the United States Constitution. The House's primary charge against Johnson was with violation of the Tenure of Office Act, passed by Congress the previous year. Specifically, he had removed Edwin M. Stanton, the Secretary of War (whom the Tenure of Office Act was largely designed to protect), from office and replaced him with General Lorenzo Thomas. The House agreed to the articles of impeachment on March 2, 1868. The trial began three days later in the Senate, with Chief Justice of the United States Salmon P. Chase presiding. The trial concluded on May 16 with Johnson's acquittal. The final tally of votes for conviction was one fewer than the two-thirds required.

Period 1865-1898

PART A

DIFFICULTY LEVEL 1

1. ANSWER: A

The American Federation of Labor (AFL) was the first federation of labor unions in the United States. It was founded in Columbus, Ohio, in May 1886 by an alliance of craft unions disaffected from the Knights of Labor, a national labor association. Samuel Gompers of the Cigar Makers' International Union was elected president of the Federation at its founding convention and was reelected every year except one until his death in 1924. Their fundamentally conservative "pure and simple" approach limited the AFL to matters pertaining to working conditions and rates of pay, relegating political goals to its allies in the political sphere. The Federation favored pursuit of workers' immediate demands rather than challenging the property rights of owners, and took a pragmatic view of politics which favored tactical support for particular politicians over formation of a party devoted to workers' interests. The AFL's leadership believed the expansion of the capitalist system was seen as the path to betterment of labor, an orientation making it possible for the AFL to present itself as what one historian has called "the conservative alternative to working class radicalism."

2. ANSWER: B

John Pierpont "J.P." Morgan (April 17, 1837 – March 31, 1913) was an American financier, banker, philanthropist, and art collector who dominated corporate finance and industrial consolidation during his time. In 1892, Morgan arranged the merger of Edison General Electric and Thomson-Houston Electric Company to form General Electric. After financing the creation of the Federal Steel Company, he merged it in 1901 with the Carnegie Steel Company and several other steel and iron businesses, including Consolidated Steel and Wire Company, owned by William Edenborn, to form the United States Steel Corporation. At the height of Morgan's career during the early 1900s, he and his partners had financial investments in many large corporations and had significant influence over the nation's high finance and United States Congress members. He directed the banking coalition that stopped the Panic of 1907. He was the leading financier of the Progressive Era, and his dedication to efficiency and modernization helped transform American business.

3. ANSWER: D

Urbanization is a population shift from rural to urban areas, and the ways in which society adapts to the change. It predominantly results in the physical growth of urban areas, be it horizontal or vertical. The onset of the industrial revolution in the late 18th century caused an unprecedented growth in urban population that took place over the course of the 19th century, both through continued migration from the countryside and due to the tremendous demographic expansion that occurred at that time. In England, the urban population jumped from 17% in 1801 to 72% in 1891 (for other countries the figure was: 37% in France, 41% in Prussia and 28% in the United States).

4. ANSWER: D

Social Darwinism is a modern name given to various theories of society that emerged in the United Kingdom, the United States, and Western Europe in the 1870s, and which sought to apply biological concepts of natural selection and survival of the fittest to sociology and politics. Social Darwinists generally argue that the strong should see their wealth and power increase while the weak should see their wealth and power decrease. Different social Darwinists have different views about which groups of people are the strong and the weak, and they also hold different opinions about the precise mechanism that should be used to promote strength and punish weakness. Many such views stress competition between individuals in laissez-faire capitalism, while others motivated ideas of eugenics, racism, imperialism, fascism, Nazism, and struggle between national or racial groups.

DIFFICULTY LEVEL 2

5. ANSWER: D

During the late nineteenth century, the American labor movement was involved in a number violent strikes, including the Great Railroad Strike, the Haymarket Riot, The Homestead Strike, and the Pullman Strike. Common to all of these strikes were the wage cuts that precipitated them, the violence between workers and strikebreakers, and the tendency of the federal government to side with big business over labor.

6. ANSWER: A

To eliminate economic competition in the late nineteenth century, American industries created pools, trusts, and holding companies. Railroad pools in the United States were associations of competing railroads "for the purpose of a proper division of the traffic at competitive points and the maintenance of equitable rates that may be agreed upon." Congress prohibited pooling agreements between railroads with the enactment of the Interstate Commerce Act of 1887. In the 19th century industries created monopolistic trusts by entrusting their shares to a board of trustees in exchange for shares of equal value with dividend rights; these boards could then enforce a monopoly. However, trusts were used in this case because a corporation could not own other companies' stock and thereby become a holding company without a "special act of the legislature." Holding companies were used after the restriction on owning other companies' shares was lifted. Congress attempted to restore economic competition by passing antitrust legislation.

7. **ANSWER: D**

The Knights of Labor was the largest and one of the most important American labor organizations of the 1880s. Its most important leader was Terence V. Powderly. The Knights promoted the social and cultural uplift of the workingman, rejected Socialism and radicalism, demanded the eight-hour day, and promoted the producers ethic of republicanism. It was also inclusive in its membership, allowing skilled and unskilled workers, women, African Americans, and immigrants. In some cases it acted as a labor union, negotiating with employers, but it was never well organized, and after a rapid expansion in the mid-1880s, it suddenly lost its new members and became a small operation again.

8. **ANSWER: A**

The Gilded Age was an era of rapid economic growth, especially in the North and West. American wages, especially for skilled workers, were much higher than in Europe, which attracted millions of immigrants. The increase of industrialization meant, despite the increasing labor force, real wages in the US grew 60% from 1860 to 1890, and continued to rise after that. However, the Gilded Age was also an era of poverty as very poor European immigrants poured in. Railroads were the major industry, but the factory system, mining, and finance increased in importance. In addition, attempts to regulate industry, either by the United States government or by labor unions, met resistance from powerful business leaders who had a stronghold on industry and public policy.

9. **ANSWER: A**

(use of evidence)

The First Transcontinental Railroad was a 1,907-mile contiguous railroad line constructed between 1863 and 1869 across the western United States to connect the Pacific coast at San Francisco Bay with the existing Eastern U.S. rail network at Council Bluffs, Iowa, on the Missouri River. Opened for through traffic on May 10, 1869, with the ceremonial driving of the "Last Spike" (later often called the "Golden Spike") with a silver hammer at Promontory Summit, the road established a mechanized transcontinental transportation network that revolutionized the settlement and economy of the American West by bringing these western states and territories firmly and profitably into the "Union" and making goods and transportation much quicker, cheaper, and more flexible from coast to coast.

10. **ANSWER: B**

(historical causation)

Because of the completion of the Transcontinental Railroad, the public reaped great benefits. Eastern businessmen could now sell their goods to California citizens. As a result of improved transportation all Americans had access to more goods at a cheaper price. The westward movement was greatly accelerated. Those seeking a new start in life could much more easily "go west." No industrial revolution can occur without a transport web. The nation was now bound together by this enormous network and its citizens were ready to reap the rewards.

11. **ANSWER: D**

(contextualization)

The cartoon above depicts William Jennings Bryan, who ran for president in 1896 on a fusion ticket that combined the Democratic Party and Populist Party, or Peoples Party. The People's Party grew out of a large mood of agrarian unrest in response to low agricultural prices in the South and the trans-Mississippi West.[1] The Farmers' Alliance, formed in 1876, promoted collective economic action by farmers and achieved widespread popularity in the South and Great Plains. The Farmers' Alliance ultimately did not achieve its wider economic goals of collective economic action against brokers, railroads, and merchants, and many in the movement advocated for changes in national policy. By the late 1880s, the Alliance had developed a political agenda that called for regulation and reform in national politics, most notably an opposition to the gold standard to counter the high deflation in agricultural prices in relation to other goods such as farm implements.

12. ANSWER: B

(comparison/contextualization)

The intended audience of the cartoon above were members of the Republican Party, which opposed Populist ideas. The Populist Party's platform, commonly known as the Omaha Platform, called for the abolition of national banks, a graduated income tax, direct election of Senators, civil service reform, a working day of eight hours and Government control of all railroads, telegraphs, and telephones. By 1896, the Democratic Party took up many of the People's Party's causes at the national level, and the party began to fade from national prominence. In that year's presidential election, the Democrats nominated William Jennings Bryan, who focused (as Populists rarely did) on the free silver issue as a solution to the economic depression and the maldistribution of power. One of the great orators of the day, Bryan generated enormous excitement among Democrats with his "Cross of Gold" speech, and appeared in the summer of 1896 to have a good chance of winning the election, if the Populists voted for him. Bryan's strength was based on the traditional Democratic vote (minus the middle class and the Germans); he swept the old Populist strongholds in the west and South, and added the silverite states in the west, but did poorly in the industrial heartland. He lost to Republican William McKinley by a margin of 600,000 votes, and lost again in a rematch in 1900 by a larger margin.

13. ANSWER: C

(continuity and change; synthesis)

In U.S. politics, a third party is a political party other than the Democrats or Republicans. The term "minor party" is also used in a similar manner. Such political parties rarely win elections, as proportional representation is not used in federal or state elections, but only in some municipal elections. A similar situation occurs with the presidential Electoral College, where Electoral College votes are often given the candidate who receives a plurality of the vote, thus bringing up accusations that certain third party presidential candidates are "spoiling" the election or splitting up segments of voters. Among the other challenges that third parties face in the United States, is the frequent exclusion from major debates and media coverage, denial of ballot access and the difficulty in raising campaign contributions large enough to compete with the two major political parties. Third parties, such as the Populist Party, have succeeded in introducing new ideas into the political arena, some of which later become Democratic or Republican policies.

14. ANSWER: B

(contextualization)

"The Gospel of Wealth" is an article written by Andrew Carnegie in 1889 that describes the responsibility of philanthropy by the new upper class of self-made rich. Carnegie proposed that the best way of dealing with the new phenomenon of wealth inequality was for the wealthy to redistribute their surplus means in a responsible and thoughtful manner. This approach was contrasted with traditional bequest (patrimony), where wealth is handed down to heirs, and other forms of bequest e.g. where wealth is willed to the state for public purposes. Carnegie argued that surplus wealth is put to best use (i.e. produces the greatest net benefit to society) when it is administered carefully by the wealthy. Carnegie also argues against wasteful use of capital in the form of extravagance, irresponsible spending, or self-indulgence, instead promoting the administration of said capital over the course of one's lifetime toward the cause of reducing the stratification between the rich and poor. As a result, the wealthy should administer their riches responsibly and not in a way that encourages "the slothful, the drunken, the unworthy."

15. ANSWER: A

(historical causation)

Carnegie put his philosophy into practice through a program of gifts to endow public libraries, known as 'Carnegie libraries' in cities and towns throughout the United States and the English-speaking world, with the idea that he was thus providing people with the tools to better themselves. In order to ensure that his gifts would not be wasted, he stipulated that the municipality must pass an ordinance establishing a tax to support the library's ongoing operating costs after the initial grant provided the costs for building and equipping the library.

After several communities squandered their grants on extravagant buildings, Carnegie established a system of architectural guidelines that mandated simplicity and functionality. When it became obvious that Carnegie could not give away his entire fortune within his lifetime, he established the Carnegie Foundation to continue his program of giving.

16. ANSWER: D

(contextualization)

The cartoon above is a critical depiction of John D. Rockefeller, founder of Standard Oil and one of the leading business magnates in the late nineteenth and early twentieth centuries. Laissez-faire capitalism, or lack of government interference, allowed him to consolidate his business empire and eliminate competition. Social Darwinian views of the time dictated that those at the top of the economic ladder deserved to be there because they had worked the hardest, despite the many unscrupulous and illegal business tactics Rockefeller employed. Finally, he utilized vertical integration to purchase other businesses, such as railroad companies, that helped make his business model successful.

DIFFICULTY LEVEL 3

17. ANSWER: D

The Sherman Antitrust Act is a landmark federal statute in the history of United States antitrust law (or "competition law") passed by Congress in 1890. It prohibits certain business activities that federal government regulators deem to be anti-competitive, and requires the federal government to investigate and pursue trusts. The Act was aimed at regulating businesses. However, its application was not limited to the commercial side of business. Its prohibition of the cartel was also interpreted to make illegal many labor union activities. This is because unions were characterized as cartels as well (cartels of laborers). This persisted until 1914, when the Clayton Act created exceptions for certain union activities.

18. ANSWER: B

Horatio Alger was a prolific 19th-century American author, best known for his many juvenile novels about impoverished boys and their rise from humble backgrounds to lives of middle-class security and comfort through hard work, determination, courage, and honesty. His writings were characterized by the "rags-to-riches" narrative, which had a formative effect on America during the Gilded Age. Alger's name is often invoked incorrectly as though he himself rose from rags to riches, but that arc applied to his characters, not to the author. Essentially, all of Alger's novels share the same theme: a young boy struggles through hard work to escape poverty.

PART B

DIFFICULTY LEVEL 1

1. ANSWER: B

Jane Addams (September 6, 1860 – May 21, 1935) was a pioneer American settlement social worker, public philosopher, sociologist, author, and leader in women's suffrage and world peace. The settlement house as Addams understood it was a space within which unexpected cultural connections could be made and where the narrow boundaries of culture, class, and education could be expanded. They doubled up as community arts centers and social service facilities. They laid the foundations for American civil society, a neutral space within which different communities and ideologies could learn from each other and seek common grounds for collective action. In 1889, Addams and Ellen Gates Starr co-founded a settlement house, the Hull House, in Chicago, Illinois. In an era when presidents such as Theodore Roosevelt and Woodrow Wilson identified themselves as reformers and social activists, Addams was one of the most prominent reformers of the Progressive Era. She helped turn America to issues of concern to mothers, such as the needs of children, local public health, and world peace. Addams became a role model for middle-class women who volunteered to uplift their communities. In 1931 she became the first American woman to be awarded the Nobel Peace Prize and is recognized as the founder of the social work profession in the United States.

DIFFICULTY LEVEL 2

2. ANSWER: B

In the 19th century, the incessant westward expansion of the United States incrementally compelled large numbers of Native Americans to resettle further west, often by force, almost always reluctantly. The West was an emerging patchwork of homestead farmers, miners, and cattle ranchers. While Easterners tried to make their way in these and other professions, Native Americans desperately clung to the hopes of maintaining their tribal traditions. Conflict between whites and Native Americans was as old as the earliest settlements, but there were clear patterns of waxing and waning intensity. The Transcontinental Railroad became the catalyst for much of the new conflict. Now thousands more could migrate much more quickly, cheaply, and comfortably. As the numbers of white settlers from the East increased dramatically, conflicts with the native tribes did so as well (*http://www.ushistory.org/us/40.asp*).

3. **ANSWER: A**

The Dawes Act of 1887 authorized the President of the United States to survey Native American tribal land and divide it into allotments for individual Indians. Those who accepted allotments and lived separately from the tribe would be granted United States citizenship.The stated objective of the Dawes Act was to stimulate assimilation of Indians into mainstream American society. Individual ownership of land on the European-American model was seen as an essential step. The act also provided what the government would classify as "excess" Indian reservation lands remaining after allotments, and sell those lands on the open market, allowing purchase and settlement by non-Native Americans. During the ensuing decades, many Native American tribes and individuals suffered dispossession of lands and other social ills.

4. **ANSWER: C**

A Century of Dishonor is a non-fiction book by Helen Hunt Jackson first published in 1881 that chronicled the experiences of Native Americans in the United States, focusing on injustices.

Jackson wrote A Century of Dishonor in an attempt to change government ideas/policy toward Native Americans at a time when effects of the 1871 Indian Appropriations Act (making the entire Native American population wards of the nation) had begun to draw the attention of the public. Her book brought to light the moral injustices enacted upon the Native Americans as it chronicled the ruthlessness of white settlers in their greed for land, wealth, and power.

5. **ANSWER: D**

The first significant Chinese immigration to North America began with the California Gold Rush of 1848-1855 and continued with subsequent large labor projects, such as the building of the First Transcontinental Railroad. During the early stages of the gold rush, when surface gold was plentiful, the Chinese were tolerated, if not well received. As gold became harder to find and competition increased, animosity toward the Chinese and other foreigners increased. As time passed and more and more Chinese migrants arrived in California, violence would often break out in cities such as Los Angeles. The Chinese Exclusion Act was signed by President Chester A. Arthur on May 6, 1882. It prohibited all immigration of Chinese laborers. The act was initially intended to last for 10 years, but was renewed in 1892 and made permanent in 1902. It was finally repealed by the Magnuson Act on December 17, 1943.

6. ANSWER: C

For much of American history, most immigrant groups coming to the United States by choice seemed distinct, but in fact had many similarities. Most had come from Northern and Western Europe. Most had some experience with representative democracy. With the exception of the Irish, most were Protestant. Many were literate, and some possessed a fair degree of wealth. During the Gilded Age, however, this changed, as more immigrants arrived from Eastern and Southern Europe. Their nationalities included Greek, Italian, Polish, Slovak, Serb, Russian, Croat, and others. Until cut off by federal decree, Japanese and Chinese settlers relocated to the American West Coast. None of these groups were predominantly Protestant. The vast majority were Catholic. However, due to increased persecution of Jews in Eastern Europe, many Jewish immigrants sought freedom from torment. Very few newcomers spoke any English, and large numbers were illiterate in their native tongues. None of these groups hailed from democratic regimes. The American form of government was as foreign as its culture.

7. ANSWER: B

Becoming mayor of a big city in the Gilded Age was like walking into a cyclone. Demands swirled around city leaders. Better sewers, cleaner water, new bridges, more efficient transit, improved schools, and suitable aid to the sick and needy were some of the more common demands coming from a wide range of interest groups. To cope with the city's problems, government officials had a limited resources and personnel. Democracy did not flourish in this environment. To bring order out of the chaos of the nation's cities, many political bosses emerged who did not shrink from corrupt deals if they could increase their power bases. The people and institutions the bosses controlled were called the political machine .City politics can at once seem simple and complex. To maintain power, a city boss had to keep his constituents happy. Most political bosses appealed to the newest, most desperate part of the growing populace — the immigrants. Occasionally bosses would provide relief kitchens to receive votes. Individuals who were leaders in local neighborhoods were sometimes rewarded city jobs in return for the loyalty of their constituents. Bosses knew they also had to placate big business, and did so by rewarding them with lucrative contracts for construction of factories or public works. These industries would then pump large sums into keeping the political machine in office. It seemed simple: "You scratch my back and I'll scratch yours." However, bringing diverse interests together in a city as large as New York, Philadelphia, or Chicago required hours of legwork and great political skill *http://www.ushistory.org/us/38d.asp).*

8. **ANSWER: B**

(contextualization; chronological reasoning)

The Woman's Christian Temperance Union (WCTU) was the first mass organization among women devoted to social reform with a program that "linked the religious and the secular through concerted and far-reaching reform strategies based on applied Christianity." The WCTU was originally organized on December 23, 1873, in Hillsboro, Ohio, and officially declared at a national convention in Cleveland, Ohio in 1874. It operated at an international level and in the context of religion and reform, including missionary work as well as matters of social reform such as suffrage. Two years after its founding, the American WCTU sponsored an international conference at which the International Women's Christian Temperance Union was formed. The connections and contradictions between the two parts of its purpose—Christianity and Temperance—meant that the women involved confronted ideological, philosophical, political and practical dilemmas in their efforts to improve society around the world. Although some labelled the Union as gender-biased, others disagreed by pointing out the many male supporters behind the scenes.

9. **ANSWER: C**

(chronological reasoning)

The WCTU's work extended across a range of efforts to bring about personal and social moral reform. Between 1900 and 1920, much of their budget was given to their center on Ellis Island, which helped to start the Americanization process for international migrants. The WCTU felt that immigrants were more prone to alcoholism. The fiction they created greatly centered on Irish and German immigrants' partaking of alcohol and being drunk.

10. **ANSWER: B**

(continuity and change)

Hostility toward international migrants, or nativism, is the political position of demanding a favored status for certain established inhabitants of a nation as compared to claims of newcomers or immigrants. Nativism typically means opposition to immigration, and support of efforts to lower the political or legal status of specific ethnic or cultural groups who are considered hostile or alien to the natural culture, upon the assumption that they cannot be assimilated.

11. **ANSWER: C**

(comparison; synthesis)

Between 1890 and 1920, nativists and labor unions campaigned for immigration restriction for fear that immigrants were driving down wages and taking jobs from native-born Americans. A favorite plan was the literacy test to exclude workers who could not read or write their own foreign language. Congress passed literacy tests, but presidents—responding to business needs for low-wage workers—vetoed them.

12. ANSWER: B

(contextualization)

Historians estimate that fewer than 1 million immigrants came to the United States from Europe between 1600 and 1799. From 1836 to 1914, over 30 million Europeans migrated to the United States. The peak year of European immigration was in 1907, when 1,285,349 persons entered the country. By 1910, 13.5 million immigrants were living in the United States. In 1921, the Congress passed the Emergency Quota Act, followed by the Immigration Act of 1924. The 1924 Act was aimed at further restricting the Southern and Eastern Europeans, especially Jews, Italians, and Slavs, who had begun to enter the country in large numbers beginning in the 1890s.

13. ANSWER: C

(contextualization)

In the years prior to the Wounded Knee conflict, the U.S. government had continued to seize the Lakota's lands. The once large bison herds (an indigenous peoples' Great Plains staple) had been hunted to near-extinction by white settlers. Promises to protect reservation lands from encroachment by settlers and gold miners were not implemented as dictated by treaty. As a result, there was unrest on the reservations. It was during this time that news spread among the reservations of a Paiute prophet named Wovoka, founder of the Ghost Dance religion. He had a vision that the Christian Messiah, Jesus Christ, had returned to earth in the form of a Native American. White Americans were alarmed by the sight of the many Great Basin and Plains tribes performing the Ghost Dance, worried that it might be a prelude to armed attack. On the morning of December 29, the troops went into the camp to disarm the Lakota. Specific details of what triggered the massacre are debated, but by the time it was over, more than 200 men, women, and children of the Lakota had been killed and 51 were wounded.

14. ANSWER: B

(use of evidence)

There is a long tradition of injustice against Native Americans by the United States government. As Americans moved farther West, conflicts with Native Americans continued, and the United States attempted to Americanize the Indians with the Dawes Act and Indian Boarding Schools. When Native Americans attempted to reclaim their culture, as the Lakota did with the Ghost Dance, they were met with massacre. Wounded Knee is generally considered to be the end of the collective multi-century series of conflicts between colonial and U.S. forces and American Indians, known collectively as the Indian Wars.

DIFFICULTY LEVEL 3

15. ANSWER: A

The Frontier Thesis or Turner Thesis, is the argument advanced by historian Frederick Jackson Turner in 1893 that American democracy was formed by the American frontier. He stressed the process—the moving frontier line—and the impact it had on pioneers going through the process. He also stressed results, especially that American democracy was the primary result, along with egalitarianism, a lack of interest in high culture, and violence. "American democracy was born of no theorist's dream; it was not carried in the Sarah Constant to Virginia, nor in the Mayflower to Plymouth. It came out of the American forest, and it gained new strength each time it touched a new frontier," said Turner. In the thesis, the American frontier established liberty by releasing Americans from European mindsets and eroding old, dysfunctional customs. Many believed that the end of the frontier represented the beginning of a new stage in American life and that the United States must expand overseas, representing a nationalistic and jingoistic application of Turner's ideas. Historians who focus scholarship on minorities, especially Native Americans and Latinos, started in the 1970s to criticize the frontier thesis because it did not attempt to explain the evolution of those groups.

PART C

DIFFICULTY LEVEL 2

1. ANSWER: B

The Social Gospel movement is a Protestant Christian intellectual movement that was most prominent in the early 20th century United States and Canada. The movement applied Christian ethics to social problems, especially issues of social justice such as economic inequality, poverty, alcoholism, crime, racial tensions, slums, unclean environment, child labor, inadequate labor unions, poor schools, and the danger of war.

2. ANSWER: C

Many intellectuals of the Gilded Age were critical of the impact industrialization had on Americans, particularly the growing gap between rich and poor. For example, Whitman's *Leaves of Grass* responded to the negative impact that recent urbanization in the United States had on the masses. In addition, an important theme of Adams's *The Education of Henry Adams* is its author's bewilderment and concern at the rapid advance in science and technology over the course of his lifetime.

3. ANSWER: A

Wabash, St. Louis & Pacific Railway Company v. Illinois, also known as the *Wabash Case*, was a Supreme Court decision that severely limited the rights of states to control interstate commerce. It led to the creation of the Interstate Commerce Commission, a regulatory agency created by the Interstate Commerce Act of 1887 to regulate railroads (and later trucking) to ensure fair rates, to eliminate rate discrimination, and to regulate other aspects of common carriers, including interstate bus lines and telephone companies.

4. ANSWER: B

(contextualization)

The Jim Crow laws were racial segregation laws enacted after the Reconstruction period in Southern United States, at state and local levels, and which continued in force until 1965, which mandated *de jure* racial segregation in all public facilities in Southern states of the former Confederacy. Jim Crow laws mandated the segregation of public schools, public places and public transportation, and the segregation of restrooms, restaurants and drinking fountains for whites and blacks. In the case of *Plessy v. Ferguson,* the Supreme Court decided that these laws were constitutional, as long as the separate facility were equal.

5. **ANSWER: B**

(use of evidence; compare/contrast; synthesis)

Plessy legitimized the state laws establishing racial segregation in the South and provided an impetus for further segregation laws. Legislative achievements won during the Reconstruction Era were erased through means of the "separate but equal" doctrine. The prospect of greater state influence in matters of race worried numerous advocates of civil equality, including Supreme Court Justice John Harlan who wrote in his dissent of the *Plessy* decision, "we shall enter upon an era of constitutional law, when the rights of freedom and American citizenship cannot receive from the nation that efficient protection which heretofore was unhesitatingly accorded to slavery and the rights of the master." Harlan's concerns about the entrenchment on the 14th Amendment, which provides equal protection and due process for all citizens, would prove well founded; states proceeded to institute segregation-based laws that became known as the Jim Crow system. In addition, from 1890 to 1908, Southern states passed new or amended constitutions including provisions that effectively disfranchised blacks and thousands of poor whites.

6. **ANSWER: C**

(use of evidence; synthesis; compare/contrast)

Brown v. Board of Education of Topeka (1954) was a landmark United States Supreme Court case in which the Court declared state laws establishing separate public schools for black and white students to be unconstitutional. The decision overturned the *Plessy v. Ferguson* decision of 1896, which allowed state-sponsored segregation, insofar as it applied to public education. Handed down on May 17, 1954, the Warren Court's unanimous (9–0) decision stated that "separate educational facilities are inherently unequal." As a result, *de jure* racial segregation was ruled a violation of the Equal Protection Clause of the Fourteenth Amendment of the United States Constitution. This ruling paved the way for integration and was a major victory of the civil rights movement

7. **ANSWER :B**

(contextualization)

Ida Bell Wells-Barnett (July 16, 1862 – March 25, 1931) was an African-American journalist, newspaper editor, suffragist, sociologist, and an early leader in the civil rights movement. She documented lynching in the United States, showing how it was often a way to control or punish blacks who competed with whites, often under the guise of rape charges. Wells-Barnett has been called the "single most powerful leader in the anti-lynching campaign in America. A dynamic, controversial, temperamental, uncompromising race woman, she broke bread and crossed swords with some of the movers and shakers of her time: Frederick Douglass, Susan B. Anthony, Marcus Garvey, Booker T. Washington, W. E. B. Du Bois, Frances Willard, and President McKinley. By any fair assessment, she was a seminal figure in Post-Reconstruction America."

8. **ANSWER: D**

(use of evidence; argumentation)

The Tuskegee Institute has recorded 3,446 blacks and 1,297 whites being lynched between 1882 and 1968, with the annual peak occurring in the late 1800s, when Democrats acted to enforce white supremacy.

9. **ANSWER: D**

(contextualization)

Upper-middle-class women of the late 19th century were not content with the cult of domesticity of the early 1800s. Many had become college educated and yearned to put their knowledge and skills to work for the public good. The values of care-taking, piety, purity would be taken out of the home and placed in the public life. The result was a broad reform movement that transformed America. One way women promoted the values of women's sphere into the public arena was through the Settlement House Movement. A Settlement House was a home where destitute immigrants could go when they had nowhere else to turn. Settlement Houses provided family-style cooking, lessons in English, and tips on how to adapt to American culture. The first America settlement house began in 1889 in Chicago and was called Hull House. Its organizer, Jane Addams, intended Hull House to serve as a prototype for other settlement houses. By 1900 there were nearly 100 settlement houses in the nation's cities. Jane Addams was considered the founder of a new profession — social work

10. **ANSWER: B**

(contextualization)

The Social Gospel movement is a Protestant Christian intellectual movement that was most prominent in the early 20th century United States and Canada. The movement applied Christian ethics to social problems, especially issues of social justice such as economic inequality, poverty, alcoholism, crime, racial tensions, slums, unclean environment, child labor, inadequate labor unions, poor schools, and the danger of war.

DIFFICULTY LEVEL 3

11. ANSWER: D

In 1895, Booker T. Washington delivered a famous speech at the Atlanta Exposition, in which he called on African Americans to focus on vocational education and to abandon their short-term hopes of social and political equality. Washington argued that when whites saw African Americans contributing as productive members of society, equality would naturally follow. DuBois disagreed. Although he admired Washington's intellect and accomplishments, he strongly opposed the position set forth by Washington in his Atlanta Exposition address. He saw little future in agriculture as the nation rapidly industrialized. DuBois felt that renouncing the goal of complete integration and social equality, even in the short run, was counterproductive and exactly the opposite strategy from what best suited African Americans. DuBois was a staunch proponent of a classical education and condemned Washington's suggestion that blacks focus only on vocational skills. Without an educated class of leadership, whatever gains were made by blacks could be stripped away by legal loopholes.

12. ANSWER: A

The Whiskey Ring was a scandal, exposed in 1875, involving diversion of tax revenues in a conspiracy among government agents, politicians, whiskey distillers, and distributors. The Whiskey Ring began in St. Louis but was also organized in Chicago, Milwaukee, Cincinnati, New Orleans, and Peoria. Before they were caught, a group of mostly Republican politicians were able to siphon off millions of dollars in federal taxes on liquor; the scheme involved an extensive network of bribes involving distillers, storekeepers, and Treasury Department agents.

13. ANSWER: B

The Crédit Mobilier scandal of 1872 involved the Union Pacific Railroad and the Crédit Mobilier of America construction company in the building of the eastern portion of the First Transcontinental Railroad. The scandal's origins dated back to the Abraham Lincoln presidency, when the Union Pacific Railroad was chartered in 1864 by the federal government and the associated Crédit Mobilier was established. In 1868 Congressman Oakes Ames had distributed Crédit Mobilier shares of stock to other congressmen, in addition to making cash bribes, during the Andrew Johnson presidency. The story was broken by the New York newspaper, *The Sun*, during the 1872 presidential campaign, when Ulysses S. Grant was running for re-election.

14. ANSWER: C

The Pendleton Civil Service Reform Act of United States is a federal law established in 1883 that stipulated that government jobs should be awarded on the basis of merit. The act provided selection of government employees by competitive exams, rather than ties to politicians or political affiliation. It also made it illegal to fire or demote government officials for political reasons and prohibited soliciting campaign donations on Federal government property. To enforce the merit system and the judicial system, the law also created the United States Civil Service Commission. A crucial result was the shift of the parties to reliance on funding from business, since they could no longer depend on patronage hopefuls. Started during the Chester Alan Arthur administration, the Pendleton Act served as a response to the massive public support of civil service reform that grew following President James Garfield's assassination by Charles J. Guiteau, who was upset after not receiving a patronage position.

15. ANSWER: A

Henry George was an American writer, politician, and political economist, who was the most influential proponent of the land value tax and the value capture of land/natural resource rents, an idea known at the time as Single-Tax. His immensely popular writing is credited with sparking several reform movements of the Progressive Era and ultimately inspiring the broad economic philosophy often referred to today as Georgism, the main tenet of which is that people legitimately own value they fairly create, but that resources and common opportunities, most importantly the value of land, belongs equally to all humanity. His most famous work, *Progress and Poverty* (1879), sold millions of copies worldwide, probably more than any other American book before that time. It is a treatise on inequality, the cyclic nature of industrialized economies, and the use of the Single-Tax as a remedy.

Period 1890-1945

PART A

DIFFICULTY LEVEL 1

1. ANSWER: C

The Federal Reserve Act created and established the Federal Reserve System, the central banking system of the United States of America. Creating the Federal Reserve gave the federal government control to regulate inflation and interest rates. Some of the most prominent implications include the internationalization of the U.S. Dollar as a global currency, the impact from the perception of the Central Bank structure as a public good by creating a system of financial stability, and the Impact of the Federal Reserve in response to economic panics. The Federal Reserve Act also permitted national banks to make mortgage loans for farmland, which had not been permitted previously. During our most recent economic downturn, the Great Recession, the Federal Reserve helped to re-stabilize the economy by keeping interest rates low and purchasing bonds—a policy known as Quantitative Easing—to maintain a reasonable level of inflation.

2. ANSWER: B

How the Other Half Lives: Studies among the Tenements of New York (1890) was an early publication of photojournalism by Jacob Riis, documenting squalid living conditions in New York City slums in the 1880s. It served as a basis for future "muckraking" journalism by exposing the slums to New York City's upper and middle classes.

3. ANSWER: A

Perhaps no muckraker caused as great a stir as Upton Sinclair. An avowed Socialist, Sinclair hoped to illustrate the horrible effects of capitalism on workers in the Chicago meatpacking industry. His bone-chilling account, *The Jungle*, detailed workers sacrificing their fingers and nails by working with acid, losing limbs, catching diseases, and toiling long hours in cold, cramped conditions. He hoped the public outcry would be so fierce that reforms would soon follow. The clamor that rang throughout America was not, however, a response to the workers' plight. Sinclair also uncovered the contents of the products being sold to the general public. Spoiled meat was covered with chemicals to hide the smell. Skin, hair, stomach, ears, and nose were ground up and packaged as head cheese. Rats climbed over warehouse meat, leaving piles of excrement behind. Sinclair said that he aimed for America's heart and instead hit its stomach. Even President Roosevelt, who coined the derisive term "muckraker," was propelled to act. Within months, Congress passed the Pure Food and Drug Act and the Meat Inspection Act to curb these sickening abuses (*http://www.ushistory.org/us/42b.asp*).

4. **ANSWER: C**

The term muckraker refers to reform-minded journalists who wrote largely for all popular magazines and continued a tradition of investigative journalism reporting; muckrakers often worked to expose social ills and corporate and political corruption. Muckraking magazines—notably *McClure's* of publisher S. S. McClure—took on corporate monopolies and crooked political machines while raising public awareness of chronic urban poverty, unsafe working conditions, and social issues like child labor.

DIFFICULTY LEVEL 2

5. **ANSWER: B**

During the early twentieth century, the Progressive Era yielded Constitutional amendments that established a federal income tax (Sixteen), allowed for the direct election of United States Senators (Seventeen), prohibited the manufacture and sale of alcohol (Eighteen), and extended voting rights to women (Nineteen). The banning of poll taxes, which disenfranchised many African Americans in the South, did not come until the 1960s with the Twenty-Fourth Amendment.

6. **ANSWER: C**

The United States is one of few countries to select candidates through popular vote in a primary election system; most countries rely on party leaders to vet candidates, as was previously the case in the U.S. In modern politics, primary elections have been described as a significant vehicle for taking decision-making from political insiders to the voters. The selection of candidates for federal, state, and local general elections takes place in primary elections organized by the public administration for the general voting public to participate in for the purpose of nominating the respective parties' official candidates; state voters start the electoral process for governors and legislators through the primary process, as well as for many local officials from city councilors to county commissioners.

The candidate who moves from the primary to be successful in the general election takes public office.

7. **ANSWER: D**

During the Progressive Era, reformers actively sought to expand democracy and correct the problems that resulted from industrialization. For example, the Seventeenth and Nineteenth amendments to the Constitution, which allowed, respectively, for the direct election of U.S. Senators and suffrage rights for women, expanded democracy. In addition, trust busting at the executive level, legislative regulation of railroads, and efforts to outlaw child labor represented a response to the negative results of industrialization. Socialism, while it was espoused by some intellectuals and members of the working class, was never seen as a viable alternative to republican capitalism in the United States.

8. **ANSWER: C**

At the end of the 1920s, the United States boasted the largest economy in the world. But the stock market crash of 1929 touched off a chain of events that plunged the United States into its longest, deepest economic crisis of its history. It is far too simplistic to view the stock market crash as the single cause of the Great Depression. A healthy economy can recover from such a contraction. Long-term underlying causes sent the nation into a downward spiral of despair. First, American firms earned record profits during the 1920s and reinvested much of these funds into expansion. By 1929, companies had expanded to the bubble point. Workers could no longer continue to fuel further expansion, so a slowdown was inevitable. While corporate profits, skyrocketed, wages increased incrementally, which widened the distribution of wealth. There were fundamental structural weaknesses in the American economic system. Banks operated without guarantees to their customers, creating a climate of panic when times got tough. Few regulations were placed on banks and they lent money to those who speculated recklessly in stocks. Agricultural prices had already been low during the 1920s, leaving farmers unable to spark any sort of recovery. When the Depression spread across the Atlantic, Europeans bought fewer American products, worsening the slide (*http://www.ushistory.org/us/48.asp*). The United States did not abandon the gold standard until 1933, four years after the Great Depression began.

9. **ANSWER: B**

In the tradition of modern Republican economic policies, President Hoover did not believe the federal government should take an active role in regulating the economy. As a result, he espoused a hands-off approach in responding to the problems of the Great

Depression. Although he supported some public works programs, such as the Hoover Dam and the Golden Gate Bridge, Hoover general advocated "rugged individualism," and he called on businesses and private charities to voluntarily assist with the collapsing economy and growing unemployment. His minimalist approach to government intervention made little impact. The economy shrank with each successive year of his Presidency. As middle class Americans stood in the same soup lines previously graced only by the nation's poorest, the entire social fabric of America was forever altered.

10. ANSWER: C

The American people were extremely dissatisfied with the crumbling economy, mass unemployment, declining wages and profits and especially Hoover's policies such as the Smoot–Hawley Tariff Act and the Revenue Act of 1932. Roosevelt entered office with enormous political capital. Americans of all political persuasions were demanding immediate action, and Roosevelt responded with a remarkable series of new programs in the "first hundred days" of the administration, in which he met with Congress for 100 days. During those 100 days of lawmaking, Congress granted every request Roosevelt asked, including relief for the unemployed, for banks, for homeowners, and for the agricultural and industrial sectors of the economy. Long-term, permanent reform programs, such as the Social Security Act—which established a system of federal insurance for the elderly, disabled, and unemployed—came later in his presidency.

11. ANSWER: C

New Deal economists argued that cut-throat competition had hurt many businesses and that with prices having fallen 20% and more, "deflation" exacerbated the burden of debt and would delay recovery. They rejected a strong move in Congress to limit the workweek to 30 hours. Instead their remedy, designed in cooperation with big business, was the NIRA. It sought to raise prices, give more bargaining power for unions (so the workers could purchase more), and reduce harmful competition. At the center of the NIRA was the National Recovery Administration (NRA), headed by former General Hugh S. Johnson, who had been a senior economic official in World War I. Johnson called on every business establishment in the nation to accept a stopgap "blanket code": a minimum wage of between 20 and 45 cents per hour, a maximum workweek of 35–45 hours, and the abolition of child labor. Johnson and Roosevelt contended that the "blanket code" would raise consumer purchasing power and increase employment.

12. ANSWER: B

The Agricultural Adjustment Act created the Agricultural Adjustment Administration (AAA) in May 1933. The AAA aimed to raise prices for commodities through artificial scarcity. The AAA used a system of domestic allotments, setting total output of corn, cotton, dairy products, hogs, rice, tobacco, and wheat. The farmers themselves had a voice in the process of using government to benefit their incomes. The AAA paid landowners subsidies for leaving some of their land idle with funds provided by a new tax on food processing. To force up farm prices to the point of "parity" 10 million acres of growing cotton was plowed up, bountiful crops were left to rot, and six million pigs were killed and discarded.

13. ANSWER: D

When Roosevelt took office, a majority of the nine judges of the Supreme Court were appointed by Republican Party presidents. Four especially conservative judges (nicknamed the Four Horsemen) often managed to convince the fifth judge Owen Roberts to strike down progressive legislation. After the Court rule unconstitutional the Agricultural Adjustment Act and the National Industrial Recovery Act, Roosevelt increasingly saw the issue of the Supreme Court as one of unelected officials stifling the work of a democratically elected government. Early in the year 1937, he asked Congress to pass the Judiciary Reorganization Bill of 1937. That proposal would have given the president the power to appoint a new justice whenever an existing judge reached the age of 70 and failed to retire within six months. In that way Roosevelt hoped to preserve the New Deal legislation. But he had stirred up a hornet's nest since many congressmen feared he might start to retire them at 70 next. Many congressmen considered the proposal unconstitutional. In the end the proposal failed.

14. ANSWER: C

(contextualization; causation)

The assembly line developed for the Ford Model T began operation on December 1, 1913. It had immense influence on the world. Despite oversimplistic attempts to attribute it to one man or another, it was in fact a composite development based on logic that took 7 years and plenty of intelligent men. The basic kernel of an assembly line concept was introduced to Ford Motor Company by William "Pa" Klann upon his return from visiting Swift & Company's slaughterhouse in Chicago and viewing what was referred to as the "disassembly line," where carcasses were butchered as they moved along a conveyor. The efficiency of one person removing the same piece over and over caught his attention. He reported the idea to Peter E. Martin, soon to be head of Ford production, who was doubtful at the time but encouraged him to proceed. Others at Ford have claimed to have put the idea forth to Henry Ford, but Pa Klann's slaughterhouse revelation is well documented in the archives at the Henry Ford Museum and elsewhere, making him an important contributor to the modern automated assembly line concept.

15. ANSWER: C

(causation)

In general, industrialization brought an improving standard of living to the United States, despite continued problems between industrialists and members of the working class. Because the efficiency of the assembly line made automobiles cheaper, the auto industry contributed to improved standards of living for many Americans in the early 20th century. In addition, Henry Ford recognized that by paying his workers enough to buy the cars they produced could sell more cars.

16. ANSWER: D

(causation; synthesis)

Progressives tried to improve the lives of industrial workers by creating new organizations and policies that would solve the social and economic problems that emerged in the United States as it urbanized and industrialized. They supported labor unions, greater government intervention in the economy, protective legislation for women workers, and other similar reforms.

17. ANSWER: B

(contextualization;continuity/change)

The Progressive Party of 1912 was an American political party formed by former President Theodore Roosevelt, after a split in the Republican Party between him and President William Howard Taft. The party also became known as the Bull Moose Party after journalists quoted Roosevelt saying "I'm feeling like a bull moose" shortly after the new party was formed. In drafting its platform, the Party aimed to reverse the domination of politics by business interests, which allegedly controlled the Republican and Democratic parties alike. The biggest controversy at the convention was over the platform section dealing with trusts and monopolies such as Standard Oil. The convention approved a strong "trust-busting" plank, but Roosevelt had it replaced with language that spoke only of "strong National regulation" and "permanent active [Federal] supervision" of major corporations.

18. ANSWER: C

(synthesis; continuity/change)

Despite the failure of 1912, the Progressive Party did not disappear at once. 138 candidates, including women, ran for the U.S. House as Progressives in 1914, and 5 were elected. However, almost half the candidates failed to get more than 10% of the vote. When the national Progressive party disintegrated, nearly all Progressives reverted to the Republican Party, including Roosevelt, who stumped for Charles Hughes and Hiram Johnson, who was elected to the Senate as a Republican in 1916. From 1916 to 1932 the Taft wing controlled the Republican Party and refused to nominate any prominent 1912 Progressives to the Republican national ticket. Finally, Frank Knox was nominated for Vice President in 1936.

The relative domination of the Republican Party by conservatives left many former Progressives with no real affiliation until the 1930s, when most joined the New Deal Democratic Party coalition of President Franklin D. Roosevelt.

19. ANSWER: C

(continuity/change over time)

The New Deal policies drew from many different ideas proposed earlier in the 20th century. Roosevelt led efforts that hearkened back to an anti-monopoly tradition that was rooted in Progressive-era reform. Supreme Court Justice Louis Brandeis, an influential adviser to many New Dealers, argued that "bigness" (referring, presumably, to corporations) was a negative economic force, producing waste and inefficiency. Other ideas were taken from Woodrow Wilson, an economic progressive, whose techniques used to mobilize the economy for World War I, such as government controls and spending, were incorporated into the New Deal.

20. ANSWER: B

(use of evidence; comparison)

The New Deal represented a significant shift in politics and domestic policy. It especially led to greatly increased federal regulation of the economy, which ran counter to the laissez-faire policies of the Gilded Age and the 1920s. It also marked the beginning of complex social programs and growing power of labor unions. The effects of the New Deal remain a source of controversy and debate among economists and historians.

21. ANSWER: D

(synthesis; causation)

Labor unions benefitted greatly from the New Deal. The National Labor Relations Act of 1935, also known as the Wagner Act, finally guaranteed workers the rights to collective bargaining through unions of their own choice. The Act also established the National Labor Relations Board (NLRB) to facilitate wage agreements and to suppress the repeated labor disturbances. The Wagner Act did not compel employers to reach agreement with their employees, but it opened possibilities for American labor. The result was a tremendous growth of membership in the labor unions, especially in the mass-production sector, composing the American Federation of Labor. Labor thus became a major component of the New Deal political coalition.

22. ANSWER: B

(contextualization)

In February 1934, Long introduced his Share Our Wealth plan over a nationwide radio broadcast. He proposed capping personal fortunes at $50 million and repeated his call to limit annual income to $1 million and inheritances to $5 million. The resulting funds would be used to guarantee every family a basic household grant of $5,000 and a minimum annual income of $2,000–3,000, or one-third of the average family homestead value and income. Long supplemented his plan with proposals for free college education and vocational training for all able students, old-age pensions, veterans' benefits, federal assistance to farmers, public works projects, greater federal regulation of economic activity, a month's vacation for every worker and limiting the work week to thirty hours to boost employment. Denying that his program was socialist, Long stated that his ideological inspiration for the plan came not from Karl Marx but from the Bible and the Declaration of Independence. "Communism? Hell no!" he said, "This plan is the only defense this country's got against communism." In 1934, Long held a public debate with Norman Thomas, the leader of the Socialist Party of America, on the merits of Share Our Wealth versus socialism.

23. ANSWER: B

(contextualization)

In the presidential election of 1932, Long became a vocal supporter of the candidacy of Franklin Delano Roosevelt. He believed Roosevelt to be the only candidate willing and able to carry out the drastic redistribution of wealth that Long believed was necessary to end the Great Depression. At the Democratic National Convention, Long was instrumental in keeping the delegations of several wavering states in the Roosevelt camp. Aware that Roosevelt had no intention to radically redistribute the country's wealth, Long became one of the few national politicians to oppose Roosevelt's New Deal policies from the left. He considered them inadequate in the face of the escalating economic crisis. Much of the opposition to Roosevelt came from conservatives who believed FDR was going too far in expanding the scope of government. Long split with Roosevelt in June 1933 to plan his own presidential bid for 1936 in alliance with the influential Catholic priest and radio commentator Charles Coughlin, another vocal critic of Roosevelt's New Deal.

DIFFICULTY LEVEL 3

24. ANSWER: A

The United States Revenue Act of 1913, also known as the Underwood Tariff, re-imposed the federal income tax following the ratification of the Sixteenth Amendment and lowered basic tariff rates from 40% to 25%, well below the Payne-Aldrich Tariff Act of 1909. It was signed into law by President Woodrow Wilson on October 3, 1913, and was sponsored by Alabama Representative Oscar Underwood. Tariffs had been the principal source of government revenue before the establishment of a federal income tax.

25. ANSWER: C

At the beginning of the Great Depression, many economists traditionally argued against deficit spending that government spending would "crowd out" private investment and spending and thus not have any effect on the economy, a proposition known as the Treasury view. Keynesian economics rejected that view. They argued that by spending vastly more money—using fiscal policy—the government could provide the needed stimulus through the multiplier effect. Keynes visited the White House in 1934 to urge President Roosevelt to increase deficit spending. Roosevelt afterwards complained that, "he left a whole rigmarole of figures – he must be a mathematician rather than a political economist."

PART B

DIFFICULTY LEVEL 1

1. ANSWER: B

During the 1920s, American farmers were still producing crops at World War I levels, but the demand no longer existed. As a result, farm prices plummeted. When Congress tried to alleviate farmers' pain with the passage of the McNary-Haugen bill, President Calvin Coolidge vetoed because of his commitment to nonintervention in the economy. When the Dust Bowl hit the Great Plains in the late 1920s, it exacerbated farmers' problems, forcing many to abandon their land and migrate west.

2. ANSWER: B

Prohibition in the United States was a nationwide constitutional ban on the sale, production, importation, and transportation of alcoholic beverages that remained in place from 1920 to 1933. It was promoted by "dry" crusaders movement, led by rural Protestants and social Progressives in the Democratic and Republican parties, and was coordinated by the Anti-Saloon League, and the Woman's Christian Temperance Union. Prohibition was mandated under the Eighteenth Amendment to the U.S. Constitution. Enabling legislation, known as the Volstead Act, set down the rules for enforcing the ban and defined the types of alcoholic beverages that were prohibited. For example, religious uses of wine were allowed. Private ownership and consumption of alcohol was not made illegal under federal law; however, in many areas local laws were stricter, with some states banning possession outright. Nationwide Prohibition ended with the ratification of the Twenty-first Amendment, which repealed the Eighteenth Amendment, on December 5, 1933. During its existed, prohibition proved to be difficult to enforce and resulted in a rise in criminal activity, including organized crime.

3. ANSWER: C

The Harlem Renaissance was a movement that spanned the 1920s. During the time, it was known as the "New Negro Movement," named after the 1925 anthology by Alain Locke. The Movement also included the new African-American cultural expressions across the urban areas in the Northeast and Midwest United States affected by the Great Migration (African American), of which Harlem was the largest. The zenith of this "flowering of Negro literature," as James Weldon Johnson preferred to call the Harlem Renaissance, took place between 1924 (when *Opportunity: A Journal of Negro Life* hosted a party for black writers where many white publishers were in attendance) and 1929 (the year of the stock market crash and the beginning of the Great Depression).

4. ANSWER: C

Flappers were a "new breed" of young Western women in the 1920s who wore short skirts, bobbed their hair, listened to jazz, and flaunted their disdain for what was then considered acceptable behavior. Flappers were seen as brash for wearing excessive makeup, drinking, treating sex in a casual manner, smoking, driving automobiles, and otherwise flouting social and sexual norms. Flappers had their origins in the liberal period of the Roaring Twenties, the social, political turbulence and increased transatlantic cultural exchange that followed the end of World War I, as well as the export of American jazz culture to Europe.

DIFFICULTY LEVEL 2

5. ANSWER: C

The Roaring Twenties was a decade of great economic growth and widespread prosperity driven by recovery from wartime devastation and postponed spending, a boom in construction, and the rapid growth of consumer goods such as automobiles and electricity. The economy of the United States had successfully transitioned from a wartime economy to a peacetime economy. However, some sectors were stagnant, especially farming and mining. The United States augmented its standing as richest country in the world, its industry aligned to mass production, and its society acculturated into consumerism. During this time, the federal government did not intervene in the economy as it had during the previous generation, known as the Progressive Era.

6. ANSWER: A

The Teapot Dome scandal was a bribery incident that took place in the United States from 1921 to 1924, during the administration of President Warren G. Harding. Secretary of the Interior Albert B. Fall had leased Navy petroleum reserves at Teapot Dome in Wyoming and two other locations in California to private oil companies at low rates without competitive bidding. In 1922 and 1923, the leases became the subject of a sensational investigation by Senator Thomas J. Walsh. Fall was later convicted of accepting bribes from the oil companies and became the first Cabinet member to go to prison. Before the Watergate scandal, Teapot Dome was regarded as the "greatest and most sensational scandal in the history of American politics." The scandal damaged the public reputation of the Harding administration, which was already severely diminished by its poor handling of the Great Railroad Strike of 1922 and the President's veto of the Bonus Bill in 1922.

7. ANSWER: B

The Palmer Raids were attempts by the United States Department of Justice to arrest and deport radical leftists, especially anarchists, from the United States. The Russian Revolution of 1917 added special force to fear of labor agitators and partisans of ideologies like anarchism. The raids and arrests occurred in November 1919 and January 1920 under the leadership of Attorney General A. Mitchell Palmer. Though more than 500 foreign citizens were deported, including a number of prominent leftist leaders, Palmer's efforts were largely frustrated by officials at the U.S. Department of Labor who had responsibility for deportations and who objected to Palmer's methods. The Palmer Raids occurred in the larger context of the Red Scare, the term given to fear of and reaction against political radicals in the U.S. in the years immediately following World War I.

8. ANSWER: B

Marcus Garvey believed that equality for African Americans could never be achieved in the United States. He formed the Universal Negro Improvement Association to promote economic cooperation among black businesses. Garvey made fiery speeches and created uniforms and flags to symbolize a new black pride. According to Garvey, the ultimate goal for blacks across the world should be to return to the "Motherland." Only in Africa could a strong nation dedicated to promotion of black culture flourish. After amassing about 80,000 followers, Garvey founded the Black Star Steamship Company to begin transporting African Americans "Back to Africa." Closely watched by government officials, Garvey was convicted of mail fraud in 1923 and deported to Jamaica.

9. ANSWER: D

Mass production made technology affordable to the middle class. The automobile, movie, radio, and chemical industries skyrocketed during the 1920s. Of chief importance was the automobile industry. Before the war, cars were a luxury. In the 1920s, mass-produced vehicles became common throughout the U.S. and Canada. By 1927, Ford discontinued the Model T after selling 15 million of that model. Only about 300,000 vehicles were registered in 1918 in all of Canada, but by 1929, there were 1.9 million, and automobile parts were being manufactured in Ontario near Detroit, Michigan. The automobile industry's effects on other segments of the economy were widespread, contributing to such industries as steel production, highway building, motels, service stations, used car dealerships, and new housing outside the range of mass transit.

10. ANSWER: B

The Great Migration was the movement of about 1.6 million African Americans between 1910 and 1930 out of the rural Southern United States to the urban Northeast and Midwest. The Great Migration began because of a "push" and a "pull." Disenfranchisement and Jim Crow laws led many African Americans to hope for a new life up north. Hate groups and hate crimes cast alarm among African American families of the Deep South. All these factors served to push African Americans to seek better lives. The booming northern economy forged the pull. Industrial jobs were numerous, and factory owners looked near and far for sources of cheap labor. Unfortunately, northerners did not welcome African Americans with open arms. While the legal systems of the northern states were not as obstructionist toward African American rights, the prejudice among the populace was as acrimonious.

11. ANSWER: B

The Depression resulted in the mass migration of people from badly hit areas in the Great Plains and the South to places such as California and the North, respectively (e.g., Okies and the Great Migration of African Americans). An Okie is a resident or native of Oklahoma. In the 1930s in California, the term (often used in contempt) came to refer to very poor migrants from Oklahoma and nearby states. The Dust Bowl brought in over a million newly displaced people, many heading to the farm labor jobs advertised in California's Central Valley. This migration is depicted in John Steinbeck's award-winning novel *The Grapes of Wrath*.

12. ANSWER: D

(contextualization; causation)

The First Red Scare was a period during the early 20th-century history of the United States marked by a widespread fear of Bolshevism and anarchism, due to real and imagined events, real events such as the Russian Revolution as well as the publicly stated goal of a worldwide communist revolution. At its height in 1919–1920, concerns over the effects of radical political agitation in American society and the alleged spread of communism and anarchism in the American labor movement fueled a general sense of paranoia. The Red Scare had its origins in the hyper-nationalism of World War I as well as the Russian Revolution. At the war's end, following the October Revolution, American authorities saw the threat of Communist revolution in the actions of organized labor, including such disparate cases as the Seattle General Strike and the Boston Police Strike and then in the bomb campaign directed by anarchist groups at political and business leaders.

13. ANSWER: B

(causation)

The Emergency Quota Act of 1921restricted immigration into the United States. Although intended as temporary legislation, the Act proved in the long run the most important turning-point in American immigration policy because it added two new features to American immigration law: numerical limits on immigration from Europe and the use of a quota system for establishing those limits. The Emergency Quota Act restricted the number of immigrants admitted from any country annually to 3% of the number of residents from that same country living in the United States as of the U.S. Census of 1910. Based on that formula, the number of new immigrants admitted fell from 805,228 in 1920 to 309,556 in 1921-In addition, the act meant that only people of Northern and Western Europe, who had been immigrating for centuries, were likely to gain admission to the United States. Thus, it was designed to limit "New Immigrants" from Eastern and Southern Europe.

14. ANSWER: A

(synthesis)

Schenck v. United States is a United States Supreme Court decision concerning enforcement of the Espionage Act of 1917 during World War I. The United States' entry into the First World War had caused deep divisions in society, and was vigorously opposed, especially by those on the radical left and by those who had ties to Ireland or Germany. The Woodrow Wilson Administration launched a broad campaign of criminal enforcement that resulted in thousands of prosecutions. Many of these were for trivial acts of dissent. A unanimous Supreme Court, in a famous opinion by Justice Oliver Wendell Holmes, Jr., concluded that defendants who distributed leaflets to draft-age men, urging resistance to induction, could be convicted of an attempt to obstruct the draft, a criminal offense. The First Amendment did not alter the well-established law in cases where the attempt was made through expressions that would be protected in other circumstances. In this opinion, Holmes said that expressions which in the circumstances were intended to result in a crime, and posed a "clear and present danger" of succeeding, could be punished.

15. ANSWER: C

(use of evidence)

During the 1920s, the Ku Klux Klan saw a resurgence in American society. Starting in 1921, it adopted a modern business system of recruiting (which paid most of the initiation fee and costume charges as commissions to the organizers) and grew rapidly nationwide at a time of prosperity. Reflecting the social tensions of urban industrialization and vastly increased immigration, its membership grew most rapidly in cities, and spread out of the South to the Midwest and West. The KKK preached "One Hundred Percent Americanism" and demanded the purification of politics, calling for strict morality and better enforcement of prohibition. Its official rhetoric focused on the threat of the Catholic Church, using anti-Catholicism and nativism. Its appeal was directed exclusively at white Protestants.

16. ANSWER: B

(continuity/change)

Radio became the first mass-broadcasting medium. Radios were expensive, but their mode of entertainment proved revolutionary. Radio advertising became the grandstand for mass marketing. Its economic importance led to the mass culture that has dominated society since. In cultural studies, mass culture refers to the current western capitalist society that emerged and developed from the 20th century, under the influence of mass media. The term alludes to the overall impact and intellectual guidance exerted by the media (primarily TV, but also the press, radio and cinema), not only on public opinion but also on tastes and values.

17. ANSWER: C

(contextualization; causation)

The Scopes Trial, formally known as *The State of Tennessee v. John Thomas Scopes* and commonly referred to as the Scopes Monkey Trial, was an American legal case in 1925 in which a substitute high school teacher, John Scopes, was accused of violating Tennessee's Butler Act, which made it unlawful to teach human evolution in any state-funded school. The trial was deliberately staged in order to attract publicity to the small town of Dayton, Tennessee, where it was held. More than 200 newspaper reporters from all parts of the country and two from London were in Dayton. Chicago's WGN radio station broadcast the trial with announcer Quin Ryan via clear-channel broadcasts for the first on-the-scene coverage of a criminal trial.

18. ANSWER: C

(contextualization)

Langston Hughes was an American poet, social activist, novelist, playwright, and columnist. He was one of the earliest innovators of the then-new literary art form called jazz poetry. Hughes is best known as a leader of the Harlem Renaissance. He famously wrote about the period that "the negro was in vogue," which was later paraphrased as "when Harlem was in vogue." Hughes's life and work were enormously influential during the Harlem Renaissance, a flowering of African American art and literature in the 1920s, alongside those of his contemporaries, Zora Neale Hurston, Wallace Thurman, Claude McKay, Countee Cullen, Richard Bruce Nugent, and Aaron Douglas.

19. **ANSWER: C**

(causation; synthesis)

The Harlem Renaissance was successful in that it brought the Black experience clearly within the corpus of American cultural history. Not only through an explosion of culture, but on a sociological level, the legacy of the Harlem Renaissance redefined how America, and the world, viewed African Americans. This new identity led to a greater social consciousness, and African Americans became players on the world stage, expanding intellectual and social contacts internationally. The progress—both symbolic and real—during this period became a point of reference from which the African-American community gained a spirit of self-determination that provided a growing sense of both Black urbanity and Black militancy, as well as a foundation for the community to build upon for the Civil Rights struggles in the 1950s and 1960s.

DIFFICULTY LEVEL 3

20. **ANSWER: D**

The Roaring Twenties was a period of literary creativity, and works of several notable authors appeared during the period. Many of the popular works were critical of the values and consumerism of the decade, and some authors moved to Europe as part of the expatriate community. For example, *The Sun Also Rises*, by Ernest Hemingway, is about a group of expatriate Americans in Europe during the 1920s. D. H. Lawrence's novel *Lady Chatterley's Lover* was a scandal at the time because of its explicit descriptions of sex. *The Great Gatsby*, by F. Scott Fitzgerald, set up in 1922 in the vicinity of New York City, is often described as the symbolic meditation on the "Jazz Age" in American literature. *All Quiet on the Western Front*. by Erich Maria Remarque, recounts the horrors of World War I and also the deep detachment from German civilian life felt by many men returning from the front.

PART C

DIFFICULTY LEVEL 1

1. ANSWER: D

The Roosevelt Corollary was an addition to the Monroe Doctrine articulated by President Theodore Roosevelt in his State of the Union address in 1904 after the Venezuela Crisis of 1902–The corollary states that the United States will intervene in conflicts between European countries and Latin American countries to enforce legitimate claims of the European powers, rather than having the Europeans press their claims directly. Roosevelt tied his policy to the Monroe Doctrine, and it was also consistent with his foreign policy of "speak softly, and carry a big stick." Roosevelt stated that in keeping with the Monroe Doctrine, the United States was justified in exercising "international police power" to put an end to chronic unrest or wrongdoing in the Western Hemisphere. While the Monroe Doctrine had sought to prevent European intervention, the Roosevelt Corollary was used to justify US intervention throughout the hemisphere. In 1934, President Franklin D. Roosevelt renounced interventionism and established his Good Neighbor policy for the Western Hemisphere.

2. ANSWER: C

In the early days of World War I, which began in 1914, Britain and France struggled against Germany, and American leaders decided it was in the national interest to continue trade with all sides as before. A neutral nation cannot impose an embargo on one side and continue trade with the other and retain its neutral status. In addition, United States merchants and manufacturers feared that a boycott would cripple the American economy. Great Britain, with its powerful navy, had different ideas. A major part of the British strategy was to impose a blockade on Germany. American trade with the Central Powers simply could not be permitted. The results of the blockade were astonishing. Trade with England and France more than tripled between 1914 and 1916, while trade with Germany was cut by over ninety percent. It was this situation that prompted submarine warfare by the Germans against Americans at sea. After two and a half years of isolationism, America entered the Great War (*http://www.ushistory.org/us/45.asp*).

3. ANSWER: B

The Republican Party—led by Henry Cabot Lodge—controlled the U.S. Senate after the election of 1918, but the Senators were divided into multiple positions on the Versailles question. It proved possible to build a majority coalition, but impossible to build a two-thirds coalition that was needed to pass a treaty. The largest bloc—led by Senator Lodge—comprised a majority of the Republicans. They wanted a treaty with reservations, especially on Article X, which involved the power of the League of Nations to make war without a vote by the U.S. Congress. These Senators feared that the League of Nations would result in American involvement in future wars. The closest the Treaty came to passage was on 19 November 1919, as Lodge and his Republicans formed a coalition with the pro-Treaty Democrats, and were close to a two-thirds majority for a Treaty with reservations, but Wilson rejected this compromise and enough Democrats followed his lead to permanently end the chances for ratification.

4. ANSWER: C

The internment of Japanese Americans in the United States was the forced relocation and incarceration during World War II of between 110,000 and 120,000 people of Japanese ancestry who lived on the Pacific coast in camps in the interior of the country. Sixty-two percent of the internees were United States citizens. The U.S. government ordered the removal of Japanese Americans in 1942, shortly after Imperial Japan's attack on Pearl Harbor. Such incarceration was applied unequally due to differing population concentrations and, more importantly, state and regional politics: more than 110,000 Japanese Americans, nearly all who lived on the West Coast, were forced into interior camps, but in Hawaii, where the 150,000-plus Japanese Americans comprised over one-third of the population, only 1,200 to 1,800 were interned. The forced relocation and incarceration has been determined to have resulted more from racism and discrimination by whites on the West Coast, rather than any military danger posed by the Japanese Americans.

DIFFICULTY LEVEL 2

5. ANSWER: D

Many different groups pushed for American expansion overseas. Industrialists sought new markets for their products and sources for cheaper resources. Nationalists claimed that colonies were a hallmark of national prestige. The European powers had already claimed much of the globe; America would have to compete or perish. Missionaries continually preached to spread their messages of faith. Social Darwinists such as Josiah Strong believed that American civilization was superior to others and that it was an American's duty to diffuse its benefits. Alfred Thayer Mahan wrote an influential thesis declaring that throughout history, those that controlled the seas controlled the world. Acquiring naval bases at strategic points around the world was imperative (*http://www.ushistory.org/us/44.asp*).

6. **ANSWER: B**

The Spanish–American War was a conflict in 1898 between Spain and the United States, the result of American intervention in the Cuban War of Independence. American attacks on Spain's Pacific possessions led to involvement in the Philippine Revolution and ultimately to the Philippine–American War. Revolts against Spanish rule had occurred for some years in Cuba. In the late 1890s, American public opinion was agitated by anti-Spanish propaganda led by journalists such as Joseph Pulitzer and William Hearst which used yellow journalism to criticize Spanish administration of Cuba. After the mysterious sinking of the American battleship *Maine* in Havana harbor, political pressures from the Democratic Party and certain industrialists pushed the administration of Republican President William McKinley into a war he had wished to avoid. Compromise was sought by Spain, but rejected by the United States which sent an ultimatum to Spain demanding it surrender control of Cuba. First Madrid, then Washington, formally declared war.

7. **ANSWER: D**

After the United States defeated Spain in the Spanish-American War, the result was the 1898 Treaty of Paris, negotiated on terms favorable to the U.S., which allowed temporary American control of Cuba, and ceded indefinite colonial authority over Puerto Rico, Guam and the Philippine islands from Spain. The defeat and collapse of the Spanish Empire was a profound shock to Spain's national psyche, and provoked a thorough philosophical and artistic revaluation of Spanish society known as the Generation of 'The United States gained several island possessions spanning the globe and a rancorous new debate over the wisdom of expansionism.

8. **ANSWER: C**

In 1887, the United States forced the king of Hawaii to sign a Constitution of the Kingdom of Hawaii, which stripped the king of much of his authority. There was a property qualification for voting, which disenfranchised most native Hawaiians and immigrant laborers, and favored the wealthier white community. Resident whites were allowed to vote, but resident Asians were excluded. Because the 1887 Constitution was signed under threat of violence, it is known as the "Bayonet Constitution." In 1891, Queen Lili'uokalani succeeded to the throne. In 1893, Queen Lili'uokalani announced plans for a new constitution, one that would return control of the island to Native Hawaiians. On January 14, 1893, a group of mostly Euro-American business leaders and residents formed a Committee of Safety to overthrow the Kingdom and seek annexation by the United States. In January 1893, Queen Lili'uokalani was overthrown and replaced by a Provisional Government composed of members of the Committee of Safety. American lawyer Sanford B. Dole became President of the Republic in 1894.

9. ANSWER: A

Before the construction of the canal across the isthmus of Panama, trip by boat from New York to San Francisco forced a luckless crew to sail around the tip of South America — a journey amounting to some 12,000 miles. The new empire might require a fast move from the Atlantic to the Pacific by a naval squadron. Teddy Roosevelt decided that the time for action was at hand. The canal would be his legacy, and he would stop at nothing to get it. President Roosevelt infamously stated that "I took the Isthmus, started the canal and then left Congress not to debate the canal, but to debate me". Several parties in the United States opposed this act of war on Colombia: the New York Times called the support given by the United States to Mr. Bunau-Varilla an "act of sordid conquest." The New York Evening Post called it a "vulgar and mercenary venture." More recently, historian George Tindall labeled it "one of the greatest blunders in American foreign policy." It is often cited as the classic example of U.S. gunboat diplomacy in Latin America, and the best illustration of what Roosevelt meant by the old African adage, "speak softly and carry a big stick [and] you will go far." After the revolution in 1903, the Republic of Panama became a U.S. protectorate until 1939.

10. ANSWER: C

Dollar Diplomacy is the effort of the United States—particularly by President William Howard Taft—to further its aims in Latin America and East Asia through use of its economic power by guaranteeing loans made to foreign countries. Historian Thomas A. Bailey argues that Dollar Diplomacy was nothing new, as the use of diplomacy to promote commercial interest dates from the early years of the Republic. However, under Taft, the State Department was more active than ever in encouraging and supporting American bankers and industrialists in securing new opportunities abroad. Bailey finds that Dollar Diplomacy was designed to make both people in foreign lands and the American investors prosper. The term was originally coined by President Theodore Roosevelt. The concept is relevant to both Liberia, where American loans were given in 1913, and Latin America. Latin Americans tend to use the term "Dollar Diplomacy" disparagingly to show their disapproval of the role that the U.S. government and U.S.

corporations have played in using economic, diplomatic, and military power to open up foreign markets.

11. ANSWER: D

The Open Door Policy is a term in foreign affairs initially used to refer to the United States policy in the late 19th century and early 20th century outlined in Secretary of State John Hay's Open Door Note, dispatched in 1899 to his European counterparts. The policy proposed to keep China open to trade with all countries on an equal basis; thus, no international power would have total control of the country. The policy called upon foreign powers, within their spheres of influence, to refrain from interfering with any treaty port or any vested interest, to permit Chinese authorities to collect tariffs on an equal basis, and to show no favors to their own nationals in the matter of harbor dues or railroad charges. The Open Door policy was rooted in desire of American businesses to trade with Chinese markets, though it also tapped the deep-seated sympathies of those who opposed imperialism, especially as the policy pledged to protect China's territorial integrity.

12. ANSWER: C

Once support for the war was in full swing, the population was mobilized to produce war materiel. In 1917, the War Industries Board was established to coordinate production of munitions and supplies. The board was empowered to allocate raw materials and determine what products would be given high priority. Women shifted jobs from domestic service to heavy industry to compensate for the labor shortage owing to military service. African Americans flocked northward in greater and greater numbers in the hope of winning industry jobs. Herbert Hoover was appointed to head the Food Administration. Shortages of food in the Allied countries had led to shortages and rationing all across Western Europe. Hoover decided upon a plan that would raise the necessary foodstuffs by voluntary means (http://www.ushistory.org/us/45c.asp).

13. ANSWER: C

Reparations were not included in Wilson's Fourteen Points, although they were part of the Treaty of Versailles. As the war drew to a close, Woodrow Wilson set forth his plan for a "just peace." Wilson believed that fundamental flaws in international relations created an unhealthy climate that led inexorably to the World War. His Fourteen Points outlined his vision for a safer world. Wilson called for an end to secret diplomacy, a reduction of armaments, and freedom of the seas. He claimed that reductions to trade barriers, fair adjustment of colonies, and respect for national self-determination would reduce economic and nationalist sentiments that lead to war. Finally, Wilson proposed an international organization comprising representatives of all the world's nations that would serve as a forum against allowing any conflict to escalate. Unfortunately, Wilson could not impose his worldview on the victorious Allied Powers. When they met in Paris to hammer out the terms of the peace, the European leaders had other ideas (*http://www.ushistory.org/us/45d.asp*).

14. ANSWER: A

While Fascist aggressors were chalking up victories across Europe and Asia, America, Britain, and France sat on the sidelines. The desire to avoid repeating the mistakes of World War I was so strong, no government was willing to confront the dictators. Economic sanctions were unpopular during the height of the Great Depression. The Loyalists in Spain were already receiving aid from the Soviet Union; therefore, public opinion was against assisting Moscow in its "private" war against fascism. As the specter of dictatorship spread across Europe, the West feebly objected with light rebukes and economic penalties with no teeth. The United States Congress and President Roosevelt passed three important laws — all called Neutrality Acts— directly aimed at reversing the mistakes made that led to the American entry into the First World War by prohibiting loans to and trade with belligerent nations (*http://www.ushistory.org/us/50b.asp*).

15. ANSWER: B

Before the attack on Pearl Harbor, the vast majority of Americans wanted to stay out of the war. The Japanese attack on Pearly Harbor changed that. The attack on Pearl Harbor was a surprise military strike conducted by the Imperial Japanese Navy against the United States naval base at Pearl Harbor, Hawaii, on the morning of December 7, 1941. The attack led to the United States' entry into World War II. The attack was intended as a preventive action in order to keep the U.S. Pacific Fleet from interfering with military actions the Empire of Japan was planning in Southeast Asia against overseas territories of the United Kingdom, the Netherlands, and the United States. There were simultaneous Japanese attacks on the U.S.-held Philippines and on the British Empire in Malaya, Singapore, and Hong Kong.

16. ANSWER: B

(contextualization)

Josiah Strong (1847–1916) was an American Protestant clergyman, organizer, editor and author. He supported missionary work so that all races could be improved and uplifted and thereby brought to Christ. His writings served to justify the expansion of United States influence overseas in order to "civilize" non-Christian and non-European peoples.

17. **ANSWER: D**

(continuity)

Strong's statement explicitly argues that the United States should continue to expand overseas because of its superior position in the world, an argument that relates to Manifest Destiny, Social Darwinism, and American Exceptionalism.

18. **ANSWER: D**

(comparison)

An early use of the term "anti-imperialist" occurred after the United States entered the Spanish-American War in 1898. Most activists supported the war itself but opposed the annexation of new territory, especially the Philippines. The Anti-Imperialist League was founded on June 15, 1898 in Boston, in opposition of the acquisition of the Philippines, which happened anyway. The anti-imperialists opposed the expansion because they believed imperialism violated the credo of republicanism, especially the need for "consent of the governed."

19. **ANSWER: A**

(contextualization)

Article X of the Covenant of the League of Nations is the section calling for assistance to be given to a member that experiences external aggression. It was signed by the major Peacemakers (Allied Forces) following the First World War, most notably Britain and France. It was designed to prevent future wars and guarantee collective security. Due to the nature of the Article, however, U.S. President Woodrow Wilson was unable to ratify his obligation to join the League of Nations, as a result of strong objection from U.S. politicians.

20. **ANSWER: B**

(contextualization; causation)

Although Wilson had secured his proposal for a League of Nations in the final draft of the Treaty of Versailles, the U.S. Senate refused to consent to the ratification of the Treaty. For many Republicans in the Senate, Article X was the most objectionable provision. Their objections were based on the fact that, by ratifying such a document, the United States would be bound by international contract to defend a League of Nations member if it was attacked. Henry Cabot Lodge from Massachusetts and Frank B. Brandegee from Connecticut led the fight in the U.S. Senate against ratification, believing that it was best not to become involved in international conflicts. Under the United States Constitution, the President of the United States may not ratify a treaty unless the Senate, by a two-thirds vote, gives its advice and consent. Because the Senate would not support ratification, the U.S. never joined the League of Nations, hampering the League's credibility as a mediator of world conflict.

21. ANSWER: B

(contextualization)

During World War II, African-American enlistment was at an all time high, with more than 1 million serving in the armed forces. However, the U.S. military was still heavily segregated. The air force and the marines had no blacks enlisted in their ranks, and the navy only accepted blacks as cooks and waiters. The army had only five African-American officers. In addition, no African-American would receive the Medal of Honor during the war, and their tasks in the war were largely reserved to noncombat units. Black soldiers had to sometimes give up their seats in trains to the Nazi prisoners of war. It would take over 50 years and a presidential order before the U.S. Army reviewed their records in order to award any Medals of Honor to black soldiers. This war marked the end of segregation in the U.S. military. In 1948 President Truman signed Executive Order 9981, officially ending segregation and racial inequality in the military.

22. ANSWER: B

(causation)

During World War II, the African American community in the United States resolved on a Double V Campaign: victory over fascism abroad, and victory over discrimination at home. Large numbers migrated from poor Southern farms to munitions centers. Racial tensions were high in overcrowded cities like Chicago; Detroit and Harlem experienced race riots in 1943. Black newspapers created the Double V Campaign to build black morale and head off radical action. Most Black women had been farm laborers or domestics before the war. Despite discrimination and segregated facilities throughout the South, they escaped the cotton patch and took blue-collar jobs in the cities. Working with the federal Fair Employment Practices Committee, the NAACP, and CIO unions, these Black women fought a "Double V" campaign—against the Axis abroad and against restrictive hiring practices at home.

23. ANSWER: B

(causation, contextualization; use of evidence)

Women in World War II took on a variety of roles from country to country. World War II involved global conflict on an unprecedented scale; the absolute urgency of mobilizing the entire population made the expansion of the role of women inevitable. The hard skilled labor of women was symbolized in the United States by the concept of Rosie the Riveter, a woman factory laborer performing what was previously considered man's work. With this expanded horizon of opportunity and confidence, and with the extended skill base that many women could now give to paid and voluntary employment, women's roles in World War II were even more extensive than in the First World War. By 1945, more than 2.2 million women were working in the war industries, building ships, aircraft, vehicles, and weaponry. Women also worked in factories, munitions plants and farms, and also drove trucks, provided logistic support for soldiers and entered professional areas of work that were previously the preserve of men.

24. ANSWER: A

(synthesis; argumentation)

The Equal Rights Amendment (ERA) was a proposed amendment to the United States Constitution designed to guarantee equal rights for women. The ERA was originally written by Alice Paul and Crystal Eastman. In 1923, it was introduced in the Congress for the first time. In 1972, it passed both houses of Congress and went to the state legislatures for ratification.

The resolution in Congress that proposed the amendment set a ratification deadline of March 22, 1979. Through 1977, the amendment received 35 of the necessary 38 state ratifications. Five states later rescinded their ratifications before the 1979 deadline, though the validity of these rescissions is disputed. In 1978, a joint resolution of Congress extended the ratification deadline to June 30, 1982, but no further states ratified the amendment before the passing of the second deadline. Several feminist organizations, disputing the validity and/or the permanence of the ratification deadline, and also disputing the validity of the five rescissions, continue to work at the federal and state levels for the adoption of the ERA.

25. ANSWER: B

(comparison)

The Atlantic Charter was a pivotal policy statement issued in August 14, 1941 that, early in World War II, defined the Allied goals for the post-war world. Although the

United States was technically not fighting in World War II by this point, it played a pivotal role in deciding the course of the war. The Charter was drafted by the leaders of the United Kingdom and the United States, and later agreed to by all the Allies of World War II. The Charter stated the ideal goals of the war: no territorial aggrandizement; no territorial changes made against the wishes of the people; restoration of self-government to those deprived of it; reduction of trade restrictions; global cooperation to secure better economic and social conditions for all; freedom from fear and want; freedom of the seas; and abandonment of the use of force, as well as disarmament of aggressor nations.

26. ANSWER: A

(causation)

The Declaration by United Nations, on 1 January 1942, was the basis of the modern UN. The term United Nations became synonymous during the war with the Allies and was considered to be the formal name that they were fighting under. The text of the declaration affirmed the signatories' perspective "that complete victory over their enemies is essential to defend life, liberty, independence and religious freedom, and to preserve human rights and justice in their own lands as well as in other lands, and that they are now engaged in a common struggle against savage and brutal forces seeking to subjugate the world". The principle of "complete victory" established an early precedent for the Allied policy of obtaining the Axis' powers' "unconditional surrender". The defeat of "Hitlerism" constituted the overarching objective, and represented a common Allied perspective that the totalitarian militarist regimes ruling Germany, Italy, and Japan were indistinguishable. The declaration, furthermore, "upheld the Wilsonian principles of self-determination," thus linking U.S. war aims in both world wars.

27. ANSWER: B

(continuity/change)

Although the Atlantic Charter was acceptable to the international community, the decision to act on its goals involved complex questions of federal policy and public opinion, especially since the American public was still against entering World War II at the time.

DIFFICULTY LEVEL 3

28. ANSWER: B

The Root–Takahira Agreement was an agreement between the United States and the Empire of Japan negotiated between United States Secretary of State Elihu Root and Japanese Ambassador to the United States Takahira Kogorō. Signed on November 30, 1908, the agreement consisted of an official recognition of the territorial status quo as of November 1908, affirmation of the independence and territorial integrity of China (i.e., the "Open Door Policy" as proposed by John Hay), maintenance of free trade and equal commercial opportunities, Japanese recognition of the American annexation of the Kingdom of Hawaii and the Philippines and American recognition of Japan's position in northeast China. Implicit in the agreement was American acknowledgment of Japan's right to annex Korea and dominance over southern Manchuria, and Japan's acquiescence to limitations on Japanese immigration to California. Shortly after this agreement, Theodore Roosevelt order the navy, the Great White Fleet, to sail around to the world and anchor in strategic ports to demonstrate America's military might.

29. ANSWER: C

An early use of the term "anti-imperialist" occurred after the United States entered the Spanish-American War in 1898. Most activists supported the war itself but opposed the annexation of new territory, especially the Philippines. The Anti-Imperialist League was founded on June 15, 1898, in Boston, in opposition of the acquisition of the Philippines. The anti-imperialists opposed the expansion because they believed imperialism violated the credo of republicanism, especially the need for "consent of the governed." Appalled by American imperialism, the Anti-Imperialist League, which included famous citizens such as Andrew Carnegie and William James, formed a platform which stated, "imperialism is hostile to liberty and tends toward militarism, an evil from which it has been our glory to be free. We regret that it has become necessary in the land of Washington and Lincoln to reaffirm that all men, of whatever race or color, are entitled to life, liberty and the pursuit of happiness."

30. ANSWER: C

The Tampico Affair began as a minor incident involving U.S. sailors and Mexican land forces loyal to General Victoriano Huerta during the Mexican Revolution. The misunderstanding occurred on April 9, 1914, but developed into a breakdown of diplomatic relations between the two countries. As a result, the United States invaded the port city of Veracruz, occupying it for more than six months. This contributed to the fall of President Victoriano Huerta, who resigned in July 1914. The U.S. occupation of Veracruz resulted in widespread anti-American sentiment among Mexican residents, and other U.S. warships were used to evacuate American citizens from both the Gulf Coast and the west coast of Mexico, taking them to refugee centers in San Diego, Texas, and New Orleans. As a result of anti-American sentiment, Mexico maintained neutrality during World War I, refusing to support the U.S. in Europe, all the while continuing to do business with Germany. With the U.S. threatening to invade in 1918 to take control of Tampico oil fields, Mexican President Venustiano Carranza had them destroyed to prevent their falling under U.S. control.

31. ANSWER: D

The bracero program (named for the Spanish term bracero, meaning "manual laborer") was a series of laws and diplomatic agreements, initiated by an August 1942 exchange of diplomatic notes between the United States and Mexico, for the importation of temporary contract laborers from Mexico to the United States. American president Franklin D. Roosevelt met with Mexican president Manuel Ávila Camacho in Monterrey, Mexico, to discuss Mexico as part of the Allies in World War II and the bracero program. After the expiration of the initial agreement in 1947, the program was continued in agriculture under a variety of laws and administrative agreements until its formal end in 1964.

32. ANSWER: B

The Manhattan Project was a research and development project that produced the first atomic bombs during World War II. In addition to developing the atomic bomb, the Manhattan Project was charged with gathering intelligence on the German nuclear energy project. It was believed that the Japanese nuclear weapons program was not far advanced because Japan had little access to uranium ore, but it was initially feared that Germany was very close to developing its own weapons.

Period 1945-1980

PART A

DIFFICULTY LEVEL 1

1. ANSWER: C

In 1947, George Kennan was serving as U.S. ambassador to the Soviet Union. That year, he drafted in his famous "Long Telegram" from Moscow, in which he articulated a policy of containment. Kennan argue that the United States should not try to defeat the Soviet Union by conquering its existing territories, but should instead work to prevent Soviet influence from spreading beyond its then-current borders. Containment became the framework for a number of United States policies, including the Truman Doctrine, Marshall Plan, and the Berlin Airlift.

DIFFICULTY LEVEL 2

2. ANSWER: A

The Origins of the Cold War are widely regarded to lie most directly in the relations between the Soviet Union and the allies (the United States, Great Britain and France) in the years 1945–1947. Those events led to the Cold War that endured for just under half a century. Events preceding the Second World War, and even the Russian Revolution of 1917, underlay pre–World War II tensions between the Soviet Union, western European countries and the United States. A series of events during and after World War II exacerbated tensions, including the Soviet-German pact during the first two years of the war leading to subsequent invasions, the perceived delay of an amphibious invasion of German-occupied Europe, the western allies' support of the Atlantic Charter, disagreement in wartime conferences over the fate of Eastern Europe, and the Soviets' creation of an Eastern Bloc of Soviet satellite states.

3. ANSWER: B

The Truman Doctrine of containment was a United States policy to stop Soviet expansion during the Cold War. President Harry S. Truman pledged to contain communism in Europe and elsewhere and impelled the US to support any nation with both military and economic aid if its stability was threatened by communism or the Soviet Union. Truman told Congress, "it must be the policy of the United States to support free people who are resisting attempted subjugation by armed minorities or by outside pressures." Truman reasoned, because these "totalitarian regimes" coerced "free peoples," they represented a threat to international peace and the national security of the United States. Truman made the plea amid the crisis of the Greek Civil War (1946–1949). He argued that if Greece and Turkey did not receive the aid that they urgently needed, they would inevitably fall to communism with grave consequences throughout the region. Because Turkey and Greece were historic rivals, it was necessary to help both equally, even though the threat to Greece was more immediate.

4. **ANSWER: B**

After World War II, Europe's economy and infrastructure were destroyed. There was fear that some European countries would be tempted by communism's promise of an equal distribution of resources. With a plan named for Secretary of State George Marshall, the United States provided billions of dollars in aid to Europe, on a per capita basis. The goals of the United States were to rebuild war-devastated regions, remove trade barriers, modernize industry, and make Europe prosperous again. As a result, Europe saw the fastest economic growth in its history. "Marshall Plan" has become a metaphor for any large scale government program that is designed to solve a specific social problem. It is usually used when calling for federal spending to correct a perceived failure of the private sector.

5. **ANSWER: B**

NATO was signed in 1949 as a system of collective security wherein member states agree to mutual defense in response to attacks by a nonmember state or group. Currently there are 28 member states. NATO was little more than a political association until the Korean War galvanized the organization's member states, and an integrated military structure was built up under the direction of two US supreme commanders. The course of the Cold War led to a rivalry with nations of the Warsaw Pact, which formed in 1955 and included the Soviet Union, its satellite nations, and its allies.

6. **ANSWER: D**

Beginning in 1950, Senator Joseph McCarthy became the most visible public face of a period in which Cold War tensions fueled fears of widespread Communist subversion. He was noted for making claims that there were large numbers of Communists and Soviet spies and sympathizers inside the United States federal government, particularly in the State Department. Ultimately, his tactics and inability to substantiate his claims led him to be censured by the United States Senate. The term McCarthyism, coined in 1950 in reference to McCarthy's practices, was soon applied to similar anti-communist activities. Today the term is used more generally in reference to demagogic, reckless, and unsubstantiated accusations, as well as public attacks on the character or patriotism of political opponents.

7. **ANSWER: B**

The Korean War began in 1950 when communist North Korea, with Soviet support, invaded democratic South Korea. In response, the United Nations Security Council decided to dispatch U.N. Forces in Korea. The United States and other countries moved to defend South Korea. By 1951, after the U.N. and U.S. forces had successfully pushed the North Koreans back to the 38th parallel, the war was at a stalemate. After China got involved on North Korea's behalf, General MacArthur wanted to escalate the war. He sought to bomb the Chinese mainland and blockade their coast. Truman disagreed. He feared escalation of the conflict could lead to World War III, especially if the now nuclear-armed Soviet Union lent assistance to China. Disgruntled, MacArthur took his case directly to the American people by openly criticizing Truman's approach. Truman promptly fired him for insubordination.

8. **ANSWER: D**

The Gulf of Tonkin Resolution was a joint resolution that the United States Congress passed on August 7, 1964, that gave U.S. President Lyndon B. Johnson authorization, without a formal declaration of war by Congress, for the use of "conventional" military force in Southeast Asia. Specifically, the resolution authorized the President to do whatever necessary in order to assist "any member or protocol state of the Southeast Asia Collective Defense Treaty." This included involving armed forces. It was opposed in the Senate only by Senators Wayne Morse (D-OR) and Ernest Gruening (D-AK). The Johnson administration subsequently relied upon the resolution to begin its rapid escalation of U.S. military involvement in South Vietnam and open warfare between North Vietnam and the United States.

9. **ANSWER: A**

In the thirteen-day standoff that became known as the Cuban Missile Crisis, the United States responded to the Soviet Union's positioning of nuclear weapons on the island of Cuba, well within striking distance of major American cities. After an initial blockade, the United States was able to avert a scheduled airstrike in Cuba by negotiated the removal of Soviet missiles from the island. In return, the United States would remove missiles from Turkey, which were within striking distance of Soviet cities.

10. ANSWER: C

Détente was a policy developed by Richard Nixon and his National Security Advisor Henry Kissinger in attempt to ease tensions with the communist bloc countries. Examples of this policy included engaging the Soviets in nuclear arms talks, expanding trade with the Soviet Union, and lifting trade and travel embargos on China.

11. ANSWER: C

The Kent State shootings involved the shooting of unarmed college students by the Ohio National Guard on Monday, May 4, 1970. The guardsmen fired 67 rounds over a period of 13 seconds, killing four students and wounding nine others. Some of the students who were shot had been protesting the Cambodian Campaign, which President Richard Nixon announced during a television address on April There was a significant national response to the shootings: hundreds of universities, colleges, and high schools closed throughout the United States due to a student strike of four million students, and the event further affected public opinion—at an already socially contentious time—over the role of the United States in the Vietnam War.

12. ANSWER: B

The Camp David Accords, a peace agreement between Egypt and Israel broken by President Jimmy Carter, was one of the few highlights of his battered presidency. Egypt became the first Middle Eastern country to officially recognize Israel's statehood.

13. ANSWER: A

(contextualiation)

The map above demonstrates the first example of collective security under the United Nations Security Council, which deployed troops to South Korea in 1950 to fight against a North Korean invasion. Although containment was the dominant United States foreign policy at this time, there are better examples to demonstrate this policy, such as the Truman Doctrine and Marshall Plan.

14. ANSWER: C

(use of evidence; comparison)

Since World War II, there has been no formal war declaration on another state, but rather Congressional approvals of troop deployment. The Korean War was the first test of collective security through the United Nations Security Council, which authorized the use of troops with General Douglas MacArthur in charge.

15. ANSWER: C

(compare/contrast; continuity/change)

Prior to World War II, the United States had assumed an isolationist stance, best evidenced by its rejection of the League of Nations and the passage of Neutrality Acts throughout the 1930s. Following the war, however, the United States became a global superpower and assumed an interventionist stance, leading organizations such as the United Nations and NATO to preserve democracy and capitalism around the globe.

16. ANSWER: B

(contextualization; use of evidence)

Of all the lessons learned from Vietnam, one rings louder than all the rest — it is impossible to win a long, protracted war without popular support. When the war in Vietnam began, many Americans believed that defending South Vietnam from communist aggression was in the national interest. Communism was threatening free governments across the globe. Any sign of non-intervention from the United States might encourage revolutions elsewhere. As the war dragged on, more and more Americans grew weary of mounting casualties and escalating costs. The small antiwar movement grew into an unstoppable force, pressuring American leaders to reconsider its commitment (*http://www.ushistory.org/us/55d.asp*).

17. ANSWER: B

(continuity/change)

Many of the tactics of the anti-war movement were borrowed from the Civil Rights Movement, which had adopted the civil disobedience tactics of Henry David Thoreau, Mohandas Gandhi, and organized labor.

18. ANSWER: B

(contextualization)

The Soviet Union's successful launch of *Spunik*, a space satellite, caused a fear that the United States was falling behind the Soviet Union in science and technology. As a result, the United States established NASA and passed the National Defense Education Act, designed to emphasize science in American classrooms. President Kennedy's speech about going to the Moon can best be understood in the Space Race that results from the launch of *Sputnik*.

19. ANSWER: C

(use of evidence; causation)

During the 1950s and 1960s, the United States was struggling to maintain global leadership, especially in light of fears that they were falling behind the Soviet Union in both the space race and arms race.

20. ANSWER: B

(contextualization; use of evidence)

Decolonization is the undoing of colonialism, where a nation establishes and maintains dependent territory. The Oxford English Dictionary defines decolonization as "the withdrawal from its colonies of a colonial power; the acquisition of political or economic independence by such colonies." The term refers particularly to the dismantlement, in the years after World War II, of the colonial empires established prior to World War I throughout the world. The United Nations Special Committee on Decolonization has stated that in the process of decolonization there is no alternative to the colonizer's allowance of self-determination, but in practice decolonization may involve either nonviolent revolution or national liberation wars by pro-independence groups.

21. ANSWER: B

(causation)

The Non-Aligned Movement (NAM) is a group of states which are not formally aligned with or against any major power bloc. The organization was founded in Belgrade in 1961, and was largely conceived by India's first prime minister, Jawaharlal Nehru; Burma's first Prime Minister U Nu; Indonesia's first president, Sukarno; Egypt's second president, Gamal Abdel Nasser; Ghana's first president Kwame Nkrumah; and Yugoslavia's president, Josip Broz Tito. All six leaders were prominent advocates of a middle course for states in the Developing World between the Western and Eastern blocs in the Cold War. While many of the Non-Aligned Movement's members were actually quite closely aligned with one or another of the super powers, the movement still maintained cohesion throughout the Cold War.

22. ANSWER: B

The CIA succeeded the Office of Strategic Services (OSS), formed during World War II to coordinate secret espionage activities against the Axis Powers for the branches of the United States Armed Forces. The National Security Act of 1947 established the CIA as one of the principal intelligence-gathering agencies of the United States federal government. On the other hand, HUAC, the McCarran Act, and the Loyalty Review Board were designed to detect and identify potential radical and/or communist threats in the United States.

23. ANSWER: C

In 1948, President Harry S. Truman's Executive Order 9981 ordered the integration of the armed forces shortly after World War II, a major advance in civil rights. Using the Executive Order meant that Truman could bypass Congress. Representatives of the Solid South, all white Democrats, would likely have stonewalled related legislation. In response, southern Democrats formed the Dixiecrat Party and ran their own candidate, Strom Thurmond of South Carolina, in the 1948 presidential election.

24. ANSWER: B

The military–industrial complex comprises the policy and monetary relationships that exist between government, national armed forces, and the defense industry that supports them. These relationships include political contributions, political approval for military spending, lobbying to support bureaucracies, and oversight of the industry. It is a type of iron triangle. The term is most often used in reference to the system behind the military of the United States, where it gained popularity after its use in the farewell address of President Dwight D. Eisenhower on January 17, 1961, though the term is applicable to any country with a similarly developed infrastructure.

Period 1945-1980

PART B

DIFFICULTY LEVEL 1

1. ANSWER: C

The case of *Brown v. Board of Education* was a landmark Supreme Court decision that helped usher in the modern Civil Rights Movement. Drawing on the Fourteenth Amendment's provisions for equal protection under the law, *Brown* declared unconstitutional the case of *Plessy v. Ferguson*, which in 1896 had ruled constitutional the segregationist Jim Crow laws. The decision in *Brown* declared that segregated facilities were inherently unequal, bringing an end to *de sure* segregation in the South.

DIFFICULTY LEVEL 2

2. ANSWER: D

The Southern Christian Leadership Conference (SCLC) is an African-American civil rights organization. SCLC was closely associated with its first president, Dr. Martin Luther King, Jr. The SCLC had a large role in the American Civil Rights Movement.

3. ANSWER: A

The Student Nonviolent Coordinating Committee (SNCC) was one of the most important organizations of the American Civil Rights Movement in the 1960s. It emerged from a student meeting organized by Ella Baker held at Shaw University in April 1960. SNCC grew into a large organization with many supporters in the North who helped raise funds to support SNCC's work in the South, allowing full-time SNCC workers to have a $10 per week salary. Many unpaid volunteers also worked with SNCC on projects in Mississippi, Alabama, Georgia, Arkansas, and Maryland. SNCC played a major role in the sit-ins and freedom rides, a leading role in the 1963 March on Washington, Mississippi Freedom Summer, and the Mississippi Freedom Democratic Party over the next few years. SNCC's major contribution was in its field work, organizing voter registration drives all over the South, especially in Georgia, Alabama, and Mississippi.

4. ANSWER: D

Malcolm X is perhaps the best known leader of the Nation of Islam. While in prison he became a member of the Nation of Islam, and after his parole in 1952 quickly rose to become one of its leaders. For a dozen years he was the public face of the controversial group; in keeping with the Nation's teachings he espoused black supremacy, advocated the separation of black and white Americans and scoffed at the civil rights movement's emphasis on integration. By March 1964, Malcolm X had grown disillusioned with the Nation of Islam and its leader Elijah Muhammad. He ultimately repudiated the Nation and its teachings.

5. ANSWER: C

Black Power is a political slogan and a name for various associated ideologies aimed at achieving self-determination for people of African/Black descent in the United States. The movement was prominent in the late 1960s and early 1970s, emphasizing racial pride and the creation of black political and cultural institutions to nurture and promote black collective interests and advance black values. It expresses a range of political goals, from defense against racial oppression, to the establishment of social institutions and a self-sufficient economy.

6. ANSWER: C

The Great Society was a set of domestic programs in the United States launched by President Lyndon B. Johnson in 1964-The main goal was the elimination of poverty and racial injustice. President Johnson first used the term "Great Society" during a speech at Ohio University, then unveiled the program in greater detail at an appearance at University of Michigan. New major spending programs that addressed education, medical care, urban problems, and transportation were launched during this period. The program and its initiatives were subsequently promoted by him and fellow Democrats in Congress in the 1960s and years following. The Great Society in scope and sweep resembled the New Deal domestic agenda of Franklin D. Roosevelt, whose administration passed the Social Security Act.

7. ANSWER: C

NOW was founded on June 30, 1966, in Washington, D.C., by women's rights activists who were frustrated with the way in which the federal government was not enforcing new anti-discrimination laws. Even after measures like the Equal Employment Opportunity Commission (EEOC) and Title VII of the Civil Rights Act of 1964, employers were still discriminating against women in terms of hiring women and unequal pay with men. NOW was created in order to mobilize women, give women's rights advocates the power to put pressure on employers and the government, and to promote full equality of the sexes. It hoped to increase the amount of women attending colleges and graduate schools, employed in professional jobs instead of domestic or secretarial work, and appointed to federal offices.

8. **ANSWER: C**

Cesar Chavez was an American farm worker, labor leader and civil rights activist, who, with Dolores Huerta, co-founded the National Farm Workers Association (later the United Farm Workers union, UFW). A Mexican American, Chavez became the best known Latino American civil rights activist, and was strongly promoted by the American labor movement, which was eager to enroll Hispanic members. His public-relations approach to unionism and aggressive but nonviolent tactics made the farm workers' struggle a moral cause with nationwide support. By the late 1970s, his tactics had forced growers to recognize the UFW as the bargaining agent for 50,000 field workers in California and Florida.

9. **ANSWER: B**

The Stonewall riots were a series of spontaneous, violent demonstrations by members of the gay community against a police raid that took place in the early morning hours of June 28, 1969, at the Stonewall Inn, located in the Greenwich Village neighborhood of Manhattan, New York City. They are widely considered to constitute the single most important event leading to the gay liberation movement and the modern fight for LGBT rights in the United States.

10. **ANSWER: B**

(causation)

The Feminine Mystique is a 1963 book by Betty Friedan which is widely credited with sparking the beginning of second-wave feminism in the United States. It is widely regarded as one of the most influential nonfiction books of the 20th century. Alvin Toffler declared that it "pulled the trigger on history." Friedan received hundreds of letters from unhappy housewives after its publication, and she herself went on to help found, and become the first president of the National Organization for Women, an influential feminist organization.

11. **ANSWER: C**

(continuity/change)

Swann v. Charlotte-Mecklenburg Board of Education was an important United States Supreme Court case dealing with the busing of students to promote integration in public schools, but it does not relate to the struggle for equal rights for women. The U.S. Equal Employment Opportunity Commission (EEOC) is a federal law enforcement agency that enforces laws against workplace discrimination. Title IX maintains, "No person in the United States shall, on the basis of gender, be excluded from participation in, be denied the benefits of, or be subjected to discrimination under any education program or activity receiving federal financial assistance." And, finally, *Roe v. Wade* (1973) is a landmark decision that a right to privacy under the due process clause of the 14th Amendment extended to a woman's decision to have an abortion

12. ANSWER: C

Phyllis Schlafly is an American constitutional lawyer, conservative activist, author, and founder of the Eagle Forum. She is known for her staunch social and political conservatism, her opposition to modern feminism, and her successful campaign against ratification of the Equal Rights Amendment.

13. ANSWER: A

(synthesis)

Both the Declaration of Sentiments, which was drafted at the Seneca Falls Convention in 1848, and *The Feminine Mystique* address the issue of women's equality in the United States.

14. ANSWER: A

(use of evidence)

Tinker v. Des Moines Independent Community School District (1969) was a decision by the United States Supreme Court that defined the constitutional rights of students in U.S. public schools. The Tinker test is still used by courts today to determine whether a school's disciplinary actions violate students' First Amendment rights.

15. ANSWER: D

(contextualization)

In 1965, Des Moines, Iowa, residents John F. Tinker (15 years old), his siblings Mary Beth Tinker (13 years old), Hope Tinker (11 years old), and Paul Tinker (8 years old), along with their friend Christopher Eckhardt (16 years old) decided to wear black armbands to their schools in protest of the Vietnam War and supporting the Christmas

Truce called for by Senator Robert F. Kennedy. The principals of the Des Moines schools learned of the plan and met on December 14 to create a policy that stated that school children wearing an armband would be asked to remove it immediately. Violating students would be suspended and allowed to return to school after agreeing to comply with the policy. The participants decided to violate this policy. Mary Beth Tinker and Christopher Eckhardt were suspended from school for wearing armbands on December 16th, and John Tinker was suspended for doing the same on the following day.

16. ANSWER: B

(synthesis)

The American Civil Liberties Union (ACLU) is a nonpartisan non-profit organization whose stated mission is "to defend and preserve the individual rights and liberties guaranteed to every person in this country by the Constitution and laws of the United States." It works through litigation, lobbying, and community education.

17. ANSWER: B

(causation)

Head Start began as part of President Lyndon B. Johnson's Great Society campaign. Its justification came from the staff of the President's Council of Economic Advisors. It provides comprehensive early childhood education, health, nutrition, and parent involvement services to low-income children and their families. The program's services and resources are designed to foster stable family relationships, enhance children's physical and emotional well-being, and establish an environment to develop strong cognitive skills. The transition from preschool to elementary school imposes diverse developmental challenges that include requiring the children to engage successfully with their peers outside of the family network, adjust to the space of a classroom, and meet the expectations the school setting provides.

18. ANSWER: C

(contextualization)

The War on Poverty is the unofficial name for legislation first introduced by United States President Lyndon B. Johnson during his State of the Union address on January 8, 1964. This legislation was proposed by Johnson in response to a national poverty rate of around nineteen percent. The speech led the United States Congress to pass the Economic Opportunity Act, which established the Office of Economic Opportunity (OEO) to administer the local application of federal funds targeted against poverty. As a part of the Great Society, Johnson believed in expanding the federal government's roles in education and health care as poverty reduction strategies. These policies can also be seen as a continuation of Franklin D. Roosevelt's New Deal, which ran from 1933 to 1935, and the Four Freedoms of 1941. The legacy of the War on Poverty policy initiative remains in the continued existence of such federal programs as Head Start, Volunteers in Service to America (VISTA), and Job Corps.

19. ANSWER: D

(use of evidence)

The author is addressing the federal government's attack against Native Americans on the Pine Ridge Reservation in South Dakota. In June 1975, in what has been called the "Pine Ridge shootout," two FBI agents were killed near Jumping Bull Ranch, and found to have been shot execution style. Three American Indian Movement members were eventually indicted for the murders: Darryl Butler, Robert Robideau and Leonard Peltier, who had escaped to Canada. Darryl and Robideau were tried in 1975 and acquitted. After extradition, Peltier was tried separately and convicted in 1976. He is serving two consecutive life sentences.

20. ANSWER: D

(causation)

The successes of the African American Civil Rights Movement served as an inspiration for other marginalized groups to fight for justice and equality. The American Indian Movement (AIM) is a Native American advocacy group in the United States, founded in July 1968 in Minneapolis, Minnesota. AIM was initially formed to address American Indian sovereignty, treaty issues, spirituality, and leadership, while simultaneously addressing incidents of police harassment and racism against Native Americans. The various specific issues concerning Native American urban communities like the one in Minneapolis (disparagingly labeled "red ghettos") include unusually high unemployment levels, overt and covert racism, police harassment and neglect, epidemic drug abuse (mainly alcoholism), crushing poverty, domestic violence and substandard housing. AIM's paramount objective is to create "real economic independence for the Indians."

DIFFICULTY LEVEL 3

21. ANSWER: D

Barry Goldwater, the Republican candidate for president in the 1964 election, was very ideologically conservative and would not have supported government intervention on behalf of social justice causes. The other individuals, however, would be considered modern-day muckrakers for raising awareness about social problems. Rachel Carson, author of *Silent Spring*, wrote about the dangers of the chemical DDT, common in pesticides. Michael Harrington wrote *The Other America*, which influenced President Johnson to declare "war" on poverty. Ralph Nader wrote *Unsafe at Any Speed* about auto mobile safety.

22. ANSWER: D

In the United States, the "New Left" was the name loosely associated with liberal, radical, Marxist political movements that took place during the 1960s, primarily among college students, who rejected the Democratic Party and the "Old Left." At the core of this was the Students for a Democratic Society (SDS). The New Left can be defined as "a loosely organized, mostly white student movement that advocated for democracy, civil rights, and various types of university reforms, and protested against the Vietnam war".

23. ANSWER: B

New Federalism is a political philosophy of devolution, or the transfer of certain powers from the United States federal government back to the states. The primary objective of New Federalism, unlike that of the eighteenth-century political philosophy of Federalism, is the restoration to the states of some of the autonomy and power which they lost to the federal government as a consequence of President Franklin Roosevelt's New Deal. As a policy theme, New Federalism typically involves the federal government providing block grants to the states to resolve a social issue. The federal government then monitors outcomes but provides broad discretion to the states for how the programs are implemented.

PART C

DIFFICULTY LEVEL 1

1. ANSWER: D

The need to always have more and better goods emerged rapidly in the West during the 1950s. Consumerism became a key component of Western society. People bought big houses in the new suburbs and bought new time-saving household appliances. This buying trend was influenced by many American cultural and economic aspects such as advertising; television; cars; new offerings from banks (loans and credit); immediately being able to have what one wanted; and achieving a perceived better life. In addition, the popularity of television skyrocketed, particularly in the US, where 77% of households purchased their first TV set during the decade. Finally, comic book audiences grew during and after World War II. Charles Schulz's *Peanuts*, appeared for the first time on October 2, 1950, in seven US newspapers. This and comic strips such as *Hi & Lois* and *Dennis the Menace* marked a revival of humor strips, a genre that had largely disappeared in the previous decade.

DIFFICULTY LEVEL 2

2. ANSWER: D

President Harry Truman desegregated the United States Armed Forces by executive order in 1948. During Eisenhower's presidency, the post-war baby boom peaked and the American economy expanded. In addition, to create a network of highways throughout the country, Eisenhower signed the Interstate Highway Act, the largest public works program in United States history.

3. ANSWER: C

Beatniks and the Beat Generation, a culture of teenage and young adults who rebelled against social norms, appeared towards the end of the decade and were criticized by older generations. They are seen as a predecessor for the counterculture and hippie movements. The Beat Generation, an anti-materialistic literary movement whose name was invented by Jack Kerouac in 1948 and stretched on into the early-mid-1960s, was at its zenith in the 1950s. Such groundbreaking literature from the beats includes William S. Burroughs' *Naked Lunch*, Allen Ginsberg's *Howl*, and Jack Kerouac's *On the Road*.

4. **ANSWER: C**

Nixon was a late convert to the conservation movement. Environmental policy had not been a significant issue in the 1968 election; the candidates were rarely asked for their views on the subject. He saw that the first Earth Day in April 1970 presaged a wave of voter interest on the subject, and sought to use that to his benefit; in June he announced the formation of the Environmental Protection Agency (EPA). Nixon broke new ground by discussing environment policy in his State of the Union speech; other initiatives supported by Nixon included the Clean Air Act of 1970 and Occupational Safety and Health Administration (OSHA); the National Environmental Policy Act required environmental impact statements for many Federal projects. Nixon vetoed the Clean Water Act of 1972—objecting not to the policy goals of the legislation but to the amount of money to be spent on them, which he deemed excessive. After Congress overrode his veto, Nixon impounded the funds he deemed unjustifiable.

5. **ANSWER: D**

From 1950 to the 1970s, women's expectations of future employment changed. Women began to see themselves going on to college and working through their marriages and even attending graduate school. Many however still had brief and intermittent work force participation, without necessarily having expectations for a "career."Although more women attended college, it was often expected that they attended to find a spouse—the so-called "M.R.S. degree". Nevertheless, Labor force participation by women still grew significantly. Beginning in the 1970s women began to flood colleges and grad schools. They began to enter profession like medicine, law, dental and business. More women were going to college and expected to be employed at the age of 35, as opposed to past generations that only worked intermittently due to marriage and childbirth.

6. **ANSWER: A**

The Watergate scandal was a major political scandal that occurred in the United States in the 1970s as a result of the June 17, 1972, break-in at the Democratic National Committee (DNC) headquarters at the Watergate office complex in Washington, D.C., and the Nixon administration's attempted cover-up of its involvement. Watergate led Congress to pass legislation that changed campaign financing, to amend the Freedom of Information Act, as well as to require financial disclosures by key government officials (via the Ethics in Government Act). Other types of disclosures, such as releasing recent income tax forms, became expected albeit not legally required. Presidents since Franklin D. Roosevelt had recorded many of their conversations but the practice purportedly ended after Watergate. Presidential term limits had already been established in 1951 with the 22nd Amendment to the Constitution.

7. ANSWER: B

According to the United States Census, about 12% of the American population is over the age of However, the elderly are not evenly distributed throughout the United States . There are higher concentrations of the elderly in the Midwest and in the South, particularly in Florida. The high concentration of elderly in Florida is partially attributable to the fact that many retirees move to Florida for the good weather. In contrast, few elderly people move to the Midwest. Instead, the high concentration of elderly people in the Midwest is due to the fact that the young are moving out of there. While the effects of an increasingly aging population on society are complex, there is a specific concern about the impact on healthcare demand. Older people generally incur more health-related costs than do younger people, and in the workplace can also cost more in worker's compensation and pension liabilities. (Source: Boundless. "The Graying of America." Boundless Sociology. Boundless, 07 Jan. 2015. Retrieved 18 Jan. 2015 from *https://www.boundless.com/sociology/textbooks/boundless-sociology-textbook/aging-18/aging-in-global-perspective-127/the-graying-of-america-720-4619/*)

8. ANSWER: A

(contextualization)

There was a large-scale expansion of the middle class in the 1950s. Unions were strong, comprising almost half the American work force. Politics tended to be moderate, with extremist positions being out of favor. The need to always have more and better goods emerged rapidly in the West during the 1950s. Consumerism became a key component of Western society. People bought big houses in the new suburbs and bought new time-saving household appliances. With the difficulties of World War II now in the past, the decade also gave birth to what might be referred to as "the suburban dream" (the typical 1950s housewife would eventually become a universally recognized stereotype). This buying trend was influenced by many American cultural and economic aspects such as advertising; television; cars; new offerings from banks (loans and credit); immediately being able to have what one wanted; and achieving a perceived better life.

9. ANSWER: D

(contextualization; use of evidence)

Television sitcoms offered a romanticized view of middle-class suburban American life with *The Adventures of Ozzie and Harriet* (1952–1966), *Father Knows Best* (1954–1960), and ABC's *The Donna Reed Show* (1958–1966) exemplifying the genre. Archetypal suburban life was limned in *Leave It to Beaver* (1957–1963), purportedly the first sitcom to be told from a child's point of view and the first to strike a blow for television realism by displaying a toilet in an early episode.

10. ANSWER: C

(compare/contrast)

Suburbs and suburban living have been the subject for a wide variety of films, books, television shows and songs. The American photojournalist Bill Owens documented the culture of suburbia in the 1970s, most notably in his book *Suburbia*. The 1962 song "Little Boxes" by Malvina Reynolds lampoons the development of suburbia and its perceived bourgeois and conformist values, while the 1982 song "Subdivisions" by the Canadian band Rush also discusses suburban conformity. The 2010 album *The Suburbs* by the Canadian-based alternative band Arcade Fire dealt with aspects of growing up in suburbia, suggesting aimlessness, apathy and endless rushing are ingrained into the suburban culture and mentality. *Over the Hedge* is a syndicated comic strip written and drawn by Michael Fry and T. Lewis. It tells the story of a raccoon, turtle, a squirrel, and their friends who come to terms with their woodlands being taken over by suburbia, trying to survive the increasing flow of humanity and technology while becoming enticed by it at the same time.

11. ANSWER: A

(use of evidence; periodization)

1950s artists and intellectuals were the most visible challengers to the ideal of middle-class suburban family life in the 1950s. David Riesman, William Whyte, Vance Packard, the Beats, and others criticized American conformity, consumerism, and patriotism and promoted a wider spectrum of values in American life.

12. ANSWER: B

(contextualization; causation)

The Elementary and Secondary Education Act (ESEA) was passed as a part of President Lyndon B. Johnson's "War on Poverty" and has been the most far-reaching federal legislation affecting education ever passed by Congress. The act is an extensive statute that funds primary and secondary education. It also emphasizes equal access to education and establishes high standards and accountability. In addition, the bill aims to shorten the achievement gaps between students by providing each child with fair and equal opportunities to achieve an exceptional education. As mandated in the act, the funds are authorized for professional development, instructional materials, for resources to support educational programs, and for parental involvement promotion. The act was originally authorized through 1965; however, the government has reauthorized the act every five years since its enactment. The current reauthorization of ESEA is the No Child Left Behind Act of 2001, named and proposed by President George W. Bush.

13. ANSWER: C

(causation)

The National Defense Education Act (NDEA) was signed into law on September 2, 1958, providing funding to United States education institutions at all levels. It was one of a suite of science initiatives inaugurated by President Dwight D. Eisenhower in 1958 motivated to increase the technological sophistication and power of the United States alongside, for instance DARPA and NASA. It followed a growing national anxiety that U.S. scientists were falling behind scientists in the Soviet Union, catalyzed, arguably, by early Soviet success in the Space Race, notably the launch of the first-ever satellite, Sputnik, the previous year. The act authorized funding for four years, increasing funding per year: for example, funding increased on eight program titles from $183 million in 1959 to $222 million in 1960. However, in the aftermath of McCarthyism, a mandate was inserted in the act that all beneficiaries must complete an affidavit disclaiming belief in the overthrow of the U.S. government. This requisite loyalty statement stirred concern and protest from the American Association of University Professors and over 153 institutions.

14. ANSWER: A

(contextualization)

In the United States, affirmative action refers to equal opportunity employment measures that Federal contractors and subcontractors are legally required to adopt. These measures are intended to prevent discrimination against employees or applicants for employment on the basis of "color, religion, sex, or national origin." The impetus toward affirmative action is to redress the disadvantages associated with overt historical discrimination.[8] Further impetus is a desire to ensure public institutions, such as universities, hospitals, and police forces, are more representative of the populations they serve. Affirmative action is a subject of controversy. Some policies adopted as affirmative action, such as racial quotas or gender quotas for collegiate admission, have been criticized as a form of reverse discrimination.

15. ANSWER: D

(continuity/change)

Regents of the University of California v. Bakke was a landmark decision by the Supreme Court of the United States. It upheld affirmative action, allowing race to be one of several factors in college admission policy. However, the court ruled that specific quotas, such as the 16 out of 100 seats set aside for minority students by the University of California, Davis School of Medicine, were impermissible. Although the Supreme Court had outlawed segregation in schools, and had even ordered school districts to take steps to assure integration, the question of the legality of voluntary affirmative action programs initiated by universities was unresolved. Proponents deemed such programs necessary to make up for past discrimination, while opponents believed they were illegal and a violation of the Equal Protection Clause of the Fourteenth Amendment to the United States Constitution.

16. ANSWER: B

(contextualization; causation)

The Affluent Society is a 1958 book by Harvard economist John Kenneth Galbraith. The book sought to clearly outline the manner in which the post-World War II United States was becoming wealthy in the private sector but remained poor in the public sector, lacking social and physical infrastructure, and perpetuating income disparities. The book sparked much public discussion at the time, and it is widely remembered for Galbraith's popularizing of the term "conventional wisdom." Galbraith argued that the "central tradition" in economics, created by Adam Smith and expanded by David Ricardo and Thomas Robert Malthus in the late eighteenth and early nineteenth centuries, is poorly suited to the affluent post-World War II U.S. society. This is so because the "central tradition" economists wrote during a time of widespread poverty where production of basic goods was necessary. U.S. society, at the time of Galbraith's writing, was one of widespread affluence, where production was based on luxury goods and wants.

17. ANSWER: C

The post–World War II economic expansion, also known as the postwar economic boom, the long boom, and the Golden Age of Capitalism, was a period of economic prosperity in the mid-20th century which occurred, following the end of World War II in 1945, and lasted until the early 1970s. According to Galbraith, using production, or gross domestic product, as a measure of U.S. society's well-being omits important measures of social and personal well-being. GDP also neglects differences in output. For example, "An increased supply of educational services has a standing in the total not different in kind from an increased output of television receivers." Production has risen to its paramount but unwarranted status because it is held in grace by both Democrats and Republicans.

18. ANSWER: C

(use of evidence; causation)

The ERA was written in 1923 by Alice Paul, suffragist leader and founder of the National Woman's Party. She and the NWP considered the ERA to be the next necessary step after the 19th Amendment (affirming women's right to vote) in guaranteeing "equal justice under law" to all citizens. The ERA was introduced into every session of Congress between 1923 and 1972, when it was passed and sent to the states for ratification. The seven-year time limit in the ERA's proposing clause was extended by Congress to June 30, 1982, but at the deadline, the ERA had been ratified by 35 states, leaving it three states short of the 38 required for ratification. It has been reintroduced into every Congress since that time, with liberals supporting it and conservatives opposing it.

19. ANSWER: D

(comparison; synthesis)

During the Gilded Age, many middle-class reformers supported the idea of women's equality, and most called for increased federal power to address the problems of inequality and injustice.

DIFFICULTY LEVEL 3

20. ANSWER: B

One of the most influential works of the 1950s was David Reisman's *The Lonely Crowd: A Study of the Changing American Character.* The book is largely a study of modern conformity, which postulates the existence of the "inner-directed" and "other-directed" personalities. Riesman argues that the character of post-World War II American society impels individuals to "other-directedness," the preeminent example being modern suburbia, where individuals seek their neighbors' approval and fear being outcast from their community. This lifestyle has a coercive effect, which compels people to abandon "inner-direction" of their lives, and induces them to take on the goals, ideology, likes, and dislikes of their community.

21. ANSWER: B

Wallace ran for President in the 1968 election as the American Independent Party candidate, with Curtis LeMay as his candidate for Vice President. Wallace hoped that southern states could use their clout to end federal efforts at desegregation. His platform also contained generous increases for beneficiaries of Social Security and Medicare. In addition, Wallace's foreign policy positions set him apart from the other candidates in the field. "If the Vietnam War was not winnable within 90 days of his taking office, Wallace pledged an immediate withdrawal of U.S. troops ... Wallace described foreign aid as money 'poured down a rat hole' and demanded that European and Asian allies pay more for their defense." In Wallace's 1998 obituary, *The Huntsville Times* political editor John Anderson summarized the impact from the 1968 campaign: "His startling appeal to millions of alienated white voters was not lost on Richard Nixon and other GOP strategists." Nixon and the Republican party subsequently adopted a "Southern Strategy" to appeal to Southern whites.

22. ANSWER: D

In the mid-1970s much of America suffered a collective malaise. Nothing fuels a strong case of malaise like a sputtering economy. The United States had grown accustomed to steady economic growth since the end of World War II. Recessions were short and were followed by robust economic growth. For the first time since the Great Depression, Americans faced an economy that could result in a lower standard of living for their children. Inflation, which crept along at one to three percent for the previous two decades, exploded into double digits. Full employment, defined as five percent or less, had been achieved in most years since 1945. Now the unemployment rate was nearing the dangerous ten percent line. Americans asked the question: what went wrong? Economists had long held that inflation and unemployment were polar forces. High inflation meant a great deal of spending; therefore, many jobs would be created. Unemployment created jobless Americans with less money to spend; therefore, prices would stay the same or fall. Surprisingly, the United States experienced high unemployment and high inflation simultaneously in the 1970s — a phenomenon called stagflation. Experts and commoners debated the roots of this problem with differing opinions. One possibility was the price of oil. When Israel defeated its Arab neighbors in the Yom Kippur War of 1973, Arab oil producers retaliated against Israel's allies by leading the Organization of Oil Producing Countries (OPEC) to enact an embargo. Oil prices skyrocketed immediately in the United States as the demand outstripped the supply (*http://www.ushistory.org/us/58b.asp*).

23. ANSWER: D

During the 1970s, more women began to hold public office, although still not in proportion to their composition of the overall population. Christian fundamentalism became a driving force in politics, especially with the Republican Party, in part as a response to 1960s liberalism and the recent *Roe v. Wade* (1973) Supreme Court decision, which legalized abortion. Americans began to live long, leading to a trend called the "Graying of America," which has had implications for programs like Social Security and Medicare. Finally, with a rising divorce rate in the United States, more children were raised in single-parent households.

24. ANSWER: D

The Three Mile Island accident was a partial nuclear meltdown that occurred on March 28, 1979, in one of the two Three Mile Island nuclear reactors in Dauphin County, Pennsylvania, United States. It was the worst accident in U.S. commercial nuclear power plant history. The incident was rated a five on the seven-point International Nuclear Event Scale: Accident With Wider Consequences. The accident crystallized anti-nuclear safety concerns among activists and the general public, resulted in new regulations for the nuclear industry, and has been cited as a contributor to the decline of a new reactor construction program that was already underway in the 1970s.

Period 1980-present

PART A

DIFFICULTY LEVEL 2

1. ANSWER: A

After the Watergate Scandal, Americans had less faith in government, especially in those who worked in Washington, DC. This cynicism led to a distrust of politicians, so Jimmy Carter and Ronald Reagan highlighted their experiences outside Washington, as governors of Georgia and California, respectively.

2. ANSWER: C

The Iran–Contra affair was a political scandal in the United States that occurred during the second term of the Reagan Administration. Senior administration officials secretly facilitated the sale of arms to Iran, the subject of an arms embargo. Some U.S. officials also hoped that the arms sales would secure the release of several hostages and allow U.S. intelligence agencies to fund the Nicaraguan Contras. Several investigations ensued, including those by the U.S. Congress and the three-person, Reagan-appointed Tower Commission. Neither found any evidence that President Reagan himself knew of the extent of the multiple programs. Ultimately the sale of weapons to Iran was not deemed a criminal offense but charges were brought against five individuals for their support of the Contras. Those charges, however, were later dropped because the administration refused to declassify certain documents. The indicted conspirators faced various lesser charges instead. In the end, fourteen administration officials were indicted, including then-Secretary of Defense Caspar Weinberger. Eleven convictions resulted, some of which were vacated on appeal. The rest of those indicted or convicted were all pardoned in the final days of the presidency of George H. W. Bush, who had been vice-president at the time of the affair.

3. ANSWER: B

Bill Clinton, the 42nd President of the United States, was impeached by the House of Representatives on two charges, one of perjury and one of obstruction of justice, on December 19, 1998. Two other impeachment articles, a second perjury charge and a charge of abuse of power, failed in the House. He was acquitted of both charges by the Senate on February 12, 1999. Independent Counsel Ken Starr alleged that Clinton had broken the law during his handling of the Lewinsky scandal and the Paula Jones lawsuit. Four charges were considered by the full House of Representatives; only two passed, and those on a nearly party-line vote. It was only the second time in history that the House had impeached the President of the United States, and only the third that the full House had considered such proceedings. The trial in the United States Senate began right after the seating of the 106th Congress, in which the Republicans began with 55 senators. A two-thirds vote (67 senators) was required to remove Clinton from office. Fifty senators voted to remove Clinton on the obstruction of justice charge and 45 voted to remove him on the perjury charge; no Democrat voted guilty on either charge. Thus, he was acquitted an allowed to remain in office.

4. **ANSWER: B**

(contextualization)

Jerry Falwell, Sr. (August 11, 1933 – May 15, 2007) was an American evangelical Southern Baptist pastor, televangelist, and a conservative political commentator. He was the founding pastor of the Thomas Road Baptist Church, a megachurch in Lynchburg, Virginia. He founded Lynchburg Christian Academy (now Liberty Christian Academy) in 1967, Liberty University in 1971, and co-founded the Moral Majority in 1979. Falwell strongly advocated beliefs and practices he believed were taught by the Bible. The church, Falwell asserted, was the cornerstone of a successful family. During his time as head of the Moral Majority, Falwell consistently pushed for Republican candidates and for conservative politics.

5. **ANSWER: A**

(change over time; contextualization; compare/contrast)

With the election of President Bill Clinton, many conservatives feared a return to an active federal government. In response, the Contract with America was a document released by the United States Republican Party during the 1994 Congressional election campaign. Written by Newt Gingrich and Richard Armey, and in part using text from former President Ronald Reagan's 1985 State of the Union Address, the Contract detailed the actions the Republicans promised to take if they became the majority party in the United States House of Representatives for the first time in 40 years. Proponents say the Contract was revolutionary in its commitment to offering specific legislation for a vote, describing in detail the precise plan of the Congressional Representatives, and broadly nationalizing the Congressional election. Furthermore, its provisions represented the view of many conservative Republicans on the issues of shrinking the size of government, promoting lower taxes and greater entrepreneurial activity, and both tort reform and welfare reform. Critics of the Contract describe it as a political ploy and election tool designed to have broad appeal while masking the Republicans' real agenda and failing to provide real legislation or governance.

6. ANSWER: C

(causation; contextualization)

Evangelical Christians overwhelmingly supported conservative principles and politicians, whom they saw as promoting traditional American values.

7. ANSWER: C

(causation)

The economic policy of the George W. Bush administration was a combination of tax cuts, expenditures for fighting two wars, and a free-market ideology intended to de-emphasize the role of government in the private sector. He advocated the ownership society, premised on the concepts of individual accountability, less government, and the owning of property.

During his first term (2001–2005), he sought and obtained Congressional approval for tax cuts: the Economic Growth and Tax Relief Reconciliation Act of 2001, the Job Creation and Worker Assistance Act of 2002 and the Jobs and Growth Tax Relief Reconciliation Act of 2003. These acts decreased all tax rates, reduced the capital gains tax, increased the child tax credit and eliminated the so-called "marriage penalty", and were set to expire in 2011. The last two years of his presidency were characterized by the worsening subprime mortgage crisis, which resulted in government intervention to bail out damaged financial institutions and a weakening economy.

The U.S. national debt grew significantly from 2001 to 2009, both in dollar terms and relative to the size of the economy (GDP), due to a combination of tax cuts and wars in both Afghanistan and Iraq. Budgeted spending under President Bush averaged 19.9% of GDP, similar to his predecessor President Bill Clinton, although tax receipts were lower at 17.9% versus 19.1%.

DIFFICULTY LEVEL 3

8. ANSWER: C

Reaganomics refers to the economic policies promoted by U.S. President Ronald Reagan during the 1980s. These policies are commonly associated with supply-side economics, referred to as trickle-down economics by political opponents and free market economics by political advocates. The four pillars of Reagan's economic policy were to reduce the growth of government spending, reduce the federal income tax and capital gains tax, reduce government regulation, and tighten the money supply in order to reduce inflation. Spending during Reagan's two terms (FY 1981–88) averaged 22.4% GDP, well above the 20.6% GDP average from 1971 to 2009. In addition, the public debt rose from 26% GDP in 1980 to 41% GDP by 1988. In dollar terms, the public debt rose from $712 billion in 1980 to $2.052 trillion in 1988, a roughly three-fold increase. The unemployment rate rose from 7% in 1980 to 10.8% in 1982, then declined to 5.4% in 1988. The inflation rate declined from 10% in 1980 to 4% in 1988.

9. **ANSWER: C**

(synthesis)

Planned Parenthood v. Casey (1992) was a case decided by the Supreme Court of the United States in which the constitutionality of several Pennsylvania state regulations regarding abortion were challenged. The Court's plurality opinion upheld the constitutional right to have an abortion and altered the standards for analyzing restrictions of that right, invalidating one regulation but upholding the other four.

PART B

DIFFICULTY LEVEL 1

1. ANSWER: A

The Cold War period of 1985–1991 began with the rise of Mikhail Gorbachev as leader of the Soviet Union. Gorbachev was a revolutionary leader for the USSR, as he was the first to promote liberalization of the political landscape (Glasnost) and capitalist elements into the economy (Perestroika); prior to this, the USSR had been strictly prohibiting liberal reform and maintained an inefficient centralized economy. The USSR, facing massive economic difficulties, was also greatly interested in reducing the costly arms race with the U.S. President Ronald Reagan, although peaceful confrontation and arms buildups throughout much of his term prevented the USSR from cutting back its military spending as much as it might have liked. Regardless, the USSR began to crumble as liberal reforms proved difficult to handle and capitalist changes to the centralized economy were badly transitioned and caused major problems. After a series of revolutions in Soviet Bloc states, and a failed coup by conservative elements opposed to the ongoing reforms, the Soviet Union collapsed in 1991.

2. ANSWER: D

The War on Terror refers to the international military campaign that started after the September 11, 2001, terrorist attacks on the United States. The United States led a coalition of other NATO and non-NATO nations participating in the campaign to attack al-Qaeda and other militant organizations. U.S. President George W. Bush first used the term. The Bush administration and the western media have since used the term to argue a global military, political, legal, and conceptual struggle against both organizations designated terrorist and regimes accused of supporting them. It was originally used with a particular focus Islamic terrorism organizations including al-Qaeda and like-minded organizations. The War on Terror has resulted in wars in Afghanistan and Iraq, as well as domestic policies like the Patriot Act.

DIFFICULTY LEVEL 2

3. ANSWER: C

The Gulf War, codenamed Operation Desert Shield for operations leading to the buildup of troops and defense of Saudi Arabia, and Operation Desert Storm in its combat phase, was a war waged by coalition forces from 34 nations led by the United States against Iraq in response to Iraq's invasion and annexation of Kuwait.

4. ANSWER: B

With the collapse of the Soviet Union in 1991, containment no longer made sense, so in the past two decades, the United States has been redefining its foreign policy. What are its responsibilities, if any, to the rest of the world, now that it has no incentive of luring them to the American "side" in the Cold War? Does the United States still need allies? What action should be taken, if any, when a "hot spot" erupts, causing misery to the people who live in the nations involved? The answers are not easy. Since 2001, the dominant issue has been prevent terrorist attacks against the United States and around the world. Many, but not all, of these attacks have involved stateless Islamist extremists that operate in many parts of the world.

5. ANSWER: C

The USA PATRIOT Act is an Act of Congress that was signed into law by President George W. Bush on October 26, 2001. Its title is a ten-letter backronym (USA PATRIOT) that stands for "Uniting and Strengthening America by Providing Appropriate Tools Required to Intercept and Obstruct Terrorism Act of 2001." On May 26, 2011, President Barack Obama signed the PATRIOT Sunsets Extension Act of 2011, a four-year extension of three key provisions in the USA PATRIOT Act: roving wiretaps, searches of business records (the "library records provision"), and conducting surveillance of "lone wolves"—individuals suspected of terrorist-related activities not linked to terrorist groups. The USA PATRIOT Act has generated a great deal of controversy since its enactment. Opponents of the Act have been quite vocal in asserting that it was passed opportunistically after the September 11 attacks, believing that there would have been little debate. Several parts of the Act clearly violate civil liberties protected by the Bill of Rights.

6. ANSWER: B

(continuity/change)

After WWII, the United States took a policy of interventionism in order to contain communist influence abroad. Such forms of interventionism included giving aid to European nations to rebuild, having an active role in the UN, NATO, and police actions around the world, and involving the CIA in several coup take overs in Latin America and the Middle

East. The US was not merely non-isolationist (i.e. the US was not merely abandoning policies of isolationism), but actively intervening and leading world affairs. (Source: Boundless. "Interventionism." Boundless Political Science. Boundless, 03 Jul. 2014. Retrieved 18 Jan. 2015 from *https://www.boundless.com/political-science/textbooks/boundless-political-science-textbook/foreign-policy-18/history-of-american-foreign-policy-110/interventionism-585-4258*)

7. ANSWER: D

(contextualization)

President Clinton assumed office shortly after the fall of the Soviet Union and end of the Cold War, but nevertheless was forced to confront numerous international conflicts. Shortly after taking office, Clinton had to decide whether the United States, as a world superpower, should have a say in the conflicts and violence occurring in Somalia, Rwanda, Bosnia and Herzegovina, Kosovo, and Haiti. Clinton also spent much of his foreign policy on the conflicts in the former Yugoslavia, East Timor, Northern Ireland, and the Middle East, with the Israeli-Palestinian conflict in particular. Although Clinton sent troops to Haiti, Bosnia, and Somalia, no action was undertaken in Rwanda, despite the fact that the global community knew a genocide was taking place there.

8. ANSWER: A

(contextualization)

Reagan significantly increased public expenditures, primarily the Department of Defense, which rose (in constant 2000 dollars) from $267.1 billion in 1980 (4.9% of GDP and 22.7% of public expenditure) to $393.1 billion in 1988 (5.8% of GDP and 27.3% of public expenditure); most of those years military spending was about 6% of GDP, exceeding this number in 4 different years. All these numbers had not been seen since the end of U.S. involvement in the Vietnam War in 1973.

9. ANSWER: D

(causation)

Of the $2.4 trillion budgeted for 2005, about $450 billion was planned to be spent on defense. This level was generally comparable to the defense spending during the Cold War. Congress approved $87 billion for U.S. involvement in Iraq and Afghanistan in November, and had approved an earlier $79 billion package the previous spring. Most of the funds were for military operations in the two countries. The ratio of defense spending of the U.S. and its allies to its potential adversaries, for the year 2000, was about 6 to 1.

10. ANSWER: A

(continuity/change; evidence; synthesis)

The military–industrial complex, or military–industrial–congressional complex, comprises the policy and monetary relationships which exist between legislators, national armed forces, and the arms industry that supports them. These relationships include political contributions, political approval for military spending, lobbying to support bureaucracies, and oversight of the industry. It is a type of iron triangle. The term is most often used in reference to the system behind the military of the United States, where it gained popularity after its use in the farewell address of President Dwight D. Eisenhower on January 17, 1961, though the term is applicable to any country with a similarly developed infrastructure.

DIFFICULTY LEVEL 3

11. ANSWER: B

Under the Reagan Doctrine, the United States provided overt and covert aid to anti-communist guerrillas and resistance movements in an effort to "roll back" Soviet-backed communist governments in Africa, Asia, and Latin America. The doctrine was designed to diminish Soviet influence in these regions as part of the administration's overall Cold War strategy. Operation Urgent Fury was a 1983 United States-led invasion of Grenada that resulted in a U.S. victory within a matter of weeks. Triggered by the house arrest and murder of the leader of the coup which had brought a revolutionary government to power for the preceding four years, the invasion resulted in a restoration of the pre-revolutionary regime.

PART C

DIFFICULTY LEVEL 2

1. ANSWER: C

Although the United States continues to import fossil fuels, it has increased its own domestic drilling for oil and natural gas. While this has resulted in greater energy independence, it has also resulted in environmental hazards and catastrophes, including the BP oil spill in the Gulf of Mexico, water pollution from Hydraulic Fracturing, or "fracking," and a rise in carbon emissions that contribute to climate change.

2. ANSWER: C

The civil rights movement of the 1960s led to the replacement of immigration quotas with per-country limits.Since then, the number of first-generation immigrants living in the United States has quadrupled, from 9.6 million in 1970 to about 38 million in 2007. Nearly 14 million immigrants entered the United States from 2000 to 2010, and over one million persons were naturalized as U.S. citizens in 2008. Since the per-country limit applies the same maximum on the number of visas to all countries regardless of their population, it has had the effect of severely restricting the legal immigration of persons born in Mexico, China, India, and the Philippines – currently the leading countries of origin of immigrants to the United States. Family reunification accounts for approximately two-thirds of legal immigration to the US every year. As of 2009, 66% of legal immigrants were admitted on this basis, along with 13% admitted for their employment skills and 17% for humanitarian reasons. Migration is difficult, expensive, and dangerous for those who enter the US illegally across the Mexico–United States border. Virtually all undocumented immigrants have no avenues for legal entry to the United States due the restrictive legal limits on green cards, and lack of immigrant visas for low skilled workers. Participants in debates on immigration in the early twenty-first century called for increasing enforcement of existing laws governing illegal immigration to the United States, building a barrier along some or all of the 2,000-mile U.S.-Mexico border, or creating a new guest worker program. Through much of 2006 the country and Congress was immersed in a debate about these proposals. As of April 2010 few of these proposals had become law, though a partial border fence had been approved and subsequently canceled.

3. ANSWER: B

(causation; use of evidence)

The Patient Protection and Affordable Care Act, commonly called the Affordable Care Act (ACA) or "Obamacare," is a United States federal statute signed into law by President Barack Obama on March 23, 2010. It represents the most significant regulatory overhaul of the U.S. healthcare system since the passage of Medicare and Medicaid in 1965. The ACA was enacted with the goals of increasing the quality and affordability of health insurance, lowering the uninsured rate by expanding public and private insurance coverage, and reducing the costs of healthcare for individuals and the government. It introduced a number of mechanisms—including mandates, subsidies, and insurance exchanges—meant to increase coverage and affordability. The law also requires insurance companies to cover all applicants within new minimum standards and offer the same rates regardless of pre-existing conditions or sex. Additional reforms aimed to reduce costs and improve healthcare outcomes by shifting the system towards quality over quantity through increased competition, regulation, and incentives to streamline the delivery of healthcare. In 2011 the Congressional Budget Office projected that the ACA would lower both future deficits and Medicare spending.

4. **ANSWER: B**

(contextualization)

The Netherlands was the first country to allow same-sex marriage in 2001. As of 2014, same-sex marriages are also recognized in Sweden, Argentina, Belgium, Canada, Iceland, Norway, South Africa, Spain, Portugal, Denmark, Uruguay, Brazil, France, New Zealand, Mexico, and Israel (though not performed there), along with twenty five states in the United States: Massachusetts, Iowa, Connecticut, Vermont, New Hampshire, New York, Maine, Maryland, Washington, Minnesota, New Mexico, Rhode Island, Delaware, California, New Jersey, Hawaii, Illinois, New Mexico, Utah, Oklahoma, Virginia, Oregon, Pennsylvania, Wisconsin, Indiana and Colorado as well as the District of Columbia. In 2003, in the case *Lawrence v. Texas,* the Supreme Court of the United States struck down sodomy laws in fourteen states, making consensual homosexual sex legal in all 50 states, a significant step forward in LGBT activism and one that had been fought for by activists since the inception of modern LGBT social movements. The "Don't ask, don't tell" 1993 law forbidding homosexual people from serving openly in the United States military, was repealed in 2010. This meant that gays and lesbians could now serve openly in the military without any fear of being discharged because of their sexual orientation. In 2012, the United States Department of Housing and Urban Development's Office of Fair Housing and Equal Opportunity issued a regulation to prohibit discrimination in federally-assisted housing programs. The new regulations ensure that the Department's core housing programs are open to all eligible persons, regardless of sexual orientation or gender identity. In early 2014 a series of protests organized by Add The Words, Idaho and former state senator Nicole LeFavour, some including civil disobedience and concomitant arrests,[63] took place in Boise, Idaho which advocated adding the words "sexual orientation" and "gender identity" to the state's Human Rights act

DIFFICULTY LEVEL 3

5. ANSWER: C

As a result of free-trade agreements, such as NAFTA, more American jobs are being outsourced by companies wishing to pay their workers less money. Unions, which used to be the backbone of industrialized jobs, have declined in strength and membership over the past 30 years. Although wages of top earners have increased, middle-class wages have barely kept pace with inflation. Finally, the mechanization of certain jobs has increased, not decreased.

6. ANSWER: D

The American population almost quadrupled during the 20th century—at a growth rate of about 1.3% a year—from about 76 million in 1900 to 281 million in 2000. It reached the 200 million mark in 1968, and the 300 million mark on October 17, 2006. Population growth is fastest among minorities as a whole, and according to the Census Bureau's estimation for 2012, 50.4% of American children under the age of 1 belonged to minority groups. Hispanic and Latino Americans accounted for 48% of the national population growth of 2.9 million between July 1, 2005, and July 1, 2006. Immigrants and their U.S.-born descendants are expected to provide most of the U.S. population gains in the decades ahead. The birth rate is 12.5 births/1,000 population, estimated as of 2013. This was the lowest since records began. In 2009, *Time* magazine reported that 40% of births were to unmarried women.

74577679R00185

Made in the USA
Columbia, SC
12 September 2019